Samuel Johnson

The Beauties of Samuel Johnson

Consisting of maxims and observations, moral, critical, and miscellaneous to which are now added, biographical anecdotes of the doctor, selected from the works of Mrs. Piozzi; his life, recently published by Boswell

Samuel Johnson

The Beauties of Samuel Johnson
Consisting of maxims and observations, moral, critical, and miscellaneous to which are now added, biographical anecdotes of the doctor, selected from the works of Mrs. Piozzi; his life, recently published by Boswell

ISBN/EAN: 9783337011321

Printed in Europe, USA, Canada, Australia, Japan

Cover: Foto ©ninafisch / pixelio.de

More available books at **www.hansebooks.com**

A NEW EDITION, being the EIGHTH,
WHEREIN THE TWO VOLUMES ARE COMPRISED IN
ONE, AND ARRANGED UNDER ONE ALPHABET,
WITH VERY CONSIDERABLE ADDITIONS.

THE

BEAUTIES

OF

Samuel Johnson, LL. D.

CONSISTING OF

MAXIMS AND OBSERVATIONS,

MORAL, CRITICAL, and MISCELLANEOUS:

TO WHICH ARE NOW ADDED,

BIOGRAPHICAL ANECDOTES

OF THE

DOCTOR,

SELECTED FROM
THE WORKS OF MRS. PIOZZI;—HIS LIFE,
RECENTLY PUBLISHED BY MR. BOSWELL,
AND OTHER AUTHENTIC TESTIMONIES,

ALSO,
HIS WILL, AND THE SERMON HE WROTE FOR THE
LATE DOCTOR DODD.

LONDON:
PRINTED FOR C. AND G. KEARSLEY, NO. 46,
FLEET-STREET.

M,DCC,XCII.

ADVERTISEMENT

To the SEVENTH EDITION.

The former Editions of this selection have been introduced into several of the most reputable Schools, for both Sexes in the Kingdom; however, the Price of the two Volumes (viz. *Five Shillings*) has been, by some, thought too much, the whole is therefore now brought into one Volume, under one Alphabet, and the Price reduced to *Three Shillings and Sixpence*; and, in order to render it still more complete, the Editor has selected from Mrs. Piozzi's, and Mr. Boswell's late Publications, together with many authentic documents, a considerable number of Biographical and other Anecdotes, including a selection of his Bon Mots. Likewise a Copy of his Will, and the Sermon which he wrote for the unfortunate Dr. Dodd, who preached it to his Fellow Convicts, in the Chapel of Newgate, a few days before he suffered.

November 6, 1786.

This Impression (the Eighth) contains, in the Biographical Department, considerable Augmentations, extracted from the Life of the Doctor, recently published in Two 4to. Volumes, by Mr. Boswell.

Jan. 1, 1792.

PREFACE

TO THE

FIRST EDITION.

THE works of Dr. Johnson have been, occasionally, so much the object of my reading, for their fancy, judgment, and above all, the interesting and moral observations which they contain upon life and manners, that in order to impress those observations the better on my mind, I availed myself of some leisure months last summer, to select them under proper heads, and arrange them in alphabetical order. As I proceeded in this work, I found myself bringing out, into one view, a body of *maxims* and *observations*, which I imagined would be *more than useful to myself*; hence I thought it a duty incumbent on me to publish them.

Such is the origin of the present publication, a publication, that as I feel it has *benefitted* myself in the *compiling*, so I trust it will

will others in the *perufal*, and happy fhall I be, if, by any œconomy of mine in the works of fuch a writer, I can contribute to make them more generally *known* or *remembered*, as by it I am fure I fhall perform an effential fervice to mankind.

In refpect to the ufe of *felection*, (particularly as I have here applied it,) Dr. Johnfon makes the beft apology for me to the public, in his Idler, vol. ii. p. 185, and which, I hope, he will accept himfelf as an additional motive for this undertaking.

" Writers of extenfive comprehenfion, (fays he) have incidental remarks upon topics very remote from the principal fubject, which are often more valuable than formal treatifes, and which yet are not known, becaufe they are not promifed in the title. *He that collects thofe under proper heads, is very laudably employed*, for tho' he exerts no great abilities in the work, he facilitates the progrefs of others, and by making that eafy of attainment, which is already written, may give fome mind, more vigorous or more adventurous than his own, leisure for new thoughts, and original designs."

How far this selection is made with judgment, I must, however, trust to the decision of the public, well knowing that if it is negligently or ignorantly performed, any thing I can say, will not excuse me; if, on the contrary, I have done justice to my design, my telling them so will not accelerate their approbation. One thing I can assure them of, that I have made my extracts as accurately and judiciously as I could—and that whatever may be the fate of the book, I have been already repaid for my labours, by the satisfaction they have afforded me.

THE EDITOR.

November 24th, 1781.

CONTENTS.

	Page
BIOGRAPHICAL Anecdotes extracted from Mrs. Piozzi	xiv
Ditto from Mr. Boswell	xxxvii
Ditto from various Authorities	xlvi
Ditto from Mr. Boswell's Life of Johnson (just published)	li
General Rules of the Essex Head Club	lxxxii
List of the Members of ditto	lxxxiii
Authentic Copy of Dr. Johnson's Will	xcix
Speech of Dr. Dodd, previous to receiving Sentence	ciii
Dr. Dodd's Sermon to his fellow Convicts	cv
List of Dr. Johnson's Works	295

A	Page		Page
		Aphorisms	30
Ability	28	Appearances	29
Abstinence	27	Applause	ibid.
Academy	13	Army	30
Accident	28	Art	29
Actions	1	Arts	18
Address	27	Assurance	27
Admiration	26	Atheist	28
Adversary	26	Avarice	21
Adversity	22	Auction	27
Advertisement	27	Author	1
Advice	23	Axioms	30
Affectation	10		
Affection	ibid.	B	
Age	13	Beauty	33
Age Old, The Vanity of wishing for	16	Beauty, Danger of	36
		Benefits	32
Age and Youth	18	Benevolence	38
Agriculture	11	Biography	36
Agriculture of England	12	Books	31
Ambition	25	Bounties, Natural	39
Antients	21	Burlesque	33
Anger	19	Business	39
Anticipation	29	Bustlers	38

Calamity

(x)

C

	Page
Calamity	49
Calumny	69
Captivity	51
Care	50
Caution	69
Censure	46
Chance	48
Change	51
Character	47
Charity	44
Charity to Captives	45
Cheats	47
Children	61
Choice	50
City	68
Civility	52
Cleanliness	51
Commerce	41
Community	63
Companion	64
Comparison	67
Competency	52
Compilation	62
Complaint	48
Complaisance	43
Complacency (Self)	44
Compliment	67
Confidence	40
Conquests (European)	69
Conscience	51
Consolation	53
Contempt	52
Content	ibid
Controversy	68
Conveniencies	ibid.
Convict	61
Copies compared with Originals	66
Courage	63

	Page
Court	62
Credulity	61
Crimes	66
Criticism	55
Cunning	63
Curiosity	54
Custom	46

D

Death	71
Deception	77
Deception (Self)	ibid.
Delay	76
Delicacy	75
Delusion	81
Dependence	73
Desire	70
Devotion	77
Difficulty	81
Diffidence	74
Diligence	80
Disappointment	75
Disease	ibid.
Disguise	80
Distrust	76
Dulness	81
Duplicity	80
Duties	ibid.
Duty	79

E

Eating	94
Education	83
Effects not always proportioned to their Causes	91
Election	91
Elegance	92
Elegy	93
Empire	87
Employment	86

Emula-

	Page		Page
Emulation	83	Greatness	117
England	92	Guilt	115
Enquiry	83	**H.**	
Envy	81	Habits	121
Epitaph	90	Happiness	118
Equanimity	88	Happiness, Domestic	120
Error	89	Health	123
Essay-Writing	95	History	124
Esteem	91	Honour	127
Estimation	92	Hope	122
Evil	87	Humanity	123
Example	82	Humour, Good	125
Excellence	87	Humour, Good, compared with Gaiety	127
Exercise	93		
Expectation	91	Hypocrisy	ibid.
F.		**I.**	
Fable	107	Idleness	134
Faction	108	Jealousy	128
Falsehood	ibid	Jesting	ibid.
Fame	94	Ignorance	138
Fancy	107	Ignorance compared with Confidence	139
Fashion	108		
Father	95	Ignorance compared with Knowledge	138
Favour	107		
Faults	ibid	Imagination	142
Fear	103	Imitation	132
Flattery	100	Importance, Self	143
Folly	102	Imposition	142
Foreigner	103	Imprisonment	139
Forgiveness	104	Improvement, Rural	145
Fortitude	108	Imprudence	139
Fortune	103	Inclination	145
Friendship	95	Inconstancy	146
Frugality	105	Incredulity	144
G.		Indiscretion	132
Genius	109	Indolence	134
Good, Universal	116	Indulgence	145
Government	113	Industry	131
Government, Self	116	Innocence	146
Gratitude	117	Insult	144
		Integrity	

	Page		Page
Integrity	137	Maxims	183
Intelligence	143	Meanness	174
Intelligence, Foreign and Domestic	143	Memory	ibid.
		Merchant	ibid.
Interest	146	Method	183
Interest and Pride	ibid.	Mind	176
Joy	129	Mind, Progress of	179
Irresolution	143	Minuteness	180
Judgment	129	Mirth	181
Justice	130	Misery	ibid.
		Moderation	184
K.		Money	182
Kings	149	Motives	ibid.
Knowledge	147		
Knowledge, Self	149	N.	
		Nabobs, &c. English	184
L.		Narration	185
Language	158	Nations	186
Language, English	160	Nature	184
Laws	162	Negligence	185
Laws, Penal	163	Notes	186
Learning	155	Novelty	185
Letter Writing	165	Numbers	ibid.
Liberty	164	O.	
Life	151	Oaths	189
London	165	Obligation	ibid.
Love	157	Observation	190
Love, Self	ibid.	Opinion	188
Loyalty	164	Opportunity	189
M.			
Madness	174	P.	
Maids, Old	183	Pain	193
Malice	170	Painting	222
Man	ibid.	Parents	190
Manners	173	Passion	191
Marriage	166	Passions, Progress of	192
Marriage, Early	ibid.	Patience	216
Marriage, Late	169	Patriot	190
Marriage, Early and Late, Comparison between	170	Patronage	194
		Peace	214
		Pedantry	213
		Peevish-	

	Page		Page
Peevishness	211	Publications, Periodical	220
People	212	Punctuality	213
Perfection	215	**R.**	
Perfidy	ibid.	Raillery	225
Perseverance	216	Reason and Fancy	244
Philosophy	219	Rebellion	238
Physician	ibid.	Recollection	239
Piety	214	Refinement	238
Pity	218	Reflection	237
Plagiarism	224	Relaxation	240
Player	221	Religion	228
Pleasure	194	Repentance	241
Pleasures of Local Emotion	196	Reproof	245
		Reputation, Literary	243
Poets and Poetry	ibid.	Resolution	226
Poet, Dramatic, and Statesman, Comparison between	209	Respect	243
		Retaliation	240
		Retirement	239
Politeness	223	Revenge	243
Politics	205	Rhetorician	245
Poverty	203	Rhyme	244
Poverty and Idleness	205	Riches	229
Power	225	Riches and Power, Comparison between	235
Practice	214		
Praise	207	Riches & Understanding, Comparison between	235
Prayer, its proper Objects	210		
		Ridicule	236
Precipitancy	224	Right	245
Prejudice	214	Romans Antient, Character of	ib.
Pride	205		
Pride and Envy	ibid.	Rules	245
Prodigality	216	**S.**	
Promise	225	Satire	246
Prosperity	210	Satirist	ibid.
Providence	222	Scarcity	257
Prudence	213	Scepticism	249
Prudence and Justice	214	Science	259
Public	222	Scripture	255
Publications, Literary	220	Seasons	259
Publications, Occasional	221	Secrets	247
			Seduction

	Page		Pag
Seduction	249	**V.**	
Sense, Good	258	Vanity	272
Sentences	257	Vaunting	278
Separation	260	Verse, Blank	277
Shakespeare	258	Vice	ibid.
Shame	256	Virtue	274
Simile	255	Virtue, Access of	277
Singularity	253	Virtue, Intentional	276
Sobriety	257	Virtue, Romantic	ibid.
Solicitation	254		
Solitude	250	**U.**	
Sorrow	ibid.	Utility	278
Sports, Rural	258	Understanding	ibid.
Statesmen	260	Undertakings, Great	ibid.
Study	256	Unities of Time and	
Style	251	Place	279
Sublimity	259	Universality	278
Subordination	253		
Success and Miscarriage	257	**W.**	
Superfluities	258	War	280
Superiority	255	Weakness, Female	287
Suspicion	254	Wealth	288
		Wickedness	ibid.
T.		Wickedness, Splendid	290
Temptation	269	Wine	288
Theory	270	Wisdom	284
Things	ibid.	Wit	282
Thoughts	269	Women	285
Time	261	Wonder	290
Time past	263	World	285
Timidity	271	Writing Letters	289
Trade	265	Writing, Mechanical	ibid.
Tragedy	272	Writer of News	ibid.
Translation	271	Wrongs	ibid.
Travelling	264	**Y.**	
Treaties	270	Youth	290
Trifles	263	Youth, Progress of	291
Truth	265	Youth and Age	294

BIO-

Mr. Johnson sends compliments to Mr. Kempfly, and begs the favor of seeing him as soon as he can. Mr. Kempfly is desired as being acquainted with the late edition of what he has honored with the perusal of Beauties.

Mony, Dec. 17. 82

BIOGRAPHICAL ANECDOTES

OF

Dr. SAMUEL JOHNSON,

EXTRACTED FROM

The Productions of Mrs. *Piozzi* (late Mrs. *Thrale*) Mr. *Boswell*, and other authentic Papers.

WITH HIS

WILL, and a Fac-simile of his HAND-WRITING.
Also a SERMON written for Dr. DODD.

Extracts from Mrs. PIOZZI.

SAMUEL JOHNSON was the son of Michael Johnson, a bookseller, at Litchfield, in Staffordshire; a very pious and worthy man, but wrong-headed, positive, and afflicted with melancholy, as his son, from whom alone I had the information, once told me: his business, however, leading him to be much on horseback, contributed to the preservation of his bodily health, and mental sanity; which, when he staid long at home, would sometimes be about to give way; and Mr Johnson said, that when his work-shop, a detached building, had fallen half down for want of money to repair it, his father was not less diligent to lock the door every night, though he saw that any body might walk in at the back part, and knew that there was no security obtained by barring the front door. " *This*, (says his son, was madness, you may see, and would have been discoverable in other instances of the prevalence of imagination, but that poverty prevented it from playing such tricks as riches and leisure encourage."

He had an uncle, (Andrew) who kept the ring in Smithfield (where they wrestled and boxed) for a whole year,

year, and never was thrown or conquered. Mr. Johnson was very conversant in the art of attack and defence by boxing, which science he had learned from his uncle Andrew, I believe. Because he saw Mr. Thrale one day leap over a cabriolet stool, to shew that he was not tired after a chace of fifty miles or more, he suddenly jumped over it too; but in a way so strange and so unwieldy, that our terror, lest he should break his bones, took from us even the power of laughing.

Michael Johnson was past fifty years old when he married his wife, who was upwards of forty, yet I think her son told me she remained three years childless before he was born into the world, who so greatly contributed to improve it. In three years more she brought another son, Nathaniel, who lived to be twenty-seven or twenty-eight years old, and of whose manly spirit I have heard his brother speak with pride and pleasure.

Their father Michael died of an inflammatory fever, at the age of seventy-six, as Mr. Johnson told me: their mother at eighty nine, of a gradual decay. She was slight in her person, he said, and rather below than above the common size. So excellent was her character, and so blameless her life, that when an oppressive neighbour once endeavoured to take from her a little field she possessed, he could persuade no attorney to undertake the cause against a woman so beloved in her narrow circle.

At the age of two years Mr. Johnson was brought up to London by his mother, to be touched by Queen Anne for the scrophulous evil, which terribly afflicted his childhood, and left such marks as greatly disfigured a countenance naturally harsh and rugged, beside doing irreparable damage to the auricular organs, which never could perform their functions since I knew him; and it was owing to that horrible disorder, too, that one eye was perfectly useless to him; that defect, however, was not observable, the eyes looked both alike.

The trick which most parents play with their children, of shewing off their newly-acquired accomplishments, disgusted Mr. Johnson beyond expression; he had been treated so himself, he said, till he absolutely

loathed

loathed his father's carresses, because he knew they were sure to precede some unpleasing display of his early abilities; and he used, when neighbours came a visiting, to run up a tree, that he might not be found and exhibited, such, as no doubt he was, a prodigy of early understanding. His epitaph upon the duck he killed by treading on it at five years old,

> Here lies poor duck
> That Samuel Johnson trod on;
> If it had liv'd it had been good luck,
> For it would have been an odd one.

is a striking example of an early expansion of mind, and knowlege of language; yet he always seemed more mortified at the recollection of the bustle his parents made with his wit, than pleased with the thoughts of possessing it. " That, (said he to me one day) is the great misery of late marriages; the unhappy produce of them becomes the plaything of dotage: an old man's child, continued he, leads much such a life, I think, as a little boy's dog, teized with awkward fondness, and forced, perhaps, to sit up and beg as we call it, to divert a company, who at last go away complaining of their disagreeable entertainment."

Dr. Johnson first learned to read of his mother and her old maid Catharine, in whose lap he well remembered sitting while she explained to him the story of St. George and the Dragon.

At eight years old he went to school, for his health would not permit him to be sent sooner. When he was about nine years old, having got the play of Hamlet in his hand, and reading it quietly in his father's kitchen, he kept on steadily enough, till coming to the ghost scene, he suddenly hurried up stairs to the street door that he might see people about him.

Mr. Johnson was himself exceedingly disposed to the general indulgence of children, and was even scrupulously and ceremoniously attentive not to offend them: he had strongly persuaded himself of the difficulty people always find to erase early impressions either of kindness or resentment, and said, he should never have so loved his

his mother when a man, had she not given him coffee, she could ill afford, to gratify his appetite when a boy." If you had had children, Sir, said I, would you have taught them any thing? I hope (replied he) that I should have willingly lived on bread and water to obtain instruction for them.

The remembrance of what had passed in his own childhood, made Mr Johnson very solicitous to preserve the felicity of children; and when he had persuaded Dr. Sumner to remit the tasks usually given to fill up boys' time during the holidays, he rejoiced exceedingly in the success of his negociation, and told me that he had never ceased representing to all the eminent schoolmasters in England, the absurd tyranny of poisoning the hour of permitted pleasure, by keeping future misery before the children's eyes, and tempting them by bribery or falsehood to evade it.

At the age of eighteen Dr. Johnson quitted school, and escaped from the tuition of those he hated or those he despised.

Of his college life I have heard but little. Dr. Johnson delighted in his own partiality for Oxford; and one day at my house, entertained five members of the other university with various instances of the superiority of Oxford, enumerating the gigantic names of many men whom it had produced, with apparent triumph. At last I said to him, Why there happens to be no less than five Cambridge men in the room now. "I did not (said he) think of that till you told me; but the wolf don't count the sheep."

I have heard him relate how he used to sit in some coffee-house at Oxford, and turn Mason's Caracticus into ridicule for the diversion of himself and of chance comers-in. "The Elfrida (says he) was too exquisitely pretty; I could make no fun out of that." When upon some occasions he would express his astonishment that he should have an enemy in the world, while he had been doing nothing but good to his neighbours, I used to make him recollect these circumstances: "Why child (said he) what harm could that do the fellow? I always thought very well of Mason for a *Cambridge* man; he
is,

is, I believe, a mighty blameless character." Such tricks were, however, the more unpardonable in Mr. Johnson, because no one could harangue like him about the difficulty always found in forgiving petty injuries, or in provoking by needless offence.

Mr. Johnson made us all laugh one day, because I had received a remarkable fine Stilton cheese as a present from some person who had packed and directed it carefully, but without mentioning whence it came, Mr. Thrale, desirous to know who we were obliged to, asked every friend as they came in, but nobody owned it: " Depend upon it, Sir, (says Johnson) it was sent by *Junius.*"

The False Alarm, his first and favourite pamphlet, was written at our house between eight o'clock on Wednesday night and twelve o'clock on Thursday night; we read it to Mr. Thrale when he came very late home from the house of Commons.

Facility of writing, and dilatoriness ever to write, Mr. Johnson always retained, from the days that he lay a-bed, and dictated his first publication to Mr. Hector, who acted as his amanuensis, to the moment he made me copy out those variations in Pope's Homer, which were printed in the Poets Lives:—The fine Rambler on the subject of Procrastination was hastily composed, as I have heard, in Sir Joshua Reynolds's parlour, while the boy waited to carry it to press: and numberless are the instances of his writing under immediate pressure of importunity or distress. He told me that the character of *Sober* in the Idler, was by himself intended as his own portrait; and that he had his own outset into life in his eye when he wrote the eastern story of Gelaleddin. Of the allegorical papers in the Rambler, Labour and Rest were his favourite; but Serotinus, the man who returns late in life to receive honours in his native country, and meets with mortification instead of respect, was by him considered as a master-piece in the science of life and manners. The character of Prospero in the fourth volume, Garrick took to be his: and I have heard the author say, that he never forgave the offence. Sophron was likewise a picture drawn from reality; and by Gelidus

lidus the philosopher, he meant to represent Mr Coulon, a mathematician who formerly lived at Rochester. The man immortalised for purring like a cat was, as he told me, one Busby, a proctor in the Commons. He who barked so ingeniously, and then called the drawer to drive away the dog, was father to Dr. Salter of the Charterhouse. He who sung a song, and by correspondent motions of his arm chalked out a giant on the wall, was one Richardson, an attorney. The letter signed Sunday, was written by Mis Talbot; and he fancied the billets in the first volume of the Rambler, were sent him by Miss Mulso, now Mrs. Chapone. The papers contributed by Mrs. Carter, had much of his esteem, though he always blamed me for preferring the letter signed Charietta to the allegory, where religion and superstition are, indeed, most masterly delineated.

Dr. Johnson was liberal enough in granting literary assistance to others, I think; and innumerable are the prefaces, sermons, lectures, and dedications, which he used to make for people who begged of him. Mr. Murphy related in his and my hearing one day, and he did not deny it, that when Murphy joked him the week before for having been so diligent of late between Dodd's sermon and Kelly's prologue, that Dr. Johnson replied, " Why Sir, when they come to me with a dead stay-maker and a dying parson, what can a man do." He *said*, however, " that he hated to give away literary performances, or even to sell them too cheaply: the next generation shall not accuse me (added he) of beating down the price of literature: one hates, besides, ever to give that which one has been accustomed to sell; would not you, Sir, (returning to Mr. Thrale) rather give away money than porter.

When Davies printed the Fugitive Pieces without his knowledge or consent; How, said I, would Pope have raved, had he been served so? " We should never (replied he) have heard the last on't, to be sure; but then Pope was a narrow man: I will, however, added, he) storm and bluster *myself* a little this time;"—so went to London in all the wrath he could muster up. At his return I asked how the affair ended: " Why (said)

(said he) I was a fierce fellow, and pretended to be very angry, and Thomas was a good-natured fellow, and pretended to be very sorry : so *there* the matter ended.

Somebody was praising Corneille one day in opposition to Shakespeare : Corneille is to Shakespeare (replied Mr. Johnson) as a clipped hedge is to a forest."

Of a much admired poem, when extolled as beautiful, (he replied) "That it had indeed the beauty of a bubble : the colours are gay, (said he) but the substance slight."

Of James Harris's Dedication to his Hermes I have heard him observe, that though but fourteen lines long, there were six grammatical faults in it. A friend was praising the style of Dr. Swift; Mr. Johnson did not find himself in the humour to agree with him : the critic was driven from one of his performances to the other. At length you must allow me, said the gentleman, that there are *strong facts* in the account of the Four last Years of Queen Anne : " Yes, surely Sir, (replies Johnson) and so there are in the Ordinary of Newgate's Account."

When I one day lamented the loss of a first cousin, killed in America—" Prithee, my dear, (said he) have done with canting : how would the world be worse for it, I may ask if all your relations were spitted at once like larks, and roasted for Presto's supper ?" Presto was the dog that lay under the table while we talked.

I was observing to the Doctor, that an acquaintance lost the almost certain hope of a good estate that had been long expected. Such a one will grieve (said I) at her friend's disappointment. " She will suffer as much perhaps, (said he) as your horse did when your cow miscarried."

The piety of Dr. Johnson was exemplary and edifying : he was punctiliously exact to perform every public duty enjoined by the church, and his spirit of devotion had an energy that affected all who ever saw him pray in private. The coldest and most languid hearers of the word must have felt themselves animated by his manner of reading the holy scriptures; and to pray by his sick bed, required strength of body as well as of mind, so vehement were his manners, and his tones of voice so pathetic. I have many times made it my request to heaven

heaven that I might be spared the sight of his death; and I was spared it!

Mr. Johnson, though in general a gross feeder, kept fast in Lent, particularly the holy week, with a rigour very dangerous to his general health.

On some occasion, when he was musing over the fire in our drawing-room at Streatham, a young gentleman called to him suddenly, and I suppose he thought disrespectfully, in these words: Mr. Johnson, Would you advise me to marry! " I could advise no man to marry, Sir, (returns for answer in a very angry tone Dr. Johnson) who is not likely to propagate understanding;" and so left the room.

Sir Joshua Reynolds mentioned some picture as excellent. " It has often grieved me, Sir, (said Mr. Johnson) to see so much mind as the science of painting requires, laid out upon such perishing materials: why do not you oftener make use of copper? I could wish your superiority in the art you profess, to be preserved in stuff more durable than canvas." Sir Joshua urged the difficulty of procuring a plate large enough for historical subjects, and was going to raise further observations: " What foppish obstacles are these! exclaims on a sudden Dr. Johnson:) Here is Thrale has a thousand ton of copper; you may paint it all round if you will, I suppose; it will serve him to brew in afterwards: Will it not, Sir? (to my husband who sat by). Such speeches may appear offensive to many, but those who knew he was too blind to discern the perfections of an art which applies itself immediately to our eye-sight, must acknowledge he was not wrong.

He delighted no more in music than painting; he was almost as deaf as he was blind: travelling with Dr. Johnson was for these reasons tiresome enough. Mr. Thrale loved prospects, and was mortified that his friend could not enjoy the sight of those different dispositions of wood and water, hill and valley, that travelling through England and France affords a man. But when he wished to point them out to his companion: " Never heed such nonsense," would be the reply: " a blade of grass is always a blade of grass, whether
in

in one country or another: let us if we *do* talk, talk about something; men and women are my subjects of enquiry; let us see how these differ from those we have left behind."

When at Versailles the people shewed us the theatre. As we stood on the stage looking at some machinery for playhouse purposes: Now we are here, what shall we act Mr. Johnson.—The Englishman at Paris? "No, no, (replied he) we will try to act Henry the Fifth." His dislike of the French was well known to both nations, I believe.

Johnson's own notions about eating however were nothing less than delicate; a leg of pork boiled till it dropped from the bone, a veal pye with plums and sugar, or the outside of a salt buttock of beef, were his favourite dainties; with regard to drink, his liking was for the strongest, as it was not the flavour, but the effect he sought for, and professed to desire; and when I first knew him, he used to pour capillaire into his Port wine. For the last twelve years, however, he left off all fermented liquors. To make himself some amends indeed, he took his chocolate liberally, pouring in large quantities of cream, or even melted butter; and was so fond of fruit, that though he usually eat seven or eight large peaches of a morning before breakfast begun, and treated them with proportionate attention after dinner again, yet I have heard him protest that he never had quite as much as he wished of wall-fruit, except once in his life, and that was when we were all together at Omberstey, the seat of my Lord Sandys.

After a very long summer, particularly hot and dry, I was wishing naturally, but thoughtlessly, for some rain to lay the dust as we drove along the Surry roads. "I cannot bear (replied he, with much asperity and an altered look) when I know how many poor families will perish next winter for want of that bread which the present drought will deny them, to hear ladies sighing for rain, only that their complexions may not suffer from the heat, or their clothes be incommoded by the dust;—for shame! leave off such foppish lamentations, and study to relieve those whose distresses are real."

With

With advising others to be charitable, however, Dr. Johnson did not content himself. He gave away all he had, and all he ever had gotten, except the two thousand pounds he left behind; and the very small portion of his income which he spent upon himself, with all our calculation, we never could make more than seventy, or at most fourscore pounds a year, and he pretended to allow himself an hundred. He had numberless dependents out of doors as well as in, " who (as he expressed it) did not like to see him latterly, unless he brought them money." For those people he used frequently to raise contributions on his richer friends; and this (says he) is one of the thousand reasons which ought to restrain a man from drony solitude and useless retirement."

The Doctor was very athletic. Garrick told a good story of him. He said, that in their young days, when some strolling players came to Litchfield, our friend had fixed his place upon the stage, and got himself a chair accordingly; which, leaving for a few minutes, he found a man in it at his return, who refused to give it back at the first intreaty: Mr. Johnson, however, who did not think it worth his while to make a second, took chair and man and all together, and threw them all at once into the pit. I asked the Doctor if this was a fact? " Garrick has not *spoiled* it in the telling (said he) it is very *near* true to be sure."

Mr. Beauclerk too related one day, how on some occasion he ordered two large mastiffs into his parlour, to shew a friend who was conversant in canine beauty and excellence, how the dogs quarrelled, and fastening on each other, alarmed all the company except Johnson, who, seizing one in one hand by the cuff of the neck, the other in the other hand, said gravely, " Come gentlemen! where's your difficulty? put one dog out at the door, and I will shew this fierce gentleman the way out of the window;" which, lifting up the mastiff and the sash, he contrived to do very expeditiously, and much to the satisfaction of the affrighted company. We inquired as to the truth of this curious recital. " The dogs have been somewhat magnified, I believe Sir: (was the reply)

reply) they were, as I remember, two stout young pointers; but the story has gained but little."

I have forgotten the year, but it could scarely I think be later than 1765 or 1766, that he was called abruptly from our house after dinner, and returning in about three hours, said, he had been with an enraged author, whose landlady pressed him for payment within doors, while the bailiffs beset him without; that he was drinking himself drunk with Madeira to drown care, and fretting over a novel which when finished was to be his whole fortune; but he could not get it done for distraction, nor could he step out of doors to offer it to sale. Mr. Johnson therefore set away the bottle, and went to the bookseller, recommending the performance, and desiring some immediate relief; which, when he brought back to the writer, he called the woman of the house directly to partake of punch, and pass their time in merriment.

It was not till ten years after, I dare say, that something in Dr. Goldsmith's behaviour struck me with an idea that he was the very man, and then Johnson confessed that it was so: the novel was the charming Vicar of Wakefield.

There was a Mr. Boyce too, who wrote some very elegant verses printed in the Magazines of five and twenty years ago, of whose ingenuity and distress I have heard Dr. Johnson tell some curious anecdotes; particularly, that when he was almost perishing with hunger, and some money was produced to purchase him a dinner, he got a bit of roast beef, but could not eat it without ketchup, and laid out the last half guinea he possessed in truffles and mushrooms, eating them in bed too, for want of clothes, or even a shirt to set up in.

Mr. Johnson loved late hours extremely, or more properly hated early ones Nothing was more terrifying to him than the idea of retiring to bed, hich he never would call going to rest, or suffer another to call so. " I lie down (said he) that my acquaintance may sleep; but I lie down to endure oppressive misery, and soon rise again to pass the night in anxiety and pain " By this pathetic manner, which no one ever possessed in so eminent

nent a degree, he used to shock me from quitting his company, till I hurt my own health not a little by sitting up with him when I was myself far from well. I often made tea for him in London till four o'clock in the morning. At Streatham indeed I managed better, having always some friend who was kind enough to engage him in talk, and favour my retreat.

The first time I ever saw this extraordinary man was in the year 1764, when Mr. Murphy, who had been long the friend and confidential intimate of Mr. Thrale, persuaded him to wish for Johnson's conversation, extolling it in terms which that of no other person could have deserved, till we were only in doubt how to obtain his company, and find an excuse for the invitation. The celebrity of Mr. Woodhouse, a shoemaker, whose verses were at that time the subject of common discourse, soon afforded a pretence, and Mr. Murphy brought Johnson to meet him, giving me general cautions not to be surprised at his figure, dress, or behaviour. What I recollect best of the day's talk, was his earnestly recommending Addison's works to Mr. Woodhouse as a model for imitation. "Give nights and days, Sir, (said he) to the study of Addison, if you mean either to be a good writer, or what is more worth, an honest man." When I saw something like the same expression in his criticism on that author, lately published, I put him in mind of his past injunctions to the young poet, to which he replied, "That he wished the shoemaker might have remembered them as well." Mr. Johnson liked his new acquaintance so much however, that from that time he dined with us every Thursday through the winter.

In the year 1766, his health, which he had always complained of, grew so exceedingly bad, that he could not stir out of his room in the court * he inhabited, for many *weeks* together, I think *months*.

Mr. Thrale soon after prevailed on him to quit his close habitation in the court and come with us to Streatham, where I undertook the care of his health, and had the honour and happiness of contributing to its restoration. One

---

* He then lived in Johnson's Court, Fleet Street, whence he afterwards removed to Bolt Court, where he died.

One day, when he was not pleased with our dinner, I asked him if he ever huffed his wife about his dinner? "So often (replied he) that at last she called to me, and said, Nay, hold, Mr. Johnson, and do not make a farce of thanking God for a dinner which in a few minutes you will protest not eatable."

Avarice was a vice against which, however, I never much heard Mr. Johnson declaim, till one represented it to him connected with cruelty, or some such disgraceful companion. "Do not (said he) discourage your children from hoarding, if they have a taste to it: whoever lays up his penny rather than part with it for a cake, at least is not the slave of gross appetite; and shews besides a preference always to be esteemed, of the future to the present moment. Such a mind may be made a good one; but the natural spendthrift, who grasps his pleasure greedily and coarsely, and cares for nothing but immediate indulgence, is very little to be valued above a negroe." We talked of Lady Tavistock, who grieved herself to death for the loss of her husband. "She was rich, and wanted employment (says Johnson) so she cried till she lost all power of restraining her tears: other women are forced to outlive their husbands, who were just as much beloved, depend on it; but they have no time for grief: and I doubt not, if we had put my Lady Tavistock into a small chandler's shop, and given her a nurse-child to tend, her life would have been saved. The poor and the busy have no leisure for sentimental sorrow."

I pitied a friend before him, who had a whining wife that found every thing painful to her, and nothing pleasing.—"He does not know that she whimpers, (says Johnson), when a door has creaked for a fortnight together, you may observe—the master will scarcely give sixpence to get it oiled."

For a lady of quality, since dead, who received us at her husband's seat in Wales with less attention than he had long been accustomed to, he had a rougher denunciation: "That woman (cries Johnson) is like four small-beer, the beverage of her table."

Mr. Johnson's hatred of the Scotch is so well known, and so many of his *bon mots* expressive of that hatred have been already repeated in so many books and pamphlets, that it is perhaps scarcely worth while to write down the conversation between him and a friend of that nation who always resides in London, and who at his return from the Hebrides asked him, with a firm tone of voice, What he thought of his country? " That it is a very vile country to be sure, Sir; (returned for answer Dr. Johnson.) Well, Sir! replies the other somewhat mortified, God made it. " Certainly he did (answers Mr. Johnson again); but we must always remember that he made it for Scotchmen."

Mr. Johnson made Dr. Goldsmith a comical answer one day, when seeming to repine at the success of Beattie's Essay on Truth---" Here's such a stir (said he) about a fellow that has written one book, and I have written many." Ah, Doctor (says his friend) there go two-and-forty sixpences you know to one guinea.

Dr. Johnson was indeed famous for disregarding public abuse. When the people criticised and answered his pamphlets papers, &c. " Why now these fellows are only advertising my book (he would say); it is surely better a man should be abused than forgotten."

He once bade a very celebrated lady who praised him with too much zeal perhaps, (which always offended him), consider what her flattery was worth before she choaked him with it."

We were talking of Richardson, who wrote Clarissa: " You think I love flattery (says Dr. Johnson), and so I do; but a little too much always disgusts me: that fellow Richardson, on the contrary, could not be contented to sail quietly down the stream of reputation, without longing to taste the froth from every stroke of the oar."

With regard to slight insults from newspaper abuse, I have already declared his notions: They sting one (says he) but as a fly stings a horse: and the eagle will not catch flies.

Mr. Johnson hated what we call unprofitable chat; and to a gentleman who had differed some time about the natural history of the mouse—" I wonder what such a one would have said (cried Johnson), if he had ever had the luck to see a lion!"

A young fellow, less confident of his own abilities, lamenting one day that he had lost all his Greek—" I believe it happened at the same time, Sir, (said Johnson), that I lost all my large estate in Yorkshire."

But however roughly he might be suddenly provoked to treat a harmless exertion of vanity, he did not wish to inflict the pain he gave, and was sometimes very sorry when he perceived the people to smart more than they deserved. How harshly you treated that man to-day, said I once, who harrangued us about gardening,—" I am sorry (said he) if I vexed the creature for there certainly is no harm in a fellow's rattling a rattle-box, only don't let him think that he thunders."

A Lincolnshire lady shewed him a grotto she had been making: Will it not be a pretty cool habitation in summer? said she, Mr. Johnson! " I think it would, Madam (replied he) for a toad."

All desire of distinction had a sure enemy in Mr. Johnson. We met a friend driving six very small ponies, and stopped to admire them. " Why does nobody (said our doctor) begin the fashion of driving six spavined horses, all spavined of the same leg? it would have a mighty pretty effect, and produce the distinction of doing something worse than the common way."

When Mr. Johnson had a mind to compliment any one, he did it with more dignity to himself, and better effect upon the company, than any man. I can recollect but few instances indeed, though perhaps that may be more my fault than his. When Sir Joshua Reynolds left the room one day, he said, There goes a man not to be spoiled by prosperity." And when Mrs. Montague shewed him some China plates which had once belonged to Queen Elizabeth, he told her, " that they had no reason to be ashamed of their present possessor, who was so little inferior to the first."

He sometimes rode on Mr. Thrale's old hunter with a good firmness, and though he would follow the hounds fifty miles an end sometimes, would never own himself either tired or amused. He was, however, proud to be amongst the sportsmen; and I think no praise ever went so close to his heart, as when Mr. Hamilton called out one day upon Brighthelmstone Downs, Why Johnson rides as well, for ought I see, as the most illiterate fellow in England.

He said of Edmund Burke, "that you could not stand five minutes with that man beneath a shed while it rained, but you must be convinced you had been standing with the greatest man you had ever yet seen."

Dr. Johnson's knowledge of literary history was extensive and surprising: he knew every adventure of every book you could name almost, and was exceedingly pleased with the opportunity which writing the Poets Lives gave him to display it. He loved to be set at work, and was sorry when he came to the end of the business he was about. I do not feel so myself with regard to these sheets: a fever, which has preyed on me while I wrote them over for the press, will perhaps lessen my power of doing well the first, and probably the last work, I should ever have thought of presenting to the Public. I could doubtless wish so to conclude it, as at least to shew my zeal for my friend, whose life, as I once had the honour and happiness of being useful to, I should wish to record a few particular traits of, that those who read should emulate his goodness; but seeing the necessity of making even virtue and learning such as his agreeable, that all should be warned against such coarseness of manners, as drove even from him those who loved, honoured, and esteemed him.

I made one day very minute enquiries about the tale of his knocking down Tom Osborne the bookseller, with his own Dictionary in his shop. And how was that affair, in earnest? do tell me, Mr. Johnson? "There is nothing to tell, dearest Lady, but that he was insolent and I beat him, and that he was a blockhead and told of it. I have beat many a fellow, but the rest had the wit to hold their tongues."

It was a perpetual miracle that he did not set himself on fire reading a bed, as was his constant custom, when exceedingly unable to keep clear of mischief with our best help; and accordingly the fore-top of all his wigs were

were burned by the candle down to the very net-work. Mr. Thrale's valet-de-chambre, for that reason, kept one always in his own hands, with which he met him at the parlour door when the bell had called him down to dinner, and as he went up stairs to sleep in the afternoon, the same man constantly followed him with another.

No man conversed so well as he on every subject; no man so acutely discerned the reason of every fact, the motive of every action, the end of every design. He was indeed often pained by the ignorance or causeless wonder of those who knew less than himself, though he seldom drove them away with apparent scorn, unless he thought they added presumption to stupidity.

I saw Mr. Johnson in none but a tranquil uniform state, passing the evening of his life among friends, who loved, honoured, and admired him: I saw none of the things he did, except such acts of charity as have been often mentioned in this book, and such writings as are universally known. What he said is all I can relate; and from what he said, those who think it worth while to read these Anecdotes, must be contented to gather his character. Mine is a mere candle-light picture of his latter days, where every thing falls in dark shadow except the face, the index of the mind; but even that is seen unfavourably, and with a paleness beyond what nature gave it.

He had a strong aversion to four-footed favourites, notwithstanding he had for many years a cat which he called Hodge, that kept always in his room at Fleet-street; but so exact was he not to offend the human species by superfluous attention to brutes, that when the creature was grown sick and old, and could eat nothing but oysters, Mr. Johnson always went out himself to buy Hodge's dinner, that Francis the Black's delicacy might not be hurt at seeing himself employed for the conveniency of a quadruped.

No one was indeed so attentive not to offend in all such sort of things, as Dr. Johnson; nor so careful to maintain the ceremonies of life: and though he told Mr. Thrale once, that he had never sought to please till past thirty years old, considering the matter as hopeless, he had been always studious not to make enemies, by apparent preference of himself. It happened very comically, that the moment this curious conversation past, of which I was a silent auditress, was in the coach, in some distant province, either Shropshire or Derbyshire I believe, and as soon as it was over, Mr. Johnson took out of his pocket a little book and read, while a gentleman of no small distinction for his birth and elegance, suddenly rode up to the carriage, and paying us all his proper compliments, was desirous not to neglect Dr. Johnson; but observing that he did not see him, tapt him gently on the shoulder—'Tis Mr. Ch--lm-ley, says my husband;—" Well, Sir! and what if it is Mr. Ch--lm-ley!" says the other sternly, just lifting his eyes a moment from his book, and returning to it again with renewed avidity.

I enquired of him concerning his account of the state of literature in Scotland, which was repeated up and down at one time by every body—" How knowledge was divided among the Scots, like bread in a besieged town, to every man a mouthful, to no man a bellyful.' This story he likewise acknowledged, and said besides, " that some officious friend had carried it to Lord Bute, who only answered—Well, well! never mind what he says—he will have the pension all one."

Another famous reply to a Scotsman who commended the beauty and dignity of Glasgow, till Mr. Johnson stopped him by observing, " that he probably had never yet seen Brentford, was one of the jokes he owned: and said himself, " that when a gentleman of that country once mentioned the lovely prospects common in his nation, he could not help telling him, that the view of the London road was the prospect in which every Scotsman most naturally and most rationally delighted."

He loved the sight of fine forest trees, however, and detested Brighthelmstone Downs, " because it was a country so truly desolate (he said), that if one had a mind to hang one's self for desperation at being obliged to live there, it would be difficult to find a tree on which to fasten the rope." Walking in a wood when it rained, was, I think the only rural image he pleased his fancy with;

with; "for (says he) after one has gathered the apples in an orchard, one wishes them well baked, and removed to a London eating-house for enjoyment."

With such notions, who can wonder he passed his time uncomfortably enough with us, whom he often complained of for living so much in the country; feeding the chickens (as he said I did) till I starved my own understanding. Get, however, (said he) a book about gardening, and study it hard, since you will pass your life with birds and flowers, and learn to raise the *largest* turnips, and to breed the *biggest* fowls. It was vain to assure him that the goodness of such dishes did not depend on their size; he laughed at the people who covered their canals with foreign fowls, when (says he) our own geese and ganders are twice as large: if we fetched better animals from distant nations, there might be some sense in the preference; but to get cows from Alderney, or water-fowl from China, only to see nature degenerating round one, is a poor ambition indeed."

When ill, he conjured me solemnly to tell him what I thought: Sir Richard Jebb was perpetually on the road to Streatham, and Mr. Johnson seemed to think himself neglected if the physician left him for an hour only; I made him a steady, but, as I thought, a very gentle harangue, in which I confirmed all that the Doctor had been saying, how no present danger could be expected; but that his age and continued ill health must naturally accelerate the arrival of that hour which can be escaped by none: "And this (says Johnson, rising in great anger) is the voice of female friendship I suppose, when the hand of the hangman would be softer."

I commended a young lady for her beauty and pretty behaviour one day, however, to whom I thought no objection could have been made. "I saw her (says Dr. Johnson) take a pair of scissars in her left hand though; and for all her father is now become a nobleman, and as you say excessively rich, I should, were I a youth of quality ten years hence, hesitate between a girl so neglected, and a *negro*."

It really surprised me to see the victory he gained over a Lady little accustomed to contradiction, who had dressed herself for church at Streatham one Sunday morning, in a manner he did not approve, and to whom he said such sharp and pungent things concerning her hat, her gown, &c. that she hastened to change them, and returning quite another figure received his applause, and thanked him for his reproofs, much to the amazement of her husband, who could scarcely believe his own ears.

All these exactnesses in a man who was nothing less than exact himself, made him extremely impracticable as an inmate, though most instructive as a companion, and useful as a friend. Mr. Thrale too could sometimes over-rule his rigidity, by saying coldly, There, there, now we have had enough for one lecture, Dr. Johnson; we will not be upon education any more till after dinner, if you please—or some such speech; but when there was nobody to restrain his dislikes, it was extremely difficult to find any body with whom he could converse, without living always on the verge of a quarrel, or of something too like a quarrel to be pleasing.

This disposition occurred too often, and I was forced to take advantage of my lost law suit, and plead inability of purse to remain longer in London or its vicinage. I had been crossed in my intentions of going abroad, and found it convenient, for every reason of health, peace, and pecuniary circumstances, to retire to Bath, where I knew Mr. Johnson would not follow me, and where I could for that reason command some little portion of time for my own use; a thing impossible while I remained at Streatham or at London, as my hours, carriage, and servants had long been at his command, who would not rise in the morning till twelve o'clock perhaps, and oblige me to make breakfast for him till the bell rung for dinner, though much displeased if the toilet was neglected, and though much of the time we passed together was spent in blaming or deriding, very justly, my neglect of œconomy, and waste of that money which might make many families happy. The original reason of our connection, his *particularly disordered health and spirits*, had been long at an end, and he had no
other

other ailments than old age, and general infirmity, which every professor of medicine was ardently zealous and generally attentive to palliate, and to contribute all in their power for the prolongation of a life so valuable. Veneration for his virtue, reverence for his talents, delight in his conversation, and habitual endurance of a yoke my husband first put upon me, and of which he contentedly bore his share for sixteen or seventeen years, made me go on so long with Mr Johnson; but the perpetual confinement, I will own to have been terrifying in the first years of our friendship, and irksome in the last: nor could I pretend to support it without help, when my coadjutor was no more. To the assistance we gave him, the shelter our house afforded to his uneasy fancies, and to the pains we took to sooth or repress them, the world perhaps is indebted for the three political pamphlets, the new edition and correction of his Dictionary, and for the Poets Lives, which he would scarce have lived, I think, and kept his faculties entire, to have written, had not incessant care been exerted at the time of his first coming to be our constant guest in the country; and several times after that, when he found himself particularly oppressed with diseases incident to the most vivid and fervent imaginations. I shall for ever consider it as the greatest honour which could be conferred on any one, to have been the confidential friend of Dr. Johnson's health, and to have in some measure, with Mr. Thrale's assistance, saved from distress at least, if not from worse, a mind great beyond the comprehension of common mortals, and good beyond all hope of imitation from perishable beings.

It is usual, I know not why, when a character is given, to begin with a description of the person; that which contained the soul of Mr Johnson deserves to be particularly described. His stature was remarkably high, and his limbs exceedingly large: his strength was more than common I believe, and his activity had been greater I have heard than such a form gave one reason to expect: his features were strongly marked, and his countenance particularly rugged; though the original complexion had certainly been fair, a circumstance somewhat unusual: his sight was near, and otherwise imperfect; yet his eyes, though of a light-grey colour, were so wild, so piercing, and at times so fierce, that fear was I believe the first emotion in the hearts of all his beholders. His mind was so comprehensive, that no language but that he used could have expressed its contents; and so ponderous was his language, that sentiments less lofty and less solid than his were, would have been encumbered, not adorned by it.

As his purse was ever open to alms-giving, so was his heart tender to those who wanted relief, and his soul susceptible of gratitude, and of every kind impression: yet though he had refined his sensibility, he had not endangered his quiet, by encouraging in himself a solicitude about trifles, which he treated with the contempt they deserve.

No man had stronger likings or aversions. His veracity was indeed, from the most trivial to the most solemn occasions, strict, even to severity; he scorned to embellish a story with fictious circumstances, which (he used to say) took off from its real value. A story (says Johnson) should be a specimen of life and manners; but if the surrounding circumstances are false, as it is no more a representation of reality, it is no longer worthy our attention."

Though a man of obscure birth himself, his partiality to people of family was visible on every occasion; his zeal for subordination warm even to bigotry; his hatred of innovation, and reverence for the old feudal times, apparent, whenever any possible manner of shewing them occurred. I have spoken of his piety, his charity, and his truth, the enlargement of his heart, and the delicacy of his sentiments. The mind of this man was indeed expanded beyond the common limits of human nature, and stored with such variety of knowledge, that I used to think it resembled a royal pleasure-ground, where every plant, of every name and nation, flourished in the full perfection.

The account of our author from whence the foregoing passages have been extracted, abounds with interesting and entertaining

entertaining information, which the Editor of this volume begs leave to recommend to the public.

When the first Edition of these Beauties appeared, the account of Dr. Johnson, who was then living, was drawn from sources less to be depended upon: however, they were, though not so interesting, in general authentic.

These anecdotes of Mrs. PIOZZI's, *at once display close observation, great attention, a strong memory, a lively imagination and an exalted mind. In a few words, a sound understanding, and a benevolent heart.*

Doctor Johnson had some failings, from which the most perfect are not exempt; these are noticed by Mrs. P. with the delicacy of sincere friendship, whilst his virtues are most amiably displayed, as a pattern for others.

༺༺༺༺༺༺༺༺༺༺༺༺༺༺༺

We will now entertain our Readers with a few Extracts from Mr. BOSWELL's Description of a Tour to the HEBRIDES, in which he accompanied the DOCTOR.

Etxracts from Mr. BOSWELL.

LORD NORTH, at the instance of the late Mr. Thrale, had some notions of bringing Dr. Johnson into parliament; and they had two meetings for that purpose, to which it appears the Doctor " was nothing loth. His Lordship, however, doubting the success of such an experiment, afterwards declined it, which the Doctor could never forgive, " That fellow, he used sometimes to say, speaking of Lord North, has a mind as narrow as the neck of a vinegar cruit"—and at another time, when mentioned as a minister—" No, Sir, there is at present no minister in parliament—Lord North's but the agent of a minister."

Mr. Boswell telling the Doctor, that when he was young and freakish, he one night at Drury Lane theatre, entertained the audience before the play by lowing like a cow. Soon after this, differing with Dr. Johnson

Johnson, upon some subject, the latter replied, "Nay, Sir, if you cannot talk better as a man, I'd have you still bellow like a cow."

The first night Dr. Johnson got to Edinburgh, walking up the High-street, arm in arm with Boswell, at a time when the well known effluvia of that capital was pretty strong; his friend observed, "Well, now Doctor, we are at last in Scotland." "Yes, Sir, cried the Doctor, grumbling, I smell it in the dark."

Seeing a board on the great door of the Royal Infirmary at Edinburgh with this inscription, "Clean your feet" just after he had quitted the high church, which was at that time shamefully dirty, he turned about to Dr. Robertson—"There is no occasion for putting such a board as this at the doors of your churches.

Being asked to see the room at Dumferline where Charles the First was born, he replied, "No, I know that he was born, and it is no matter where."

Speaking of the superior assiduity of the Scottish over the English clergy, in *instructing* their parishioners; Johnson replied with some warmth, "I do not believe your people are better instructed; if they are, it is the blind leading the blind, for your clergy are not instructed themselves."

Having lost his oak stick in Mull, an inconsiderable little island in the Hebrides, he suspected his guide had stolen it—but his fellow-traveller endeavouring to persuade him it was not so, and that it would be restored him again, he replied—"No, Sir, it is not to be expected that any man in Mull who has got it will part with it—consider the value of *such a piece of timber here.*"

BIBLE.

Talking of Dr. Kennicott's translation of the Bible, the company expressed a wish it might be quite faithful. "Sir, I know not any crime so great that a man could contrive to commit, as poisoning the sources of eternal truth."

BIOGRAPHY.

"I do not think the life of any literary man in England well written—Beside the common incidents of life it it should tell us his studies, his mode of living——the means by which he attained to excellence, and his opinion of his own works."

He said, that Dr. Birch had more anecdotes than any man—Boswell observed, "Dr. Percy had a great many, that he flowed with them like one of the Scotch brooks."
"Sir, if Percy is like one of your brooks—Birch is like the River Thames—Birch excels Percy, as much as Percy excels Goldsmith.

CONVERSATION AND READING.

Sir, they should be mixed like eating and exercise; the one digests the other.

Q. But is not the man of conversation the *readier* and more agreeable man?

A. Sir, he may have more *money* about him, but then you are to consider he has *no fortune*.

CARDS.

I am sorry I have not learned to play at cards—it is very useful in life—as moderate play generates kindness and consolidates society.

CHARITY.

If thoughtlessly given, we may neglect the most deserving objects, and as every man has but a certain proportion to give, if it is lavished upon those who first present themselves, there may be nothing left for such who have a better claim. A man should first relieve those who are nearly connected with him by whatever ties; and then, if he has any thing to spare, he may extend his bounty to a wider circle.

LORD THURLOW.

Speaking of the present Lord Chancellor, long before he came into his present high office. "I honour Thurlow, Sir, he's a fine fellow—he looks for the truth in conversation, and in the research fairly puts his mind to yours."

SMOAKING.

" Smoaking has gone out. To be sure it is a shocking thing, blowing smoak out of our mouths into other people

people's mouth, eyes, and nofes, and having the fame thing done to us.

CLEANLINESS.

I remember when people in England changed a fhirt only once a week.

FIRE.

Formerly good tradefmen had no fire but in the kitchen, never in the parlour, but on Sunday. My father, who was a magiftrate of Litchfield, lived thus: 'They never began to have a fire in the p rlour, but on leaving off bufinefs, or fome great revolution of their life.

DR. DODDRIDGE.

Dr. Doddridge, he obferved, was the author of one of the fineft epigrams in the Englifh language—it is in Orton's Life of him, the fubject is his family motto, " Dum Vivimus Vivamus."

> " Live while you live, the Epicure would fay,
> " And feize the pleafures of the prefent day;"
> " Live while you live, the facred Preacher cries,
> " And give to God each moment as it flies,
> " Lord! in my views, let both united be,
> " I live in pleafure, when I live to thee."

FOOTE.

When he firft heard of Foote's death, he exclaimed, " Then we have loft a man who has left a chafm in fociety that will not readily be filled up."

At another time he obferved, " Foote had little or no principle—he is at times neither governed by goodmanners or difcretion—and very little by affection— but for a broad laugh the fcoundrel has no fellow."

Q. by a lady. Pray, Doctor, don't you look upon Foote as an infidel?

A. No—Madam. No other than you may call a dog an infidel, who does not know whether he believes or not.

GARRICK.

" The opinion that many people conceive of players, being in private life the characters they reprefent on the ftage, is very ftrong; Garrick told me, (Dr. Johnfon) that fome years after he came on the ftage, he received

ceived a message by an elderly looking gentlewoman who told him, there was a certain lady of rank and fortune who had a great partiality for him, and wanted to know whether he was married or not. Garrick replied in the negative. She seemed much pleased, and said he should soon hear from her again. Many months passed over without his hearing any farther about it—at last he met the woman accidentally in the street, whom he interrogated about the delay of her commission—at first she seemed to shuffle off the question, but he insisting upon knowing, she confessed to him, that the lady having first seen him in *Ranger*, she was charmed with his air and address—but soon after having appeared in *Sharp* in the Lying Valet, she thought she saw so many mean, shifting qualities about him, that she could by no means put either her person or fortune into his possession."

The other instance is equally strong. A grocer in the town of Litchfield, a neighbour of Peter Garrick's, having occasion to come up to London—Peter gave him a letter, recommending him to his brother David. The man came to town late in the evening, and seeing Garrick's name up in the bills for Abel Drugger, he went to the two shilling gallery, and then waited in anxious expectation of seeing in the person of his countryman the greatest actor of the age. On Garrick's appearance, he was for some time in doubt whether it could be him or not; at last, being convinced of it by the people around him, he felt himself so disgusted with the mean appearance and mercenary conduct of the character, which, by a foolish combination he attached to the player, that he went out of town without delivering his letter.

On his arrival in Litchfield, Peter Garrick asked him, "How he was received by his brother, and how he liked him." "To tell you the truth, says the man, I never delivered your letter." "Not delivered my letter! says Peter, how came that about?" "Why the fact is, I saw enough of him on the stage to make that unnecessary—he may be rich, as I dare say any man who

who lives like him must be, but by—— (and here, said the Doctor, the man vociferated an oath) though he is your brother, Mr. Garrick, he is one of the meanest and most pitiful fellows I ever saw in my life."

It was amongst the *memorabilia* of Garrick's petty habits. "That he kept a book of all who had either praised or abused him."

Meditations on a Pudding, by Dr. JOHNSON, *in playful fancy, ridiculing Hervey's Meditations.*

"Let us seriously reflect of what a pudding is composed. It is composed of flour that once waved in the golden grain, and drank the dews of the morning—of milk pressed from the swelling udder by the gentle hand of the beauteous milk-maid, whose beauty and innocence might have recommended a worse draught; who while she stroaked the udder indulged no ambitious thoughts of wandering in palaces, and formed no plans for the destruction of our fellow-creatures.—Milk which is drawn from the cow, that useful animal that eats the grass of the field, and supplies us with that which made the greatest part of the food of mankind, in the age which the poets have agreed to call Golden.

"It is made with an egg, that miracle of nature, which the theoretical Burnet has compared to creation; an egg contains water within its beautiful smooth surface, and an unformed mass, which, by the incubation of the parent, becomes a regular animal, furnished with bones and sinews, and covered with feathers.

"Let us consider—can there be more wanting to complete this meditation on a pudding—if more is wanting, more may be found. It contains salt which keeps the sea from putrefaction; salt, which is made the image of intellectual essence, contributes to the formation of a pudding."

LAW.

A lawyer has no business with the justice or injustice of the cause he undertakes, unless his client asks his opinion, and then he is bound to give it honestly. The justice or injustice of the cause is to be decided by the judge.

"A

"A country is in a bad state which is governed only by laws, because a thousand things occur for which laws cannot provide, and where authority ought not to interpose."

LIFE *(Its Duties)*

Speaking of the difficulty of living in the world with an abstracted mind, "Sir, Dr. Cheyne has laid down a rule to himself on this subject, which should be imprinted on every mind."

"To neglect nothing to secure my eternal peace more than if I had been certified I should die within the day, nor to mind any thing that my secular obligations and duties demanded of me, less than if I had been ensured to live fifty years."

LAZINESS.

Dr. Johnson observing upon some occasion, that laziness was worse than the tooth-ache; Mr. Boswell replied, "I cannot agree with you there; for a bason of cold water, or a horse-whip will cure laziness." "No, Sir, it will only put off the fit, it will not cure the disease; I have been trying to cure laziness all my life, and could not do it."

MIND.

The supposition of one man having more imagination—another more judgment, is not true—it is only one man has more mind than another. "Sir, the man who has vigour may walk to the East, as well as the West, if he happens to turn his head that way."

MARRIAGE.

Some cunning men choose fools for their wives, thinking to manage them, but they always fail; depend upon it, no woman is the worse for sense and knowledge.

LORD MANSFIELD.

A person in company saying, That he had heard Lord Mansfield was not a great English lawyer. "Sir, you may as well maintain, that a carrier who has driven a packhorse between Edinburgh and Berwick for thirty years, does not know the road, as that Lord Mansfield does not know the laws of England."

SARAH

SARAH, DUCHESS OF MARLBOROUGH.

The Duchess had no superior parts, but was a bold, frontless woman, who knew how to make the most of her opportunities in life.

POLITENESS.

Politeness is of great consequence to society—it is *fictitious benevolence*—it supplies the place of it amongst those who see each other often, or but little. Depend upon it the want of it never fails to produce something disagreeable to one or other. I have always applied to good-breeding what Addison in his Cato says of honour:

> " Honour's a sacred tie, the law of Kings,
> " The noble mind's distinguishing perfection,
> " That aids and strengthens Virtue where it meets her,
> " And imitates her actions where she is not."

PROSTITUTION.

On the subject of making women do penance in the church for fornication, he observed, " It is right, Sir, infamy is attached to the crime by universal opinion as soon as it is known. I would not be the man who would discover it, if I alone knew it—for a woman may reform. Nor would I commend a person who divulges a woman's first offence; but being once divulged, it ought to be infamous. Consider of what importance to society the chastity of women is; upon that all the property in the world depends. We hang a thief for stealing a sheep, but the unchastity of a woman takes sheep and farm and all from the right owner.

" I have much more reverence for a common prostitute than for a woman who conceals her guilt; the prostitute is known; she cannot deceive, she cannot bring herself into the arms of an honest man without his knowledge."

PULTNEY (of Bath)

" Pultney was as paltry a fellow as could be; he was a Whig who pretended to be honest, and you know it is ridiculous for a Whig to pretend to be honest—he cannot hold it out."

QUIN.

Q. You have heard Quin read Milton, Doctor?
A. Sir, I have heard Quin *attempt* to read Milton.
Q. What! then you do not like him?
A. Why no, Sir, he read it too much like a player; by imitating the several characters of the poem; whereas his business was that of a narrator, not an imitator.

SIR JOSHUA REYNOLDS.

Speaking of this great artist, he gave the following eulogium on him as a man:

"Reynolds, Sir, is the most invulnerable man I know; the man with whom, if you should quarrel, you would find the most difficulty how to abuse."

SUICIDE.

"There is no situation a man can possibly be in that he has a right to put himself to death." Suppose, says Mr. Boswell, that a man is absolutely sure, that if he lives a few days longer, he shall be detected in a fraud, the consequence of which will be utter disgrace and expulsion from society. What is he to do then?" "Then, Sir, says Johnson, let him go to some place where he is not known—but don't let him go to the devil where he is known."

SAILOR.

Mr. Boswell expressing his wonder, "That a man who had been pressed on board a man of war, did not chuse to continue longer than nine months." "Sir, I should rather wonder he stayed so long, if he could help it—no man will be a sailor who has contrivance enough to get into a jail, for being in a ship is being in a jail, with the chance of being drowned."

SIR ROBERT WALPOLE.

Sir Robert Walpole, on the whole was a fine fellow, —and even his enemies thought him so before his death. Lord Bath told me, " he was very sure Sir Robert was of that social pleasant temper, that he never felt any thing said against him for half an hour in his life. He then repeated Pope's character of him:

" Seen

" Seen him I have, but in his happier hour
" Of social pleasure — ill exchang'd for power;
" Seen him uncumber'd with the venal tribe,
" Smile without art, and win without a bribe."

JOHN WILKES.

"It is wonderful to think that all the force of government was required to prevent Wilkes from being chosen chief magistrate of London, without success, though the livery-men knew at the same time he would rob their shops, and debauch their daughter's.

PAUL WHITEHEAD.

Q. " Pray, Doctor, was not Whitehead prosecuted for his poem, called Manners?"

A. " No, Sir; but Dodsley his publisher was. Whitehead was a man who hung loose upon society, but Dodsley being a man who kept a shop, and being more readily found, was called before the house of Lords—and after all I think the poem but a poor performance."

EXTRACTS from various AUTHORITIES.

UPON the publication of Lord Bolingbroke's philosophical works by David Mallet, Dr. Johnson was asked his opinion of the author.—" Sir, says he, I look upon him to be both a *scoundrel* and a *coward*—a scoundrel for loading his blunderbuss up to the muzzle, against the peace and happiness of society, and a coward for leaving David Mallet to draw the trigger."

A gentleman observing to Dr. Johnson, that there were less vagrant poor in Scotland than in England, and as a proof of it, said there was no instance of a beggar dying in the streets there;—" I believe you're very right, Sir, says Johnson, but that does not arise from the want of vagrants, but *the impossibility of starving a Scotchman*."

Pray, Dr. Johnson, says a female smatterer in poetry, which was the greatest poet, Boyce or Derrick?—" Oh, Madam,

Madam (says the Doctor) there can be no great difference between a *louse and a flee*.

Dr. Johnson being at dinner at Mrs. Macauley's, the conversation turned on the *equality of mankind*, which the lady of the house contended for with all the energy of a republican. Johnson made a few short answers, in hopes to change the subject, but finding she would go on, he finished his dinner with as much haste as possible, and then giving his plate to the footman, begged he'd take his place: "Good God! what are you about, Doctor," said the lady?—"Oh! nothing, Madam, but to preserve the *equality of mankind*.

The emigration of the Scotch to London, being a conversation between the Doctor and Foote, the latter said he believed the number of Scotch in London were as great in the former as the present reign:—"No, Sir, you are certainly wrong in your belief;—but I see how you're deceived, you can't distinguish them now as formerly, for the fellows all come here *breeched* of late years."

Pray Doctor, said a gentleman to him, is Mr. Thrale a man of conversation, or is he only wise and silent?—"Why, Sir, his conversation does not shew the *minute* hand,—but he generally strikes the hour very correctly."

Pray, says Garrick's mother to Johnson, "what's your opinion of my son David?"—"Why, Madam, replied the Doctor, David will either be hanged, or become a great man."

Upon the publication of the *Poems of Offian*, being asked by the commentator on that work, whether he thought any *one man living* could write such an epic poem?—Johnson replied very gravely,—"O yes! Sir, *many men, many women*, and *many children!*"

"You knew Mr. Capel, the editor of Shakespeare, Dr. Johnson?"—"Yes, Sir, I have seen him at Garrick's!"—"And what think you of his abilities?"—"Great *application*, Sir! Were he and I to count the grains in a bushel of wheat for a wager, he would certainly prove the winner."

On Dr. Johnson's return from Scotland, a particular friend of his was saying, that now he had a view of the country,

country, he was in hopes it would cure him of many prejudices againſt that nation, particularly in reſpect to the *fruits*.—"Why yes, Sr, I have found out that gooſeberries will grow there againſt a ſouth wall, but the ſkins are ſo tough that it is death to the man who ſwallows one of them."

I remember, ſays the Doctor, to have given a *ſhilling* to a peaſant in the Iſle of Skey, for half a days attendance on me, and he was ſo ſtruck with the liberality of the reward, that he aſked with ſome ſurpriſe, whether I *meant it all for him?*—This raiſing the laugh againſt Mr. Boſwell, who was the only Scotchman in company, the Doctor went on—"I mention this circumſtance to ſhew the humility of the man's mind; but had it happened to a peaſant of your country (turning round to an Iriſh gentleman who ſat next him) the probability is, that he would not know *what a ſhilling was.*"

When Dr. Johnſon had an audience of the King, by appointment, in the Queen's library, in the courſe of converſation his Majeſty aſked him, "why he did not continue writing?—"Why, Sire," ſays Johnſon, "I thought I had done enough!" "So ſhould I too, Doctor," replied the King, "if you had not written ſo well."

Forgetting an appointment he had to ſup with Garrick, till near one o'clock in the morning, he ſallied out at that hour, and knocked at his door in Southampton-ſtreet.—Garrick putting his head out of the window, told him all the company were gone, and that he and Mrs. Garrick were going to bed.—"Open the door, David, ſays the Doctor, I have ſomething to tell you will give you ſatisfaction."—This brought down Garrick, who, after letting him in, impatiently aſked him what was the news he had that was to give him ſo much *ſatisfaction?*—"Why ſit you down there, ſays the Doctor, *and I'll flatter you.*"

An

---

* A ſhort time before the Doctor's death Mr. Kearſley, in converſation with him, enquired if that obſervation of his Majeſty's was true; he ſaid it was nearly ſo, but his memory was become very defective

An eminent carcafe butcher, as meagre in his perfon as he was in his underftanding, being one day in a bookfeller's fhop, took up a volume of Churchill's Poems, and by way of fhewing his tafte, repeated with great affectation, the following line:

"Who rules o'er freemen fhould himfelf be free.

Then turning to the Doctor,—"What think you of that, Sir?" faid he. "Rank nonfenfe, replied the other!— it is an affertion without a proof—and *you* might, with as much propriety fay,

"Who flays fat oxen fhould himfelf be fat."

When Lord Chefterfield's letters to his fon firft came out, a gentleman was afking the Doctor whether they did not contain great knowledge of the world?—"O! yes, Sir, fays Johnfon, very much of modern knowledge. They inculcate the morals of a *w*——, and the *manners of a dancing-mafter.*"—Being afked his opinion of the writings of a certain fuccefsful dramatic author, he replied, " They were fuch as a wife man fhould be afhamed to remember."

Previous to a convivial meeting on the night before the publication of his firft edition of Shakefpeare, Tonfon, the publifher, defired a gentleman to afk Johnfon for a lift of the fubfcribers?—"Why, Sir, fays the Doctor, "I have two material reafons againft it:—In the firft place I have *loft all their names*, and in the fecond, I have *fpent all the money.*"

Perhaps, faid a gentleman, talking to Dr. Johnfon on church preferments, "after all, a *Conge d'Elire* has not the force of a pofitive command, but implies only a ftrong *recommendation.*"—"Very true, Sir, fays Johnfon, but fuch a ftrong recommendation as if I fhould throw you out of a three pair of ftairs window, and *recommend you to fall to the ground.*"

Being afked his opinion of hunting, he faid, " it was the *labour* of the Savages of North America, but the *amufement* of the gentlemen of England."

When he was told of his friend Mrs. Thrale's marriage with Piozzi, the Italian finger, he was dumb with furprize, surprise for some moments, at last recovering himself, he exclaimed with great emotion,

Varium et mutabile semper fœmina.

'The author of the life of Socrates,* who was as thick as he was long, once called our author " a literary savage ;" when Johnson heard of it he replied—" Why I expected some such ridiculous observations from a *literary punchinello.*"

When Dr. Percy first published his collection of ancient English ballads, perhaps he was too lavish in commendation of the beautiful simplicity and poetic merit he supposed himself to discover in them. This circumstance provoked Johnson to observe one evening, at Miss Reynold's tea-table, that he could rhyme as well, and as elegantly in common narrative and conversation. For instance, says he,

> As with my hat upon my head
> I walk'd along the Strand,
> I there did meet another man
> With his hat in his hand.

Or to render such poetry subservient to my own immediate use,

> I therefore pray thee, Renny dear,
> That thou wilt give to me,
> With cream and sugar soften'd well,
> Another dish of tea.
>
> Nor fear that I, my gentle maid,
> Shall long detain the cup,
> When once unto the bottom I
> Have drank the liquor up.
>
> Yet hear, alas! this mournful truth,
> Nor hear it with a frown:—
> Thou can'st not make the tea so fast
> As I can gulp it down.

And thus he prceeded through several more stanzas, till the Reverend Critic cried out for quarter.

In a conversation on the infancy of the American war—a gentleman present giving some remarkable instances of the *ill-timed lenity* and *procrastination of hostilities* on our side; the Doctor observed, " that a prince who made

* Mr. Cooper.

made war upon his enemies *tenderly*, often distressed his subjects *cruelly*."

He used to say of Gray, the poet, that he was the very Torre of poetry. He played his coruscations so speciously, that his steel dust was mistaken by many for a shower of gold.

A gentleman reading to Dr. Johnson, *Garrick's Ode, on the Stratford Jubilee*, when he came to the following couplet:

 "The little loves like bees
 "Clust'ring and climbing up his knees."

Could not help exclaiming, "What damned stuff here is!" "Very bad to be sure, Sir, says the Doctor; but I should hope 'tis not my friend David's writing, but rather *Mrs. Garrick's woman*."

"I hope, Sir, says a friend, that the man I recommended to sit up with you (during his last indisposition) was both wakeful and alert. "Sir, answered the Doctor, his vigilance was that of a dormouse, and his activity that of a turnspit on his first entrance into a wheel."

ANECDOTES, &c.

EXTRACTED FROM

Mr. BOSWELL's LIFE OF JOHNSON.

JOHNSON, previous to his removing to the university, read a great deal in a desultory manner, without any scheme of study, as chance threw books in his way, and inclination directed him through them. He used to mention one curious instance of his casual reading when but a boy. Having imagined that his brother had hid some apples behind a large folio upon an upper shelf in his father's shop, he climbed up to search for them. There were no apples; but the large folio proved to be Petrarch, whom he had seen mentioned, in some preface, as one of the restorers of learning. His curiosity having been thus excited, he sat down with avidity, and read a great part of the book. What he read during these two years, he told Mr. B. was not works of mere amusement, "not voyages and travels, but all literature, Sir, all ancient writers, all manly; though but little Greek, only some of Anacreon and Hesiod; but in this irregular manner (added he) I had looked into a great many books, which were not commonly known at the universities, where they seldom read any books but what are put into their hands by their tutors; so that when I came to Oxford, Dr. Adams, master of Pembroke College, told me, I was the best qualified for the University that he had ever known come there."

No man had a more ardent love of literature, or a higher respect for it. His apartment in Pembroke College was that upon the second floor over the gateway. The enthusiasts of learning will ever contemplate it with veneration. One day, while he was sitting in it quite alone, Dr. Panting, then master of the College, whom he called " a fine Jacobite fellow," overheard him uttering this soliloquy, in his strong emphatic voice: " Well, I have a mind to see what is done in other places of learning. I'll go and visit the Universities abroad. I'll go to France and Italy. I'll go to Padua.—And I'll mind my business. For an *Athenian* blockhead is the worst of all blockheads."

The following curious account of his journey, with his wife, to church, on the nuptial morn, was given to Mr. B. by the Doctor himself. " Sir, she had read the old romances, and had got into her head the fantastical notion that a woman of spirit should use her lover like a dog. So, Sir, at first she told me that I rode too fast, and she could not keep up with me; and when I rode a little slower, she passed me, and complained that I lagged behind. I was not to be made the slave of caprice; and I resolved to begin as I meant to end. I therefore pushed on briskly till I was fairly out of her sight. The road lay between two hedges, so I was sure she could not miss it; and I contrived that she

she should soon come up with me. When she did, I observed her to be in tears."

The following beautiful ODE to FRIENDSHIP, written at an early period of his life, was never before printed:

 FRIENDSHIP, peculiar boon of Heav'n,
  The noble mind's delight and pride,
 To men and angels only giv'n,
  To all the lower world deny'd.

 While love, unknown among the blest,
  Parent of thousand wild desires,
 The savage and the human breast
  Torments alike with raging fires.

 With bright, but oft destructive, gleam,
  Alike o'er all his lightnings fly;
 Thy lambent glories only beam
  Around the fav'rites of the sky.

 Thy gentle flow of guiltless joys
  On fools and villains ne'er descend;
 In vain for thee the tyrant sighs,
  And hugs a flatt'rer for a friend.

 Directress of the brave and just,
  O guide us thro' life's darksome way!
 And let the tortures of mistrust
  On selfish bosoms only prey.

 Nor shall thine ardours cease to glow,
  When souls to blissful climes remove:
 What rais'd our virtue here below,
  Shall aid our happiness above.

A few days before the first of his Essays, intituled the Rambler, came out, there started another competitor for fame, in the same form, under the title of "The Tatler Revived," which was "born but to die." Johnson was not very happy in the choice of his title, "The Rambler," which certainly is not suited to a series of grave and moral discourses; which the Italians have literally, but ludicrously, translated by *Il Vagabondo*. He gave Sir Joshua Reynolds the following account of its getting this name: "What *muſt* be done, Sir, *will* be done. When I was to begin publiſhing that paper, I was at a loſs how to name it. I ſat down at night upon my bedſide, and reſolved that I would not go to ſleep till I had fixed its title. The Rambler ſeemed the beſt that occurred, and I took it."

With what devout and conſcientious ſentiments this Paper was undertaken, is evidenced by the following prayer, which he compoſed and offered up on the occaſion: "Almighty GOD, the giver of all good things, without whoſe help all labour is ineffectual, and without whoſe grace all wiſdom is folly; grant, I beſeech Thee, that in this undertaking thy Holy Spirit may not be with-held from me, but that I may promote thy glory, and the ſalvation of myſelf and others:—grant this, O LORD, for the ſake of thy ſon JESUS CHRIST. Amen."

The firſt paper of the Rambler was publiſhed on Tueſday the 20th of March, 1750; and its author was enabled to continue it, without interruption, every Tueſday and Friday, till Saturday the 17th of March, 1752, on which day it cloſed. Notwithſtanding his conſtitutional indolence, his depreſſion of ſpirits, and his labour in carrying on his Dictionary, he anſwered the ſtated calls of the preſs twice a week from the ſtores of his mind, during all that time having received no aſſiſtance, except four billets in No. 10, by Miſs Mulſo, now Mrs. Chapone; No. 30, by Mrs. Catherine Talbot; No 97, by Mr. Samuel Richardſon, whom he deſcribes in an introductory note, as "An author who has enlarged the knowledge of human nature, and taught the paſſions to move at the command of virtue;" and Numbers 44 and 100, by Mrs. Elizabeth Carter.

Poſterity will be aſtoniſhed when they are told, upon the authority of Johnſon himſelf, that many of theſe diſcourſes, which we ſhould ſuppoſe had been laboured with all the ſlow attention of literary leiſure, were written in haſte, as the moment preſſed, without even being read over by him before they were printed. It can be accounted for only in this way; that by reading and meditation, and a very close inspection of life, he had accumulated a great fund of miscellaneous knowledge, which, by a peculiar promptitude of mind, was ever ready at his call, and which he had constantly accustomed himself to clothe in the the most apt and energetic expression. Sir Joshua Reynolds once asked him by what means he had attained his extraordinary accuracy and flow of language, He told him, that he had early laid it down as a fixed rule to do his best on every occasion; and in every company to impart whatever he knew in the most forcible language he could put it in; and that by constant practice, and never suffering any careless expressions to escape him, or attempting to deliver his thoughts without arranging them in the clearest manner, it became habitual to him.

As the Rambler was entirely the work of one man, there was, of course, such an uniformity in its texture, as very much to exclude the charm of variety? and the grave, and often solemn cast of thinking, which distinguished it from other periodical papers, made it, for some time, not generally liked. So slowly did this excellent work, of which twelve editions have now issued from the press, gain upon the world at large, that even in the closing number the author says, "I have never been much a favourite of the public."

Johnson told Mr. B. with an amiable fondness, a little pleasing circumstance relative to this work. Mrs. Johnson, in whose judgment and taste he had great confidence, said to him, after a few numbers of the Rambler had come out, "I thought very well of you before; but I did not imagine you could have written any thing equal to this." Distant praise, from whatever quarter, is not so delightful as that of a wife whom a man loves and esteems. Her approbation may be said "to come home to his *bosom*;" and being so near, its effect is most sensible and permanent.

In 1751 we are to consider him as carrying on both his Dictionary and Rambler. But he also wrote " The Life of Cheynel," in the miscellany called " The Student;" and the Reverend Dr. Douglas having, with uncommon acuteness, clearly detected a gross forgery and imposition upon the public by William Lauder, a Scotch schoolmaster, who had, with equal impudence and ingenuity, represented Milton as a plagiary from certain modern Latin poets, Johnson, who had been so far imposed upon as to furnish a Preface and Postscript to his work, now dictated a letter for Lauder, addressed to Dr. Douglas, acknowledging his fraud in terms of suitable contrition.

This extraordinary attempt of Lauder was no sudden effort. He had brooded over it for many years; and to this hour it is uncertain what his principal motive was, unless it were a vain notion of his superiority, in being able, by whatever means, to deceive mankind. To effect this, he produced certain passages from Grotius, Masenius, and others, which had a faint resemblance to some parts of the " Paradise Lost." In these he interpolated some fragments of Hog's Latin translation of that Poem, alledging, that the mass thus fabricated, was the archetype from which Milton copied. These fabrications he published from time to time in the Gentleman's Magazine; and, exulting in his fancied success, he, in 1750, ventured to collect them into a pamphlet, entitled " An Essay on Milton's Use and Imitation of the Moderns in his Paradise Lost." To this pamphlet Johnson wrote a Preface, in full persuasion of Lauder's honesty, and a Postcript recommending, in the most persuasive terms, a subscription for the relief of a grand-daughter of Milton, of whom he thus speaks: ' It is yet in the power of a great people to reward the poet whose name they boast, and from their alliance to whose genius they claim some kind of superiority to every other nation of the earth; that poet, whose works may possibly be read when every other monument of British greatness shall be obliterated; to reward him, not with pictures, or with medals, which, if he sees, he sees with contempt, but with tokens of gratitude, which he, perhaps, may even now consider, as not unworthy the regard of an immortal spirit.'

The circle of his friends, in the year 1752, was extensive and various, far beyond what has been generally imagined, among whom was his *dulce decus*, Sir

Joshua

Joshua Reynolds, and with whom he maintained an uninterrupted intimacy to the last hour of his life.—When Johnson lived in Castle-street, Cavendish-square, he used frequently to visit two ladies, who lived opposite to him, Miss Cotterells, daughters of Admiral Cotterell. Reynolds used also to visit there, and thus they met. Mr. Reynolds had, from the first reading of his most admirable Life of Savage, conceived a very high admiration of Johnson's powers of writing. His conversation no less delighted him; and he cultivated his acquaintance with the laudable zeal of one who was ambitious of general improvement. Sir Joshua, indeed, was lucky enough at their very first meeting, to make a remark, which was so much above the common-place style of conversation, that Johnson at once perceived that Reynolds had the habit of thinking for himself. The ladies were regretting the death of a friend, to whom they owed great obligations; upon which Reynolds observed, " You have, however, the comfort of being relieved from a burthen of gratitude." They were shocked a little at this alleviating suggestion, as too selfish; but Johnson defended it in his clear and forcible manner, and was much pleased with the *mind*, the fair view of human nature, which it exhibited, like some of the reflections of Rochefaucalt.—The consequence was, that he went home with Reynolds, and supped with him.

When they were one evening together at the Miss Cotterells, the then Duchess of Argyle and another lady of high rank came in. Johnson thinking that the Miss Cotterells were too much engrossed by them, and that he and his friend were neglected as low company, of whom they were somewhat ashamed, grew angry; and resolving to shock their supposed pride, by making their great visitors imagine that his friend and he were low indeed, he addressed himself in a loud tone to Mr. Reynolds, saying, " How much do you think you and I could get in a week, if we were to *work as hard* as we could?" as if they had been common mechanics.

Soon after his acquaintance with Mr. Langton commenced, Johnson passed a considerable time at Oxford.

He at first thought it strange that Langton should associate so much with Beauclerk, one who had the character of being loose, both in his principles and practice; but by degrees, he himself was fascinated. Mr. Beauclerk's being of the St. Alban's family, and having, in some particulars, a resemblance to Charles the Second, contributed, in Johnson's imagination, to throw a lustre upon his other qualities; and, in a short time, the moral, pious Johnson, and the gay, dissipated Beauclerk, were companions. "What a coalition! (said Garrick, when he heard of this) I shall have my old friend to bail out of the round-house." Innumerable were the scenes in which Johnson was amused by these young men. Beauclerk had such a propensity to satire, that at one time Johnson said to him, "You never open your mouth but with intention to give pain; and you have often given me pain, not from the power of what you said, but from seeing your intention." At another time applying to him, with a slight alteration, a line of Pope, he said, "Thy love of folly, and thy scorn of fools—Every thing thou dost shews the one, and every thing thou say'st the other." At another time he said to him, "Thy body is all vice, and thy mind all virtue." Beauclerk not seeming to relish the compliment, Johnson said, "Nay, Sir, Alexander the Great, marching in triumph into Babylon, could not have desired to have had more said to him."

Johnson was some time with Beauclerk at his house at Windsor, where he was entertained with experiments in natural philosophy. One Sunday, when the weather was very fine, Beauclerk enticed him, insensibly, to saunter about all the morning. They went into a church-yard, in the time of divine service, and Johnson laid himself down at his ease upon one of the tomb-stones. "Now, Sir, (said Beauclerk) you are like Hogarth's Idle Apprentice." When Johnson got his pension, Beauclerk said to him, in the humourous phrase of Falstaff, "I hope you'll now purge, and live cleanly like a gentleman."

One night when Beauclerk and Langton had supped at a tavern in London, and sat till about three in the morning,

morning, it came into their heads to go and knock up Johnson, and see if they could prevail on him to join them in a ramble. They rapped violently at the door of his chambers in the Temple, till at last he appeared in his shirt with his little black wig on the top of his head, instead of a night-cap, and a poker in his hand, imagining, probably, that some ruffians were coming to attack him, when he discovered who they were, and was told their errand, he smiled, and with great good humour agreed to their proposal: " What is it you, you dogs? I'll have a frisk with you." He was soon dressed, and they sallied forth together into Covent-Garden, where the green-grocers and fruiterers were beginning to arrange their hampers, just come in from the country. Johnson made some attempts to help them; but the honest gardeners stared so at his figure and manner, and odd interference, that he soon saw his services were not relished. They then repaired to one of the neighbouring taverns, and made a bowl of that liquor called *Bishop*, which Johnson had always liked; while in joyous contempt of sleep, from which he had been roused, he repeated the festive lines,

" Short, O short then be thy reign,
And give us to the world again."

They did not stay long, but walked down to the Thames, took a boat, and rowed to Billingsgate.—Beauclerk and Johnson were so well pleased with their amusement, that they resolved to persevere in dissipation for the rest of the day: but Langton deserted them, being engaged to breakfast with some young ladies. Johnson scolded him for " leaving his social friends, to go and sit with a set of wretched, *un-idea'd* girls. Garrick being told of this ramble, said to him smartly, " I heard of your frolic t'other night. You'll be in the Chronicle." Upon which Johnson afterwards observed, " *He* durst not do such a thing. His *wife* would not *let* him.

The following is that celebrated letter to Lord Chesterfield, on the two papers which he had written in the World, in recommendation of Johnson's Dictionary.

To the Right Hon. the EARL *of* CHESTERFIELD.

"MY LORD,   February, 1755.

"I have been lately informed, by the proprietor of the World, that two papers, in which my Dictionary is recommended to the public, were written by your Lordship. To be so distinguished, is an honour, which, being very little accustomed to favours from the great, I know not well how to receive, or in what terms to acknowledge.

"When, upon some slight encouragement, I first visited your Lordship, I was overpowered, like the rest of mankind, by the enchantment of your address; and could not forbear to wish that I might boast myself *Le vainqueur du vainqueur de la terre* ;—that I might obtain that regard for which I saw the world contending; but I found my attendance so little encouraged, that neither pride nor modesty would suffer me to continue it.— When I had once addressed your Lordship in public, I had exhausted all the art of pleasing which a retired and uncourtly scholar can possess. I had done all that I could; and no man is well pleased to have his all neglected, be it ever so little.

"Seven years, my Lord, are now past, since I waited in your outer rooms, or was repulsed from your door; during which time I have been pushing on my work through difficulties, of which it is useless to complain, and have brought it, at last, to the verge of publication, without one act of assistance*, one word of encouragement, or one smile of favour. Such treatment I did not expect, for I never had a Patron before.

---

* The following note is subjoined by Mr. Langton. "Dr. Johnson, when he gave me this copy of his letter, desired that I would annex to it his information to me, that whereas it is said in the letter, that 'no assistance has been received,' he did once receive from Lord Chesterfield the sum of ten pounds; but as that was so inconsiderable a sum, he thought the mention of it could not properly find place in a letter of the kind that this was."

"The

"The shepherd in Virgil grew at last acquainted with Love, and found him a native of the rocks.

"Is not a Patron, my Lord, one who looks with unconcern on a man struggling for life in the water, and when he has reached ground, encumbers him with help? The notice which you have been pleased to take of my labours, had it been early, had been kind; but it has been delayed till I am indifferent, and cannot enjoy it; till I am solitary, and cannot impart it; till I am known, and do not want it. I hope it is no very cynical asperity not to confess obligations where no benefit has been received, or to be unwilling that the public should consider me as owing that to a Patron, which Providence has enabled me to do for myself.

"Having carried on my work thus far, with so little obligations to any favourer of learning, I shall not be disappointed though I shall conclude it, if less be possible, with less; for I have been long wakened from that dream of hope, in which I once boasted myself with so much exultation,

My Lord,
Your Lordship's most humble,
Most obedient servant,
SAMUEL JOHNSON."

Johnson having now explicitly avowed his opinion of Lord Chesterfield, did not refrain from expressing himself concerning that nobleman with pointed freedom: "This man (said he) I thought had been a Lord among wits; but, I find, he is only a wit among Lords!" And when his Letters to his natural son were published, he observed, that "they teach the morals of a whore, and the manners of a dancing-master."

In 1756 he resumed his scheme of giving an edition of Shakespeare with notes. He issued proposals of considerable length, in which he shewed that he perfectly well knew what a variety of research such an undertaking required; but his indolence prevented him from pursuing it with that diligence which alone can collect those scattered facts that genius, however acute, penetrating, and luminous, cannot discover by its own force. It is remarkable, that at this time his fancied activity was for the moment so vigorous, that he promised his work should be published before Christmas, 1757. Yet nine years elapsed before it saw the light. His throes in bringing it forth had been severe and remittent, and at last we may almost conclude that the Cæsarian operation was performed by the knife of Churchill.

> "He for subscribers bates his hook,
> And takes your cash; but where's the book?
> No matter where; wise fear, you know,
> Forbids the robbing of a foe;
> But what, to serve our private ends,
> Forbids the cheating of our friends?"

Sunday, July 31, 1763, Mr. B. told him he had been that morning at a meeting of the people called Quakers, where he had heard a woman preach. Johnson said, "Sir, a woman's preaching is like a dog's walking on his hinder legs. It is not done well; but you are surprized to find it done at all."

The year 1765 was distinguished by his being introduced into the family of Mr. Thrale, one of the most eminent brewers in England, and Member of Parliament for the Borough of Southwark. Foreigners are not a little amazed when they hear of brewers, distillers, and men in similar departments of trade, held forth as persons of considerable consequence. Johnson used to give this account of the rise of Mr. Thrale's father. "He worked at six shillings a week for twenty years in the great brewery which was afterwards his own. The proprietor of it had an only daughter, who was married to a nobleman. It was not fit that a Peer should continue the business. On the old man's death, therefore, the brewery was to be sold. To find a purchaser for so large a property was a difficult matter; and, after some time, it was suggested, that it would be adviseable to treat with Thrale, a sensible, active, honest man, who had been long employed in the house, and to transfer the whole to him for thirty thousand pounds, security being taken upon the property. This was accordingly settled. In eleven years Thrale paid the purchase-money. He acquired a large fortune, and lived to be Member of Parliament for Southwark. But what was most remarkable was the liberality with which he used his riches. He gave his son and daughters the best education. The esteem which his good conduct procured him from the nobleman who had married his master's daughter, made him be treated with much attention; and his son, both at school and at the university of Oxford, associated with young men of the first rank. His allowance from his father, after he left college, was splendid; no less than a thousand a year. This, in a man who had risen as old Thrale did, was a very extraordinary instance of generosity. He used to say, "If this young dog does not find so much after I am gone as he expects, let him remember that he has had a great deal in my own time."

Mr. Thrale had married Miss Hesther Lynch Salusbury, of good Welch extraction, a lady of lively talents, improved by education. That Johnson's introduction into Mr. Thrale's family, which contributed so much to the happiness of his life, was owing to her desire for his conversation, is the most probable and general supposition. But it is not the truth. Mr. Murphy, who was intimate with Mr. Thrale, having spoken very highly of Dr. Johnson, he was requested to make them acquainted. This being mentioned to Johnson, he accepted of an invitation to dinner at Thrale's, and was so much pleased with his reception, both by Mr. and Mrs. Thrale, and they so much pleased with him, that his invitations to their house were more and more frequent, till at last he became one of the family, and an apartment was appropriated to him, both in their house in Southwark, and in their villa at Streatham.

Nothing could be more fortunate for Johnson than this connection. He had at Mr. Thrale's all the comforts and even luxuries of life; his melancholy

was

was diverted, and his irregular habits leſſened, by aſſociation with an agreeable and well-ordered family. He was treated with the utmoſt reſpect, and even affection. The vivacity of Mrs. Thrale's literary talk rouſed him to cheerfulneſs and exertion even when they were alone. But this was not often the caſe; for he found here a conſtant ſucceſſion of what gave him the higheſt enjoyment, the ſociety of the learned, the witty, and the eminent in every way, who were aſſembled in numerous companies, called forth his wonderful powers, and gratified him with admiration, to which no man could be inſenſible.

In the October of this year he at length gave to the world his edition of Shakſpeare, which, if it had no other merit but that of producing his Preface, in which the excellencies and defects of that immortal bard are diſplayed with a maſterly hand, the nation would have had no reaſon to complain. A blind, indiſcriminate admiration of Shakſpeare had expoſed the Britiſh nation to the ridicule of foreigners. Johnſon, by candidly admitting the faults of his poet, had the more credit in beſtowing on him deſerved and indiſputable praiſe; and doubtleſs none of all his panegyriſts have done him half ſo much honour.

Trinity College, Dublin, at this time ſurpriſed Johnſon with a ſpontaneous compliment of the higheſt academical honours, by creating him Doctor of Laws.

This unſolicited mark of diſtinction, conferred on ſo great a literary character, did much honour to the judgment and liberal ſpirit of that learned body.

He uſed to ſay of Goldſmith's Traveller, " There has not been ſo fine a poem ſince Pope's time."

And here it is proper to ſettle, with authentic preciſion, what has long floated in public report, as to Johnſon's being himſelf the author of a conſiderable part of that poem. But in the year 1783, he marked with a pencil the lines which he had furniſhed, which are only line 420,

" To ſtop too fearful, and too faint to go;"

and

and the concluding ten lines, except the last couplet but one, distinguished by the Italic character:

"How small of all that human hearts endure,
"That part which kings or laws can cause or cure.
"Still to ourselves in every place consign'd,
"Our own felicity we make or find;
"With secret course, which no loud storms annoy,
"Glides the smooth current of domestic joy.
"*The lifted axe, the agonizing wheel,*
"*Luke's iron crown, and Damien's bed of steel,*
"To men remote from power, but rarely known,
"Leave reason, faith, and conscience all our own."

Of the "Deserted Village," he furnished the four following, which are the last:

"That trade's proud empire hastes to swift decay,
"As ocean sweeps the the labour'd mole away:
"While self-dependent power can time defy,
"As rocks resist the billows and the sky."

Mr. Cuthbert Shaw, alike distinguished by his genius, misfortunes, and misconduct, published in 1766, a Poem, called "The Race, by Mercurius Spur, Esq." in which he whimsically made the living poets of England contend for pre-eminence of fame by running:

"Prove by their heels the prowess of the head."

In this Poem there was the following portrait of Johnson:

"Here Johnson comes,---unblest with outward grace,
"His rigid morals stamp'd upon his face.
"While strong conceptions struggle in his brain;
"(For even wit is brought to bed with pain):
"To view him, porters with their loads would rest,
"And babes cling frighted to the nurse's breast.
"With looks convuls'd, he roars in pompous strain,
"And like an angry lion shakes his mane.
"The Nine, with terror struck, who ne'er had seen
"Aught human with so horrible a mien,
"Debating whether they should stay or run,
"Virtue steps forth, and claims him for her son.

" With gentle speech she warns him now to yield,
" Nor stain his glories in the doubtful field ;
" But wrapt in conscious worth, content sit down,
" Since fame resolv'd his various pleas to crown,
" Though forc'd his present claim to disavow,
" Had long reserv'd a chaplet for his brow.
" He bows, obeys ; for Time shall first expire,
" Ere Johnson stay, when Virtue bids retire."

Dr Johnson repeatedly talked of the heinousness of the crime of adultery, by which the peace of families was destroyed. "He said confusion of progeny constitutes the essence of the crime ; and therefore a woman who breaks her marriage vows is much more criminal than a man who does it. A man, to be sure, is criminal in the sight of God : but he does not do his wife a very material injury, if he does not insult her ; if, for instance, from mere wantonness of appetite, he steals privately to her chambermaid. Sir, a wife ought not greatly to resent this. I would not receive home a daughter who had run away from her husband on that account. A wife should study to reclaim her husband by more attention to please him. Sir, a man will not, once in a hundred instances, leave his wife and go to a harlot, if his wife has not been negligent of pleasing."

Being asked if it was not hard that one deviation from chastity should absolutely ruin a young woman. Johnson. "Why no, Sir ; it is the great principle which she is taught. When she has given up that principle, she has given up every notion of female honour and virtue, which are all included in chastity."

When Mr. B. once censured a gentleman of his acquaintance for marrying a second time, as it shewed a disregard of his first wife, he said, "Not at all, Sir. On the contrary, were he not to marry again, it might be concluded that his first wife had given him a disgust to marriage ; but by taking a second wife he pays the highest compliment to the first, by shewing that she made him so happy as a married man, that he wishes to be so a second time."

As a proof that Dr. Johnson possessed great personal courage, Mr. B. gives the following instances.

On being told one day of the danger there was that a gun might burst if charged with many balls, he put in six or seven, and fired it off against a wall. Mr. Langton, when swimming with the Doctor near Oxford, cautioned him against a pool, which was reckoned particularly dangerous; upon which Johnson directly swam into it.

One night he was attacked in the street by four men, to whom he would not yield, but kept them all at bay, till the watch came up, and carried both him and them to the round-house.

Foote, who so successfully revived the old comedy, by exhibiting living characters, had resolved to imitate Johnson on the stage, expecting great profits from his ridicule of so celebrated a man. Johnson being informed of his intention, and being at dinner at Mr. Thomas Davies's the bookseller, he asked Mr. Davies "What was the common price of an oak-stick;" and being answered six-pence, "Why then, Sir, (said he) give me leave to send your servant to purchase me a shilling one. I'll have a double quantity; for I am told Foote means to *take me off*, as he calls it, and I am determined the fellow shall not do it with impunity." Davies took care to acquaint Foote of this, which effectually checked the wantonness of the mimic. Mr. Macpherson's menaces made Johnson provide himself with the same implement of defence; and had he been attacked he would have made his corporal prowess be felt as much as his intellectual.

His "Journey to the Western Islands of Scotland," is a most valuable performance. It abounds in extensive philosophical views of society, and in ingenious sentiments and lively description. A considerable part of it, indeed, consists of speculations, which many years before he saw the wild regions which we visited together, probably had employed his attention, though the actual sight of those scenes undoubtedly quickened and augmented them. Mr. Orme, the very able historian, agreed with Mr. B. in this opinion,

which

which he thus strongly expressed:—" There are in that book thoughts, which, by long revolution in the great mind of Johnson, have been formed and polished like pebbles rolled in the ocean!"

In the year 1776 an Epitaph, which Dr. Johnson had written for the monument of Dr. Goldsmith in Westminster Abbey, gave occasion to a remonstrance to the Monarch of Literature.

Sir William Forbes, who gave Mr. B. an account of this circumstance, writes to him thus—" I enclose the Round Robin. This *jeu d'esprit* took its rise one day at dinner at our friend Sir Joshua Reynolds's. All the company present, except myself, were friends and acquaintance of Dr. Goldsmith. The Epitaph, written for him by Dr. Johnson, became the subject of conversation, and various emendations were suggested, which it was agreed should be submitted to the Doctor's consideration.—But the question was; who should have the courage to propose them to him? At last it was hinted, that there could be no way so good as that of a Round Robin, as the sailors call it, which they make use of when they enter into a conspiracy, so as not to let it be known who puts his name first or last to the paper. This proposition was instantly assented to, and Dr. Barnard, Dean of Derry, now Bishop of Killaloe, drew up an address to Dr. Johnson on the occasion, replete with wit and humour, but which it was feared the Doctor might think treated the subject with too much levity. Mr. Burke then proposed the address as it stands in the paper in writing, of which the following is a copy:

"*We the circumscribers, having read with great pleasure, an intended Epitaph for the Monument of Dr. Goldsmith, which, considered abstractedly, appears to be, for elegant composition, and masterly style, in every respect worthy of the pen of its learned author, are yet of opinion, that the character of the deceased as a writer, particularly as a Poet, is perhaps not delineated with all the exactness which Dr. Johnson is capable of giving it. We therefore, with deference to his superior judgment,*

ment, humbly requeſt that he would at leaſt take the trouble of reviſing it, and of making ſuch additions and alterations as he ſhall think proper, upon a further peruſal: But if we might venture to expreſs our wiſhes, they would lead us to requeſt, that he would write the Epitaph in Engliſh, rather than in Latin: as we think that the memory of ſo eminent an Engliſh writer ought to be perpetuated in that language to which his works are likely to be ſo laſting an ornament, which we alſo know to have been the opinion of the late Doctor himſelf.

Thos. Franklin.   T. Barnard.
Ant. Channier.   R. B. Sheridan.
G. Colman,   P. Metcalf.
Wm. Vackell,   E. Gibbon.
J. Reynolds,   Jos. Warton.
W. Forbes.   Edm. Burke.

"Sir Joſhua agreed to carry it to Dr. Johnſon, who received it with great good humour, and deſired Sir Joſhua to tell the gentlemen, that he would alter the Epitaph in any manner they pleaſed, as to the ſenſe of it; *but he would never conſent to diſgrace the walls of Weſtminſter Abbey with an Engliſh inſcription.*"

Tom Davies, the bookſeller, in 1778, unfortunately failed in his circumſtances, and much indebted to Dr. Johnſon's kindneſs for obtaining for him many alleviations of his diſtreſs. Johnſon blamed his folly in quitting the ſtage, by which he and his wife got five hundred pounds a year. Mr B. told the Doctor he believed it was owing to Churchill's attack upon him;

"He mouths a ſentence as curs mouth a bone."

Johnſon replied, "I believe ſo too, Sir. But what a man is he who is to be driven from the ſtage by a line! Another line would have driven him from his ſhop."

Mr. Thomas Davies was ſoon to have a benefit at Drury-lane theatre, as ſome relief to his unfortunate circumſtances. Dr. Johnſon, Mr. Boſwell, and

and their friends, were all warmly interested for his success, and had contributed towards it. However, they thought there was no harm in having a joke, when he could not be hurt by it. Mr. B. proposed that he should be brought on to speak a Prologue upon the occasion; and began to mutter fragments of what it might be: as, that when now grown *old*, he was obliged to cry, "Poor Tom's *a-cold*;—that he owned he had been driven from the stage by a Churchill, but that this was no disgrace, for a Churchill had beat the French; that he had been satyrised as "mouthing a sentence as curs mouth a bone," but he was now glad of a bone to pick.—"Nay, (said Johnson,) I would have him to say,

"Mad Tom is come to see the world again."

Goldsmith being mentioned one day, Johnson observed that it was long before his merit came to be acknowledged. That he once complained to him, in ludicrous terms of distress, "Whenever I write any thing the public make a point to know nothing at all about it: but that his "Traveller" brought him into high reputation.

Johnson, (now in his seventieth year) said, "it is a man's own fault, it is from want of use, if his mind grows torpid in old age."

This season there was a whimsical fashion in the newspapers, of applying Shakspeare's words to describe living people well known in the world; which was done under the title of "*Modern Characters from Shakspeare*;" many of which were admirably adapted. The fancy took so much, that they were afterwards collected into a pamphlet. Somebody said to Johnson, that he had not been in those characters. "Yes, (said he) I have. I should have been sorry to be left out." He then repeated what had been applied to him.

"I must borrow GARAGANTUA's mouth."

Johnson had a noble ambition floating in his mind, and had, undoubtedly, often speculated on the possibility

bility of his super-eminent powers being rewarded in this great and liberal country by the highest honours of the state. Sir William Scott, upon the death of the late Lord Litchfield, who was Chancellor of the University of Oxford, said to Johnson, " What a pity it is, Sir, that you did not follow the profession of the law! You might have been Lord Chancellor of Great Britain, and attained to the dignity of the Peerage; and now that the title of Litchfield, your native city, is extinct, you might have had it." Johnson upon this seemed much agitated; and, in an angry tone, exclaimed, " Why will you vex me, by suggesting this, when it is too late ?"

But he did not repine at the prosperity of others.— The late Dr. Thomas Leland told Mr. Courtenay, that when Mr. Edmund Burke shewed Johnson his fine house and lands near Beaconsfield, Johnson coolly said, " *Non equidem invideo; miror magis.*"

In May 1780, Mr. Boswell, then at Edinburgh, received the following letter from Mr. Langton:

" The melancholy information you have received concerning Mr. Beauclerk's death is true. Had his talents been directed in any sufficient degree as they ought, I have always been strongly of opinion, that they were calculated to make an illustrious figure; and that opinion, as it had been in part formed by Dr. Johnson's judgment, receives more and more confirmation by hearing what, since his death, Dr. Johnson has said concerning them; a few evenings ago he was at Mr. Vesey's, where Lord Althorpe, who was one of a numerous company there, addressed Dr. Johnson on the subject of Mr. Beauclerk's death, saying, ' Our club has had a great loss since we met last.' He replied, ' A loss, that perhaps the whole nation could not repair!' The Doctor then went on to speak of his endowments, and particularly extolled the wonderful ease with which he uttered what was highly excellent. He said, that no man ever was so free when he was going to say a good thing, from a look that expressed that it was coming; or, when he had said it, from a look that expressed that it had come. At Mr. Thrale's,

Thrale's, some days before, when we were talking on the same subject, he said, referring to the same idea of his facility, 'That Beauclerk's talents were those which he had felt himself more disposed to envy, than those of any whom he had known.'

"At the evening I have spoken of above, at Mr. Vesey's, you would have been much gratified, as it exhibited an instance of the high importance in which Dr. Johnson's character is held, I think even beyond any I was ever before witness to. The company consisted chiefly of ladies, among whom were the Duchess Dowager of Portland, the Duchess of Beaufort, whom I suppose, from her rank, I must mention before her mother Mrs. Boscawen, and her elder sister Mrs. Lewson, who was likewise there; Lady Lucan, Lady Clermont, and others of note, both for their stations and understandings. Among the gentlemen were, Lord Althorpe, whom I have before named, Lord Macartney, Sir Joshua Reynolds, Lord Lucan, Mr. Wraxall, whose book you have probably seen, '*The Tour to the Northern Parts of Europe*;' a very agreeable ingenious man; Dr. Warren, Mr. Pepys, the Master in Chancery, whom I believe you know, and Dr. Barnard, the Provost of Eton. As soon as Dr. Johnson was come in and had taken a chair, the company began to collect round him, till they became not less than four or five deep; those behind standing, and listening over the heads of those that were sitting near him. The conversation for some time was chiefly between Dr. Johnson and the Provost of Eton, while the others contributed occasionally their remarks. Without attempting to detail the particulars of the conversation, which perhaps if I did, I should spin my account out to a tedious length, I thought, my dear Sir, this general account of the respect with which our valued friend was attended to, might be acceptable."

Of the extraordinary tumults this year, Dr. Johnson has given the following concise, lively, and just account, in his "Letters to Mrs. Thrale."

"On Friday the good Protestants met in St. George's Fields, at the summons of Lord George Gordon, and marching

marching to Westminster, insulted the Lords and Commons, who all bore it with great tameness. At night the outrages began by the demolition of the mass-house by Lincoln's-inn.

"An exact journal of a week's defiance of government I cannot give you. On Monday, Mr. Strahan, who had I think been insulted, spoke to Lord Mansfield, who had, I think, been insulted too, of the licentiousness of the populace; and his Lordship treated it as a very slight irregularity.

"On Tuesday night they pulled down Fielding's house, and burnt his goods in the street. They had gutted, on Monday, Sir George Savill's house, but the building was saved. On Tuesday evening, leaving Fielding's ruins, they went to Newgate to demand their companions, who had been seized demolishing the chapel. The keeper could not release them but by the Mayor's permission, which he went to ask; at his return he found all the prisoners released, and Newgate in a blaze. They then went to Bloomsbury, and fastened upon Lord Mansfield's house, which they pulled down; and as for his goods they totally burnt them. They have since gone to Caenwood, but a guard was there before them. They plundered some Papists, I think, and burnt a Mass-house in Moorfields the same night.

"On Wednesday I walked with Dr. Scott to look at Newgate, and found it in ruins, with the fire yet glowing. As I went by, the Protestants were plundering the Sessions-house at the Old Bailey. There were not, I believe, a hundred, but they did their work at leisure, in full security, without sentinels, without trepidation, as men lawfully employed in full day. Such is the cowardice of a commercial place.— On Wednesday they broke open the Fleet, and the King's Bench, and the Marshalsea, and Wood-street Compter, and Clerkenwell Bridewell, and released all the prisoners.

"At night they set fire to the Fleet, and to the King's Bench, and I know not how many other places,

places, and one might see the glare of conflagration fill the sky from many parts. The sight was dreadful. Some people were threatened: Mr. Strahan advised me to take care of myself. Such a time of terror you have been happy in not seeing.

" The King said in council, ' That the magistrates had not done their duty, but that he would do his own; and a proclamation was published, directing us to keep our servants within doors, as the peace was now to be preserved by force. The soldiers were sent out to different parts, and the town is now at quiet.

" The soldiers are stationed so as to be every where within call; there is no longer any body of rioters, and the individuals are haunted to their holes, and led to prison; Lord George was last night sent to the Tower. Mr. John Wilkes was this day in my neighbourhood, to seize the publishers of a seditious paper.

" Several chapels have been destroyed, and several inoffensive Papists have been plundered; but the high sport was to burn the gaols. This was a good rabble trick. The debtors and the criminals were all set at liberty; but of the criminals, as has always happened, many are already re taken; and two pirates have surrendered themselves, and it is expected that they will be pardoned.

Government now acts again with its proper force; and we are all again under the protection of the King and the Law. I thought that it would be agreeable to you and my master to have my testimony to the publick security: and that you would sleep more quietly when I told you that you are safe.

" There has, indeed, been an universal panick, from which the King was the first that recovered.— Without the concurrence of his ministers, or the assistance of the civil magistrate, he put the soldiers in motion, and saved the town from calamities, such a rabble's government must naturally produce.

" The publick has escaped a very heavy calamity. The rioters attempted the Bank on Wednesday-night, but in no great number, and, like other thieves, with no great resolution. Jack Wilkes headed the party that drove them away. It is agreed, that if they had seized the Bank on Tuesday, at the height of the panick, when no resistance had been prepared, they might have carried irrecoverably away whatever they had found. Jack, who was always zealous for order and decency, declares, that if he be trusted with power, he will not leave a rioter alive. There is, however, now no longer any need of heroism or bloodshed, no blue ribband is any longer worn."

At a city dinner where were present, Mr. Wilkes, Dr. Beattie, and Mr. Boswell, the Doctor gave an entertaining account of *Bet Flint*, a woman of the town, who with some eccentrick talents, and much effrontery, forced herself upon his acquaintance.— " Bet, (said he) wrote her own Life in verse, which she brought to me, wishing that I would furnish her with a Preface to it (laughing). I used to say of her, that she was generally slut and drunkard, occasionally whore and thief. She had, however, genteel lodgings, a spinnet, on which she played, and a boy that walked before her chair. Poor Bet was taken up on a charge of stealing a counterpane, and tried at the Old Bailey. Chief Justice ———, who loved a wench, summed up favourably, and she was acquitted. After which, Bet said, with a gay and satisfied air, ' Now that the counterpane is my own, I shall make a petticoat of it."

He told his friends that he had in one day written six sheets of a translation from the French, adding, " I should be glad to see it now. I wish that I had copies of all the pamphlets written against me, as it is said Pope had. Had I known that I should make so much noise in the world, I should have been at pains to collect them. I believe there is hardly a day in which there is not something about me in the newspapers."

The following curious anecdote is from Dr. Burney's own words: " Dr. Burney related to Dr. Johnson the partiality which his writings had excited in a friend of Dr. Burney's, the late Mr. Bewley, well known in Norfolk,

Norfolk, by the name of the *Philosopher of Massingham*; who, from the Ramblers, and Plan of his Dictionary, and long before the author's fame was established, by the Dictionary itself, or any other work, had conceived such a reverence for him, that he urgently begged Dr. Burney to give him the cover of the first letter he had received from him, as a relick of so estimable a writer. This was in 1755. In 1760, when Dr. Burney visited Dr. Johnson at the Temple in London, where he had then chambers, he happened to arrive there before he was up, and being shewn into the room where he was to breakfast, finding himself alone, he examined the contents of the apartment, to try whether he could, undiscovered, steal any thing to send to his friend Bewley, as another relick of the admirable Dr. Johnson. But finding nothing better to his purpose, he cut some bristles of a hearth-broom, and enclosed them in a letter to his country enthusiast, who received them with due reverence.

"The Doctor was so sensible of the honour done him by a man of genius and science, to whom he was an utter stranger, that he said to Dr. Burney, "Sir, there is no man possessed of the smallest portion of modesty, but must be flattered with the admiration of such a man. I'll give him a set of my Lives, if he will do me the honour to accept of them."

"In this he kept his word; and Dr. Burney had not only the pleasure of gratifying his friend with a present more worthy of his acceptance than the segment of a hearth-broom, but soon after of introducing him to Dr. Johnson himself in Bolt-court, with whom he had the satisfaction of conversing a considerable time, not a fortnight before his death, which happened in St. Martin's-street, during his visit to Dr. Burney, in the house where the great Sir Isaac Newton had lived and died before."

In one of his registers of the year 1782, there occurs the following curious passage: "Jan. 20. The ministry is dissolved. I prayed with Francis, and gave thanks." It has been the subject of discussion, whether there are two distinct particulars mentioned here, or that

that we are to understand the giving of thanks to be in consequence of the dissolution of the ministry. In support of the last of these conjectures, may be urged his mean opinion of that ministry, which has frequently appeared in the course of this work; and it is strongly confirmed by what he said on the subject to Mr. Seward:—" I am glad the ministry is removed. Such a bunch of imbecility never disgraced a country. If they sent a messenger into the City to take up a printer, the messenger was taken up instead of the printer, and committed by the sitting Alderman. If they sent one army to the relief of another, the first army was defeated and taken before the second arrived. I will not say what they did was always wrong; but it was always done at a wrong time."

In December, 1782, he writes to Mr. B. " Having passed almost this whole year in a succession of disorders, I went in October to Brighthelmston, whither I came in a state of so much weakness that I rested four times in walking between the inn and the lodging. By physic and abstinence I grew better, and am now reasonably easy, though at a great distance from health. I am afraid, however, that health begins, after seventy, and often long before, to have a meaning different from that which it had at thirty. But it is culpable to murmur at the established order of the creation, as it is vain to oppose it. He that lives, must grow old, and he that would rather grow old than die, has God to thank for the infirmities of old age."

The death of Mr. Thrale had made a very material alteration upon Johnson, with respect to his reception in that family. The manly authority of the husband no longer curbed the lively exuberance of the lady;— and as her vanity had been fully gratified, by having the Colossus of Literature attached to her for many years, she gradually became less assiduous to please him.

It has been observed and wondered at, that Mr. Charles Fox never talked with any freedom in the presence of Dr. Johnson, though it is well known that his conversation is various, fluent, and exceedingly agreeable. Johnson's experience, however, founded him in going on thus: "Fox never talks in private company, not from any determination not to talk, but because he has not the first motion. A man who is used to the applause of the House of Commons, has no wish for that of a private company. A man accustomed to throw for a thousand pounds, if set down to throw for sixpence, would not be at the pains to count his dice. Burke's talk is the ebullition of his mind; he does not talk from a desire of distinction, but because his mind is full."

Mr. B. and the Doctor once talked of the accusation against a gentleman for supposed delinquencies in India. JOHNSON. "What foundation there is for accusation I know not, but they will not get at him.—Where bad actions are committed at so great a distance, a delinquent can obscure the evidence till the scent becomes cold; there is a cloud between, which cannot be penetrated, therefore all distant power is bad. I am clear that the best plan for the government of India is a despotic governor; for if he be a good man, it is evidently the best government; and supposing him to be a bad man, it is better to have one plunderer than many. A governor, whose power is checked, lets others plunder that he himself may be allowed to plunder. But if despotic, he sees that the more he lets others plunder the less there will be for himself, so he restrains them; and though he himself plunders, the country is a gainer, compared with being plundered by numbers."

In the autumn of 1783, he received a visit from the celebrated Mrs. Siddons. He gives this account of it in one of his letters to Mrs. Thrale: "Mrs. Siddons, in her visit to me, behaved with great modesty and propriety, and left nothing behind her to be censured or despised. Neither praise nor money, the two powerful corrupters of mankind, seem to have depraved her. I shall be glad to see her again. Her brother Kemble calls on me, and pleases me very well. Mrs. Siddons and I talked of plays; and she told me her intention of exhibiting this winter the characters

characters of Constance, Catherine, and Isabella, in Shakspeare."

When Mrs. Siddons came into the room, there happened to be no chair ready for her, which he observing, said with a smile, "Madam, you who so often occasion a want of seats to other people, will the more easily excuse the want of one yourself."

Having placed himself by her, he with great good humour entered upon a consideration of the English drama; and, among other enquiries, particularly asked her, which of Shakspeare's characters she was most pleased with. Upon her answering that she thought the character of Queen Catherine, in Henry the Eighth, the most natural. I think so too, Madam, (said he;) and whenever you perform it, I will once more hobble out to the theatre myself." Mrs. Siddons promised she would do herself the honour of acting his favourite part for him; but many circumstances happened to prevent the representation of King Henry the Eighth during the Doctor's life.

In the course of this visit he thus gave his opinion upon the merits of some of the principal performers whom he remembered to have seen upon the stage.—
" Mrs. Porter, in the vehemence of rage, and Mrs. Clive in the sprightliness of humour, I have never seen equalled. What Clive did best, she did better than Garrick; but could not do half so many things well; she was a better romp than any I ever saw in nature. Pritchard, in common life, was a vulgar ideot; she would talk of her *gownd:* but, when she appeared upon the stage, seemed to be inspired by gentility and understanding. I once talked with Colley Cibber, and thought him ignorant of the principles of his art. Garrick, Madam, was no declaimer; there was not one of his own scene-shifters, who could not have spoken *To be, or not to be,* better than he did;— yet he was the only one whom I could call a master both in tragedy and comedy; though I liked him best in comedy. A true conception of character, and natural expression of it, were his distinguishing excellencies."

Having expatiated, with his usual force and eloquence, on Mr. Garrick's extraordinary eminence as an actor, he concluded with this compliment to his social talents:—" And after all, Madam, I thought him less to be envied on the stage than at the head of a table."

Johnson, indeed, had thought more upon the subject of acting than might be generally supposed. Talking of it one day to Mr. Kemble, he said, " Are you, Sir, one of those enthusiasts who believe yourself transformed into the very characters you represent?" Upon Mr. Kemble's answering he had never felt so strong a persuasion himself; " To be sure not, Sir, (said Johnson). The thing is impossible. And if Garrick really believed himself to be that monster Richard the Third, he deserved to be hanged every time he performed it."

After the re-establishment of his health, as mentioned by Mrs. Piozzi, he continued free from any alarming complaints till 1783, when, during the night, in the summer-season, he was attacked with a paralytic stroke, at his house in Bolt-court, Fleet-street, which deprived him of the powers of speech. He awoke with the attack, and immediately rung the bell; but on the approach of his servant could not articulate a syllable.— Feeling, however, that he retained the full use of his senses, he signified a desire for pen, ink, and paper, and wrote the following note to Mr. Allen, a printer, who lived next door to him; a very honest, virtuous, good man, who had been his intimate and confidential friend for many years.

" Dear Sir,

" It hath pleased Almighty God this morning to deprive me of the powers of speech; and as I do not know

"know but that it might be his further good pleasure
"to deprive me soon of my senses, I request you will
"on the receipt of this note, come to me, and act for
"me, as the exigencies of my case may require.

"I am sincerely your's,

"S. JOHNSON.

"To Mr. Edmund Allen."

Mr. Allen immediately attended him, and sent for his usual physicians, Drs. Heberden and Brocklesby, who, in the course of a few months, recovered him so much, that he was able to take the air, and visit his friends as usual.

He continued every day growing better; and as he found his spirits much relieved by society, it was proposed by some friends to establish a club in the neighbourhood, which would answer that purpose. The Doctor seemed highly pleased with the proposal, and after naming some friends, whom he wished to have about him, they met early in the winter of 1783, at the Essex-head, in Essex-street, for the first time, when the Doctor being unanimously called to the chair, he surprised them with a set of rules drawn by himself, as Ben. Jonson did his "*Leges Convivales*," which being read, and approved of by the rest of the members, were regularly entered in a book for that purpose.

These rules, to use his own words, are "founded in frequency and parsimony;" and as the public may have some curiosity in seeing so learned a man as Dr. Johnson in his hours of social relaxation, the following is an authentic copy of them, together with the names of the gentlemen who composed the club, as they stood "on the rota of monthly attendance."

General Rules of the Essex-Head Club, commenced the 10th of December, 1783.

" To day deep thoughts with me resolve to drench
" In mirth—which after no repenting draws."
MILTON.

I. THE Club shall consist of twenty-four members. The meetings shall be on the Monday, Wednesday[*], and Saturday of every week; but on the *week before Easter-day* there shall be no meeting.

II. Every member is at liberty to introduce a friend once in a week, but not oftener.

III. Two members shall oblige themselves to attend in their turn every night from eight to ten o'clock, or procure two to attend in their room.

IV. Every member present at the club shall spend at least sixpence; and every man who stays away, shall forfeit three-pence.

V. The master of the house shall keep an account of the absent members, and deliver to the President of the night a list of the forfeits incurred.

VI. When any member returns after absence, he shall immediately lay down his forfeits; which, if he omits to do, the President shall require them of him.

VII. There shall be no general reckoning, but every member shall adjust his own expences.

VIII. The night of indispensible attendance will come to every member once a month. Whoever shall for three months together omit to attend himself, or by substitution—nor shall make any apology on the fourth month, shall be considered as having abdicated the Club.

IX. When a vacancy is to be filled, the name of the candidate, and of the member recommending him, shall stand in the club-room three nights: on the fourth he may be chosen by ballot, six members at least being present, and two thirds of the ballot being in his favour, or the majority, should the numbers not be divisible by three.

[*] Several of the members being Fellows of the Royal Society, this night was afterwards changed to Thursday for their convenience.

X. The

X. The master of the house shall give notice, six days before, to each of those members whose turn of necessary attendance is come.

The notice may be in these words: ["Sir, On —— the —— of —— will be your turn of presiding at the Essex-head; your company is therefore earnestly requested."]

One penny shall be left by each member for the waiter.

Nightly Rules of the Essex-head Club.

I. The President will collect seven-pence from each member at his entrance, marking his attendance thus \ ; and three-pence for every preceding night which is not marked against his name in the book thus V.

II. The forfeits to be paid over to the landlord. The seven-pence to be considered as part of each member's distinct reckoning.

III. Two letters of notice are to be forwarded each night, by the Penny-post, to the Presidents of that day seven-night, as by list of the members.

IV. When the forfeits are paid, they should be noted in the book thus W.

List of the members of the Essex-head Club, when first instituted, as they stood on the rota of monthly attendance.

Dr. Johnson,
Dr. Horsley,
Dr. Brocklesby,
—— Jodderell, Esq.
William Cooke, Esq.
W. Ryland, Esq.
—— Paradise, Esq.
Dr. Burney,
John Hoole, Esq.
Francesco Sastres, Esq.
Mr. Edmund Allen, (Printer),
Hon. Daines Barrington,
James Barry, Esq.
J. Wyatt, Esq.

Mr. John Nichols, (Printer)
Edward Poore, Esq.
Rt. Hon. William Wyndham, M. P.
Thomas Tyers, Esq.
William Cruikshank, Esq.
W. Seward, Esq.
Richard Clarke, Esq. (late Lord Mayor of London.)*
William Strahan, Esq. M. P.
Arthur Murphy, Esq.
Dr. W. Scott, (now Sir W. Scott.)

The Doctor, when his health permitted it, was a constant visitor, and seemed to reserve his spirits and conversation for those meetings, to the delight and improvement of his friends. In this career of innocent relaxation, the constant bleeding which he was obliged to undergo for the necessary reduction of an asthma (with which he was afflicted many years) brought on a dropsy, which again confined him to his house for some months in the spring of 1784.

In the summer of the same year he grew so much better, that supposing the air of Italy might be the best means of re-establishing his health, he hinted in conversation his desire to undertake that journey. His old and intimate friend Sir Joshua Reynolds, eager to extend a life so dear to himself, and so valuable to the public, and yet thinking the Doctor's finances not equal to the project, mentioned the circumstance to the Lord Chancellor, adding, "that if his pension could be encreased two "hundred a-year more, it would be fully sufficient for "the purpose." His Lordship met the proposal cordially, and took the first opportunity to speak of it to the K—g.

His M——y had been previously advertised of the Doctor's intention, and seemed to think favourably of

---

* 1785.—Mr. Clarke's Mayoralty was distinguished by exemplary attendance to the duties of that high office; wisdom in his conduct, and politeness to his fellow citizens, to whom he was always easy of access. The Corporation of London unanimously voted him their thanks, in a distinguished manner, for his singular services as their Chief Magistrate; it was, however, his character as a private gentleman, which first procured him the Doctor's friendship.

it;

it; but whether he did not conceive the Lord Chancellor's application to be direct, or that he understood Dr. Johnson's physicians had no opinion of this journey, when it was mentioned to him he waved the conversation.

The Chancellor, on this, wrote to Dr. Johnson, informing him, that as the return of his health might not wait the forms of an addition to his pension, he might draw immediately upon him for 500l. which lay at his banker's for that purpose.

So liberal and unexpected an offer, from a quarter where he had no right to expect it, called forth the Doctor's gratitude, and he immediately wrote the Lord Chancellor the following letter:

"My Lord,

"After a long and not inattentive observation on mankind, the generosity of your Lordship's offer raises in me no less wonder than gratitude. Bounty so liberally bestowed I should gladly receive, if my condition made it necessary; for to such a mind who would not be proud to own his obligation? But it hath pleased God to restore me to such a measure of health, that if I should now appropriate so much of a fortune destined to do good, I could not escape from myself the charge of advancing a false claim. My journey to the continent, though I once thought it necessary, was never much encouraged by my physicians, and I was very desirous that your Lordship should be told of it by Sir Joshua Reynolds as an event very uncertain; for if I should grow much better I should not be willing, and if much worse I should not be able to migrate.

"Your Lordship was first solicited without my knowledge; but when I was told that you was pleased to honour me with your patronage, I did not expect to hear of a refusal; yet as I have had no long time to brood hope, and have not rioted in imaginary opulence, this cold reception has scarce been a disappointment; and from your Lordship's kindness I have "received

"received a benefit which men like you are able to bestow. I shall now live *mihi carior*, with a higher opinion of my own merit.

I am, my Lord,
Your Lordship's most obliged,
Most grateful,
And most humble servant,
S. JOHNSON."

To the Right Honourable
the Lord Chancellor.
Sept. 1784.

The Doctor was at Litchfield when he wrote this letter, on his return from Derbyshire, in tolerable good health. However on his arrival in town in October, Providence thought fit to make all pecuniary as well as medical application unnecessary. The dropsy returned in his legs, which swelled to such a thickness that his physicians had no hopes of his recovery. They, however, continued to visit him, and prescribe such medicines as were best calculated to compose and quiet his pains. He was likewise occasionally visited by several of his friends, and, at intervals, possessed his usual spirits, and flow of conversation.

His constant friend, as well as physician, Dr. Brocklesby, calling upon him one morning, after a night of much pain and restlessness, he suddenly repeated these lines from Macbeth:

—————————— Oh! Doctor,
"Canst thou not minister to a mind diseas'd,
"Pluck from the memory a rooted sorrow,
"Raze out the written troubles of the brain,
"And with some sweet oblivious antidote
"Cleanse the full bosom of that perilous stuff
"Which weighs upon the heart?———

And when the Doctor replied in the following words of the same author:

—————————— "Therein the patient
"Must minister unto himself."

He

He exclaimed, "well applied,—that's true,—that's more than poetically true."

On the Thursday before his death, finding himself grow worse, he insisted on knowing from Dr. B——, whether there were any hopes of his recovery? The Doctor at first waved the question; but he repeating it with great eagerness, the other told him, "that from the complication of disorders he laboured under, and the advanced state of life he was in, there were but little hopes." He received his fate with firmness; thanked him, and said he would endeavour to compose himself for the approaching scene.

The next day, a friend of his hearing the alarming sentence, and anxious to have every possible means tried for his recovery, brought Dr. Warren to him; but he would take no prescription; he said, "he felt it too late, the soul then wanted medicine and not the body." Upon the Doctor's taking his leave, he told him "he must not go till he had given him his fee, and then presenting him with a copy of *his Lives of the Poets*, begged his acceptance of it, assuring him, "that was all the fee he had ever given his other two physicians."

For some weeks before he died, he received the sacrament two, or three times in each week. An intimate friend of his coming into the room one day, after this ceremony, the Doctor exclaimed "Oh! my friend, I owe you many obligations through life; but they will all be more than amply repaid by your taking this most important advice, BE A GOOD CHRISTIAN."

The next night he was at intervals delirious; and in one of those fits, seeing a friend at his bedside, he exclaimed, "What, will that fellow never have done talking poetry to me?" He recovered his senses before morning, but spoke little after this. His heart, however, was not unemployed, as by his fixed attention, and the motion of his lips, it was evident he was pouring out his soul in prayer. He languished in this manner till seven o'clock on Monday evening, the 13th of December, 1784, and then expired without a groan, in the 75th year of his age.

Dr.

Dr. Brocklesby, who will not be suspected of fanaticism, obliged Mr. Boswell with the following account of Dr. Johnson's death:

"For some time before his death all his fears were calmed and absorbed by the prevalence of his faith, and his trust in the merits and *propitiation* of Jesus Christ.

"He talked often to me about the necessity of faith in the *sacrifice* of Jesus, as necessary beyond all good works, whatever, for the salvation of mankind.

"He pressed me to study Dr. Clarke, and to read his sermons. I asked him why he pressed Dr. Clarke, an Arian. 'Because (said he) he is fullest on the *propitiatory sacrifice.*'

Johnson having thus in his mind the true Christian scheme, at once rational and consolatory, uniting justice and mercy in the Divinity, with the improvement of human nature, while the Holy Sacrament was celebrating in his apartment, fervently uttered this prayer:

"Almighty and most merciful Father, I am now, as to human eyes it seems, about to commemorate, for the last time, the death of thy Son Jesus Christ, our Saviour and Redeemer. Grant, O Lord, that my whole hope and confidence may be in his merits, and thy mercy; enforce and accept my imperfect repentance; make this commemoration available to the confirmation of my faith, the establishment of my hope, and the enlargement of my charity; and make the death of thy Son Jesus Christ effectual to my redemption. Have mercy upon me, and pardon the multitude of my offences. Bless my friends; have mercy upon all men. Support me, by the Holy Spirit, in the days of weakness, and at the hour of death; and receive me, at my death, to everlasting happiness, for the sake of Jesus Christ. Amen."

"The Doctor, from the time that he was certain his death was near, appeared to be perfectly resigned, was seldom or never fretful or out of temper, and often said to his faithful servant, 'Attend, Francis, to the salvation

salvation of your soul, which is the object of greatest importance:" he also explained to him passages in the scripture, and seemed to have pleasure in talking upon religious subjects.

"On Monday the 13th of December, the day on which he died, a Miss Morris, daughter to a particular friend of his, called, and said to Francis, that she begged to be permitted to see the Doctor, that she might earnestly request him to give her his blessing.—Francis went into the room, followed by the young lady, and delivered the message. The Doctor turned himself in the bed, and said, 'God bless you my dear!' These were the last words he spoke.—His difficulty of breathing increased till about seven o'clock in the evening, when Mr. Barber and Mrs. Desmoulins, who were sitting in the room, observing that the noise he made in breathing had ceased, went to the bed, and found he was dead."

About two days after his death the following very agreeable account was communicated to Mr. Malone, in a letter, by the Honourable Mr. Byng:

"DEAR SIR,

"SINCE I saw you, I have had a long conversation with Cawston*, who sat up with Dr. Johnson from nine o'clock on Sunday evening till ten o'clock on Monday morning. And from what I can gather from him, it should seem, that Dr. Johnson was perfectly composed, steady in hope, and resigned to death. At the interval of each hour, they assisted him to sit up in his bed, and move his legs, which were in much pain; when he regularly addressed himself to fervent prayer; and though sometimes his voice failed him, his senses never did, during that time. The only sustenance he received was cider and water. He said his mind was prepared, and the time to his dissolution seemed long. At six in the morning he enquired the hour, and, on being informed, said that all went on regularly, and he felt he had but a few hours to live.

* A servant to the Right Hon. W. Wyndham.

"At ten in the morning he parted from Cawston, saying, 'You should not detain Mr. Windham's servant——I thank you;—bear my remembrance to your master.' Cawston says, that no man could appear more collected, more devout, or less terrified at the approaching minute.

"This account, which is so much more agreeable than, and somewhat different from your's, has given us the satisfaction of thinking that that great man died as he lived, full of resignation, strengthened in faith, and joyful in hope."

A few days before his death he had asked Sir John Hawkins, as one of his executors, where he should be buried; and on being answered "Doubtless in Westminster Abbey," seemed to feel a satisfaction very natural to a poet, and indeed very natural to every man of any imagination, who has no family sepulchre in which he can be laid with his fathers. Accordingly, upon Monday, December 20, his remains were deposited in that noble and renowned edifice; and over his grave was placed a large blue flag stone, with this inscription:

SAMUEL JOHNSON, LL.D.
Obiit xiii Die Decembris,
Anno Domini
M.DCC.LXXXIV.
Ætatis suæ LXXV.

His funeral was attended by a respectable number of his friends, particularly by many of the members of the Literary Club, who were then in town; and was also honoured by the presence of several of the Reverend Chapter of Westminster. His school fellow, Dr. Taylor, performed the mournful office of reading the service.

As Johnson had abundant homage paid to him during his life, so no writer in this nation ever had such an accumulation of literary honours after his death. A sermon upon that event was preached in St. Mary's Church, Oxford, before the University, by the Reverend Mr. Agutter, of Magdalen College.

His body was opened on Wednesday December 15, in the presence of Drs. Heberden and Brocklesby, where the causes which produced his last disorder were discoverable, but found impracticable to have been removed by medicine. His heart was *uncommonly large*, as if analogous to the extent and *liberality of his mind:* and what was very extraordinary, one of his kidneys was entirely consumed, though he never once complained of any *nephritic*, or gravelly disorder. It is, however, to be conjectured, that he had some *presentiment* of this circumstance, as a few months before his death he had an argument with his physicians, on the possibility of a man's living after the loss of one of his kidneys.

Some time previous to his death he made a will, subscribed only by two witnesses; but telling the circumstance to some friend, who knew he had a freehold of about twelve pounds a year, in Litchfield, in right of his father, another was drawn; but so tardy are some of the wisest men, even in the most necessary acts, when they awaken the fears of death—it was only a few weeks before he died, that the blanks were filled up. On the same principle of delay, the revision of many manuscripts was postponed, some of which were burned by the Doctor the week before he died, to avoid being left in an imperfect state. Among the rest was one book, out of two, wherein he had noted hints for writing his life, which he committed to the flames by mistake.

Though I have subjoined an authentic copy of the Doctor's will to these Memoirs, there are two clauses which, in justice to him, ought particularly to be explained and commented on.—By the first he has left an annuity of seventy pounds to his old, faithful black servant, Francis Barber, who lived with him for near forty years, and who, by a faithful and diligent discharge of his duty, had deserved this mark of his master's generosity and friendship. When he had determined on this legacy for him, he asked Dr. Brocklesby, who happened to be sitting with him, how much people in general left to their favourite servants? The other answered him, from twenty to fifty pounds a year, but that no nobleman gave more than the last sum: "Why then," says the

the Doctor, "I'll be *Nobilissimus*, for I have left Frank *seventy pounds* a year; and as it probably will make the poor fellow's mind easy, to know that he will be provided for after my death, I'll be obliged to you to tell him of it."

If we compare this generous action with that of his brother poet Pope, how superior Dr. Johnson rises in generous feelings and grateful remembrance of faithful services! When the bard of Twickenham died, he left but *one hundred pounds* to his faithful servant John Searle, and *one more* on the death of Mrs. Martha Blount, which was eventual; and yet he distinguishes this man, in his Epistle to Dr. Arbuthnot, under the character of *good John*.

"Shut, shut the door, good John, fatigued I said,
"Tie up the knocker, say, I'm sick, I'm dead."

And Dr. Warburton, who had an opportunity of knowing the fact, calls him, in a note upon this passage, "his old and faithful servant." But compliments pass from the head, generous actions arise from the heart.

The other clause does his memory equal honour. When Dr. Johnson's father died, which is now above thirty years ago, he owed Mr. Innys, a bookseller, who lived in Pater-noster Row, thirty pounds; after many enquiries the Doctor found out the descendant of this man, and has left him the sum of *two hundred pounds*, as a compensation for the loss of the principal, and interest, for so many years.

So anxious was this good man to discharge every part of his moral character with punctuality, that some time before his death he sat down to recollect what little sums he might owe in the early part of his life to particular friends, which were never given with a view to be restored. Among this number he sent a guinea to the son of an eminent printer, which he had borrowed of his father many years before, to pay his reckoning at a tavern.

He likewise recollected borrowing thirty pounds of Sir Joshua Reynolds at a great distance of time; "but this sum (said the Doctor to Sir Joshua, with a manliness of mind

mind which anfwered for the feelings of his friend being fimilar to his own) I intend to beftow on a charity which I know you'll approve of."

Dr. Johnfon's figure, even in his youth, could never have been calculated either " to make women falfe," or give him a preference in the fchools of manly, or military exercifes. His face was formed of large coarfe features, which, from a ftudious turn, when compofed, looked fluggifh, yet awful and contemplative. He had likewife nearly loft the fight of one of his eyes, which made him *courfe* every object he looked at in fo fingular a manner, as often to create pity, fometimes laughter. The head at the front of this book is efteemed a good likenefs; it was etched from a drawing made by Mr. Trotter after the Doctor had dined, when he was inclined to take his afternoon nap.

His face, however, was capable of great expreffion, both in refpect to *intelligence* and *mildnefs*, as all thofe can witnefs who have feen him in the glow of converfation, or under the influence of grateful feelings. I am the more confirmed in this opinion by the authority of a celebrated French phyfiognomift, who has, in a late publication on his art, given two different etchings of Dr. Johnfon's head, to fhew the correfpondence between the countenance and the mind.

In refpect to perfon, he was rather of the *heroic* ftature, being above the middle fize; but though ftrong, broad, and mufcular, his parts were flovenly put together. When he walked the ftreets, what with the conftant roll of his head, and the concomitant motion of his body, he appeared to make his way by that motion independent of his feet. At other times he was fubject to be feized with fudden convulfions, which fo agitated his whole frame, that to thofe who did not know his diforder, it had the appearance of madnefs—Indeed, to fee him in moft fituations, he was not favourably diftinguifhed either by nature or his habits.

His domeftic arrangements were always frugal, and he never afpired, even when his fame and reputation were at the higheft, to exhibit, either in his drefs or

eftablifhment,

establishment, what the world calls a genteel appearance.

He visited none of his friends so constantly as the late Mr. and Mrs. Thrale. In the family of this gentleman he lived a considerable part of the year, and they so perfectly understood his habits, and had such a proper relish for his conversation, that he seemed more *at home* there than any where else. He had a suite of apartments for himself, both at their town and country-house—formed a library principally of his own selection—directed the education of the young ladies, and was, in every respect, so much "the guide, philosopher, and friend" of the family, that Mr. Thrale, on his death, left him two hundred pounds, and appointed him one of his executors.

From the largeness of his person, the demands of nature were expected to be considerable, and nature was true to herself. He fed without much delicacy, either in choice or quantity, but then his dinner was his last meal for the day. He formerly drank his bottle, it is said, with a view to dispel that apprehension, which he dreaded through life, of approaching insanity. But afterwards suspecting danger from that habit he almost totally abandoned it. "For," said he, in that moral and philosophic strain which generally distinguished his remarks, "What ferments the spirits, may also derange the intellects; and the means employed to counteract dejection may hasten the approach of madness."

In his traffic with booksellers, he shewed no great regard to money-matters. By his Dictionary he no more than barely supported himself during the many years that he was employed in that great undertaking. By his Ramblers, I have before observed, he did not get much above two guineas per week; and tho' it is reasonable to suppose he might, on a representation of the encreasing fame of those valuable papers, have got his stipend encreased —he did not solicit it—" his wants being few, they were competently supplied."

CHARAC-

CHARACTER—BY Mr BOSWELL.

"His figure was large and well-formed, and his countenance of the cast of an ancient statue; yet his appearance was rendered strange, and somewhat uncouth, by convulsive cramps, by the scars of that distemper which it was once imagined the royal touch could cure, and by a slovenly mode of dress. He had the use only of one eye; yet so much does mind govern, and even supply the deficiency of organs, that his visual perceptions, as far as they extended, were uncommonly quick and accurate. So morbid was his temperament, that he never knew the natural joy of a free and vigorous use of his limbs; when he walked, it was like the struggling gait of one in fetters; when he rode, he had no command or direction of his horse, but was carried as if in a balloon. That with his constitution and habits of life he should have lived seventy-five years, is a proof that an inherent *vivida vis* is a powerful preservative of the human frame.

"He was prone to superstition, but not to credulity. Though his imagination might incline him to a belief of the marvellous and the mysterious, his vigorous reason examined the evidence with jealousy. He was a sincere and zealous Christian, of high Church of England and monarchical principles, which he would not tamely suffer to be questioned: and had, perhaps, at an early period, narrowed his mind somewhat too much, both as to religion and politics. His being impressed with the danger of extreme latitude in either, though he was of a very independent spirit, occasioned his appearing somewhat unfavourable to the prevalence of that noble freedom of sentiment which is the best possession of man. Nor can it be denied, that he had many prejudices, which, however frequently suggested many of his pointed sayings, that rather shewed a playfulness of fancy than any settled malignity.

"He was steady and inflexible in maintaining the obligations of religion and morality, both from a regard for the order of society, and from a veneration

for

for the great source of all order; correct, nay stern in his taste; hard to please, and easily offended; impetuous and irritable in his temper, but of a most humane and benevolent heart, which shewed itself not only in a most liberal charity, as far as his circumstances would allow, but in many instances of active benevolence.

"He loved praise when it was brought to him; but was too proud to seek for it. He was somewhat susceptible of flattery. As he was general and unconfined in his studies, he cannot be considered as a master of any one particular science; but he had accumulated a vast and various collection of learning and knowledge, which was so arranged in his mind, as to be ever in readiness to be brought forth. But his superiority over other learned men, consisted chiefly in what may be called the art of thinking, the art of using his mind; a certain continual power of seizing the useful substance of all that he knew, and exhibiting it in a clear and forcible manner; so that knowledge which we often see to be no better than lumber in men of dull understanding, was in him, true, evident, and actual wisdom.

"His moral precepts are practical; for they are drawn from an intimate acquaintance with human nature. His mind was so full of imagery that he might have been perpetually a poet; yet it is remarkable, that however rich his prose is in that respect, the poetical pieces which he wrote were in general not so, but rather strong sentiment and acute observation, conveyed in good verse,—particularly in heroick couplets.

"Though usually grave, and even aweful in his deportment, he possessed uncommon and peculiar powers of wit and humour: He frequently indulged himself in colloquial pleasantry; and the heartiest merriment was often enjoyed in his company, with this great advantage, that as it was entirely free from any poisonous tincture of vice or impiety, it was salutary to those who shared in it.

"He

"He had accustomed himself to such accuracy in his common conversation, that he at all times delivered himself with an elegant choice of expression, and a slow deliberate utterance. He united a most logical head with a fertile imagination, which gave him an extraordinary advantage in arguing; for he could reason close or wide, as he saw best for the moment. Exulting in his intellectual strength and dexterity, he could, when he pleased, be the greatest sophist that ever contended in the lists of declamation; and, from a spirit of contradiction, and a delight in shewing his powers, he would often maintain the wrong side with equal warmth and ingenuity; so that, when there was an audience, his real opinions could seldom be gathered from his talk; though when he was in company with a single friend, he would discuss a subject with genuine fairness. But he was too conscientious to make error permanent and pernicious by deliberately writing it; and in all his numerous works he earnestly inculcated what appeared to him to be the truth. His piety was constant, and was the ruling principle of all his conduct.

In answer to some insinuations of Sir John Hawkins, that the mind of Johnson was oppressed with a sense of *guilt*, Mr. Boswell is candid enough to own, " That his conduct after he came to London, and had associated with Savage and others, was not so strictly virtuous in one respect, as when he was a younger man. It was well known that his amorous inclinations were uncommonly strong and impetuous. He owned to many of his friends that he used to take women of the town to taverns, and hear them relate their history. In short, it must not be concealed, that like many other good and pious men, amongst whom we may place the Apostle Paul, upon his own authority, Johnson was not from propensities which were ever ' warring against the law of his mind,'—and that in his combats with them, he was sometimes, though rarely, overcome."

Some years since, the Doctor coming up Fleet-street, at about two o'clock in the morning, was alarmed with

with the cries of a person seemingly in great distress. He followed the voice for some time, when by the glimmer of an expiring lamp, he perceived an unhappy female, almost naked and perishing, on a truss of straw, who had just strength enough to tell him, "she was turned out by an inhuman landlord, in that condition, and to beg his charitable assistance not to let her die in the street." The Doctor, melted at her story, desired her to place her confidence in God, for that under him he would be her protector. He accordingly looked about for a coach to put her into; but there was none to be had: "His charity, however, worked too strong" to be cooled by such an accident. He kneeled down by her side, raised her in his arms, wrapped his great coat about her, placed her on his back, and in this condition carried her home to his house.

Next day, her disorder appearing to be *venereal*, he was advised to abandon her: but he replied, "that may be as much her misfortune as her fault; I am determined to give her the chance of a reformation; he accordingly kept her in his house above thirteen weeks, where she was regularly attended by a physician, who restored her to her usual health.

The Doctor, during this time learned more of her story; and finding her to be one of those unhappy women who are impelled to this miserable life more from necessity than inclination, he set on foot a subscription, and established her in a milliner's shop in the country, where she was living some years ago in very considerable repute.

Dr Johnson was buried in a public manner, in Westminster-abbey, on Monday, Dec. 20, 1784, at the foot of Shakspeare's monument, in the Poet's Corner, near the grave of his old and intimate friend David Garrick. His pall was supported by the Right Honourable Edmund Burke, Right Honourable William Wyndham, Sir Joseph Banks, Sir Charles Bunbury, George Colman, and Bennet Langton, Esqrs. His executors likewise attended, as did a considerable number of his friends and acquaintances, who sincerely paid this last tribute of affection to his memory.

Sir Joshua Reynolds, immediately after the Doctor's death, ordered Mr. Hoskins, in St. Martin's Lane, caster of figures to the Royal Academy, to make a plaister of Paris cast from his face.

The Doctor was so much pleased with these Beauties that he purchased several copies to present to his friends, and when the second edition was printing, he sat twice, at Mr. Kearsley's request, to Mr. Trotter.—The etching from that drawing, forms the frontispiece to this volume.

An authentic Copy of Dr. JOHNSON's WILL, extracted from the Prerogative Court of Canterbury.

IN the name of God. Amen. I SAMUEL JOHNSON, being in full possession of my faculties, but fearing this night may put an end to my life, do ordain this my last will and testament. I bequeath to God a soul polluted with many sins, but I hope purified by repentance, and I trust redeemed by Jesus Christ. I leave seven hundred and fifty pounds in the hands of Bennet Langton, Esq. three hundred pounds in the hands of Mr. Barclay and Mr. Perkins, brewers; one hundred and fifty pounds in the hands of Dr. Percy, Bishop of Dromore; one thousand pounds, three per cent. annuities in the public funds, and one hundred pounds now lying by me in ready money; all these before-mentioned sums and property I leave, I say, to Sir Joshua Reynolds, Sir John Hawkins, and Dr. William Scott of Doctors Commons; in trust for the following uses: That is to say, to pay to the representatives of the late William Innys, bookseller, in St. Paul's Church Yard, the sum of two hundred pounds; to Mrs. White, my female servant, one hundred pounds stock in the three per cent. annuities aforesaid. The rest of the aforesaid sums of money and property, together with my books,

books, plate, and houshold-furniture, I leave to the before-mentioned Sir Joshua Reynolds, Sir John Hawkins, and Doctor William Scott, also in trust, to be applied, after paying my debts, to the use of Francis Barber, my man servant, a negro, in such manner as they shall judge most fit and available to his benefit. And I appoint the aforesaid Sir Joshua Reynolds, Sir John Hawkins, and Doctor William Scott, sole executors of this my last will and testament, hereby revoking all former wills and testaments whatsoever. In witness whereof I hereunto subscribe my name, and affix my seal, this eighth Day of December, 1784.

SAM. JOHNSON, (L. S.)

Signed, sealed, published, declared and delivered by the said testator, as his last will and testament, in the presence of us, the word two *being first inserted in the opposite page.*

GEORGE STRAHAN.
JOHN DES MOULINS.

By way of codicil to my last will and testament, I SAMUEL JOHNSON, *give, devise, and bequeath, my messuage, or tenement, situated at Litchfield, in the county of Stafford, with the appurtenances, in the tenure or occupation of Mrs. Bond, of Litchfield aforesaid, or of Mr. Hinchman, her under tenant, to my executors in trust, to sell and dispose of the same; and the money arising from such sale I give and bequeath as follows, to Thomas and Benjamin, the sons of Fisher Johnson, late of Leicester, and ———— Whiting, daughter of Thomas Johnson, late of Coventry, and the grand daughter of the said Thomas Johnson, one full and equal fourth part each; but in case there shall be more grand-daughters than one of the said Thomas Johnson, living at the time of my decease, I give and bequeath the part or share of that one to, and equally between such grand-daughters. I give and bequeath to the Rev. Mr. Rogers, of Berkley, near Froome, in the county of Somerset, the sum of one hundred pounds, requesting him to apply the same towards the maintenance of Elizabeth Merne, a lunatic. I also give and bequeath to my god-children, the son and daughter of Mauritius Low, painter, each of them one hundred pounds* of my stock in the three per cent. consolidated annuities, to be applied and disposed of by and at the discretion of my executors, in the education or settlement in the world of them my said legatees. Also I give and bequeath to Sir John Hawkins, one of my executors, the Annales Ecclesiastici of Baronius and Hollingshed; and Stowe's Chronicles; and also an octavo Common Prayer Book. To Bennet Langton, Esq. I give and bequeath my Polyglot Bible. To Sir Joshua Reynolds, my great French Dictionary, by Martiniere, and my own copy of my folio English Dictionary of the last revision. To Dr. William Scott, one of my executors, the Dictionnaire de Commerce, and Lectius's edition of the Greek Poets. To Mr. Windham, Poeta Greci Heroici, per Henricum Stephanum. To the Rev. Mr. Strahan, Vicar of Islington, in the county of Middlesex, Mills's Greek Testament, Beza's Greek Testament by Stephens, all my Latin Bibles, and my Greek Bible, by Wechelius. To Dr. Heberden, Dr. Brocklesby, Dr. Butter, Mr. Cruickshanks, the Surgeon who attended me, Mr. Holder, my Apothecary, Gerard Hamilton, Esq. Mrs. Gardiner, of Snow-hill, Mrs. Francis Reynolds, Mr. Hoole, and the Rev. Mr. Hoole, his son, each a book at their election, to keep as a token of remembrance. I also give and bequeath to Mr. John des Moulins, two hundred pounds consolidated three per cent, annuities; and to Mr. Sastres, the Italian master, the sum of five pounds, to be laid out in books of piety for his own use. And whereas the said Bennet Langton hath agreed, in consideration of the sum of seven hundred and fifty pounds, mentioned in my will to be in his hands, to grant and secure an annuity of seventy pounds, payable during the life of me and my servant, Francis Barber, and the life of the survivor of us, to Mr. George Stubbs in trust for us; my mind and will is, that in case of my decease before the said agreement shall be perfected, the said sum of seven hundred and fifty pounds, and the bond for securing the said sum, shall go to the said Francis Barber; and I hereby give and bequeath to him the same, in lieu of the bequest in his favour contained in my said will. And I hereby empower my said Executors to deduct and retain all expences that shall or may be incurred in the execution of my said will, or of this codicil thereto, out of such estate and effects as I shall die possessed of. All the rest, residue,

residue, and remainder of my estate and effects, I give and bequeath to my said Executors, in trust for the said Francis Barber, his executors and administrators. Witness my hand and seal this ninth day of December, 1784.

SAMUEL JOHNSON, *(L. S.)*

Signed, sealed, published, declared and delivered by the said Samuel Johnson, as and for a codicil to his last will and testament, in the presence of us, who in his presence, and at his request, and also in the presence of each other, have hereunto subscribed our names as witnesses.

JOHN COPLEY.
WILLIAM GIBSON.
HENRY COTE.

Proved at London, with a Codicil, the sixteenth of December, 1784, before the worshipful George Harris, Doctor of Laws, and Surrogate, by the oath of Sir Joshua Reynolds, Knight, Sir John Hawkins, Knight, and William Scott, Doctor of Laws, the Executors named in the will, to whom administration was granted, having been first sworn duly to administer.

HENRY STEVENS,
GEO. GOSTLING,   } Deputy Registers.
JOHN GRENE,

Dec. 13, 1784.

Dr. DODD's SPEECH,

Delivered in Court on Friday the 16th of May, 1777, previous to his receiving Sentence of Death.

Written by Dr. JOHNSON.

My Lord,

I now stand before you a dreadful example of human infirmity. I entered upon publick life with the expectations common to young men whose education has been liberal, and whose abilities have been flattered; and when I became a clergyman, considered myself as not impairing the dignity of the order. I was not an idle, nor, I hope, an useless minister. I taught the truths of Christianity with the zeal of conviction, and the authority of innocence. My labours were approved, my pulpit became popular; and I have reason to believe, that of those who heard me, some have been preserved from sin, and some have been reclaimed. Condescend, my Lord, to think, if these considerations aggravate my crime, how much must they embitter my punishment!

Being distinguished and elated by the confidence of mankind, I had too much confidence in myself; and, thinking my integrity what others thought it, established in sincerity, and fortified by religion, I did not consider the danger of vanity, nor suspect the deceitfulness of my own heart. The day of conflict came, in which temptation surprised and overwhelmed me. I committed the crime which I entreat your Lordship to believe that my conscience hourly represents to me in its full bulk of mischief and malignity. Many have been overpowered by temptation, who are now among the penitent in heaven.

To an act now waiting the decision of vindictive justice, I will not presume to oppose the counterbalance of almost thirty years (a great part of the life of man) passed in exciting and exercising charity; in relieving such distresses as I now feel, in administering those consolations which I now want. I will not otherwise extenuate my offence, than by declaring, what many circumstances make probable, that I did not intend to be finally fraudulent. Nor will it become me to apportion my punishment, by alledging that my sufferings have been not much less than my guilt. I have fallen from reputation, which ought to have made me cautious; and from a fortune which ought to have given me content. I am sunk at once into poverty and scorn; my name and my crime fill the ballads in the streets, the sport of the thoughtless, and the triumph of the wicked.

It may seem strange that, remembering what I have lately been, I should still wish to continue what I am. But contempt of death, how speciously soever it might mingle with Heathen virtues, has nothing suitable to Christian penitence. Many motives impel me to beg earnestly for life. I feel the natural horror of a violent death, and the universal dread of untimely dissolution. I am desirous of recompensing the injury I have done to the clergy, to the world, and to religion, and to efface the scandal of my crime by the example of my repentance. But, above all, I wish to die with thoughts more composed, and calmer preparation. The gloom of a prison, the anxiety of a trial, and the inevitable vicissitudes of passion, leave the mind little disposed to the holy exercises of prayer and self examination. Let not a little time be denied me, in which I may, by meditation and contrition, be prepared to stand at the tribunal of Omnipotence, and support the presence of that Judge who shall distribute to all according to their works, who will receive to pardon the repenting sinner, and from whom the merciful shall obtain mercy.

For these reasons, amidst shame and misery, I yet wish to live, and most humbly intreat, that I may be recommended by your Lordship to the clemency of his Majesty.

'A SERMON.

A Sermon, written by Dr. Johnson, and preached by Dr. Dodd, before his Fellow-convicts, in the Chapel of *Newgate*.

My dear and unhappy Fellow-prisoners,

CONSIDERING my peculiar circumstances and situation, I cannot think myself justified, if I do not deliver to you, in sincere Christian love, some of my serious thoughts on our present awful state.

In the sixteenth chapter of the Acts of the Apostles, you read a memorable story respecting *Paul* and *Silas*, who, for preaching the Gospel, were cast by the magistrates into prison, verse 23,—and, after having received many stripes, were committed to the *goaler*, with a strict charge to keep them safely. Accordingly he thrust them into the inner prison, and made their feet fast in the stocks. At midnight Paul and Silas, supported by the testimony of a good conscience, prayed, and sang praises to God, and the prisoners heard them; and suddenly there was a great earthquake, so that the foundations of the prison were shaken; and immediately all the doors were opened, and every ones chains were loosed. The keeper of the prison, awaking out of his sleep, and seeing the prison doors open, in the greatest distress, as might well be imagined, drew his sword, and would have killed himself, supposing that the prisoners were fled.—But Paul cried with a loud voice, Do thyself no harm, for we are all here.—The keeper, calling for a light, and finding his prisoners thus freed from their bonds by the imperceptible agency of divine power, was irresistibly convinced that these men were not offenders against the law, but martyrs to the truth: he sprang in therefore, and came trembling, and fell down before Paul and Silas, and brought them out, and said, Sirs, What must I do to be saved?

What must I do to be saved? is the important question, which it becomes every human being to study from the first hour of reason to the last: but which we, my fellow prisoners, ought to consider with particular diligence and intenseness of meditation. Had it not been forgot-

or neglected by us, we had never appeared in this place. A little time for recollection and amendment is yet allowed us by the mercy of the law. Of this little time let no particle be lost. Let us fill our remaining life with all the duties which our present condition allows us to practise. Let us make one earnest effort for salvation! And oh! heavenly Father, who desirest not the death of a sinner, grant that this effort may not be in vain.

To teach others what *they must do to be saved*, has long been my employment and profession. You see with what confusion and dishonour I now stand before you--no more in the pulpit of instruction, but on this humble seat with yourselves.--You are not to consider me now as a man authorised to form the manners, or direct the conscience, and speaking with the authority of a pastor to his flock. I am here guilty, like yourselves, of a capital offence; and sentenced, like yourselves, to a public and shameful death. My profession, which has given me stronger convictions of my duty than most of you can be supposed to have attained, and has extended my views to the consequences of wickedness farther than your observation is likely to have reached, has loaded my sin with peculiar aggravations; and I entreat you to join your prayers with mine, that my sorrow may be proportionate to my guilt!

I am now, like you, enquiring, *what I must do to be saved?* and stand here to communicate to you what that enquiry suggests. Hear me with attention, my fellow-prisoners; and, in your melancholy hours of retirement, consider well what I offer to you from the sincerity of my good will, and from the deepest conviction of a penitent heart.

Salvation is promised to us Christians, on the terms of *Faith*, *Obedience*, and *Repentance*. I shall therefore endeavour to shew how, in the short interval between this moment and death, we may exert *faith*, perform *obedience*, and exercise *repentance*, in a manner which our heavenly Father may, in his infinite mercy, vouchsafe to accept.

I. *Faith* is the foundation of all Christian virtue. It is that *without which it is impossible to please God*. I shall
therefore

therefore confider, firſt, How *faith* is to be particularly exerted by us in our preſent ſtate.

Faith is a full and undoubting confidence in the declarations made by God in the holy Scriptures; a ſincere reception of the doctrines taught by our bleſſed Saviour, with a firm aſſurance that he died to take away the ſins of the world, and that we have, each of us, a part in the boundleſs benefits of the univerſal ſacrifice.

To this *faith* we muſt have recourſe at all times, but particularly if we find ourſelves tempted to deſpair.— If thoughts ariſe in our minds, which ſuggeſt that we have ſinned beyond the hope of pardon, and that therefore it is vain to ſeek for reconciliation by repentance; we muſt remember how God willeth that every man ſhould be ſaved, and that thoſe who obey his call, however late, ſhould not be rejected. If we are tempted to think that the injuries we have done are unrepaired, and therefore repentance is vain; let us remember that the reparation which is impoſſible is not required; that ſincerely to will, is to do, in the ſight of Him to whom all hearts are open; and that what is deficient in our endeavour is ſupplied by the merits of Him who died to redeem us.

Yet let us likewiſe be careful, leſt an erroneous opinion of the all-ſufficiency of our Saviour's merits lull us into careleſſneſs and ſecurity. His merits are indeed all-ſufficient! but he has preſcribed the terms on which they are to operate. He died to ſave ſinners, but to ſave only thoſe ſinners that repent. Peter, who denied him, was forgiven, but he obtained his pardon by *weeping bitterly*. They who have lived in perpetual regularity of duty, and are free from any groſs or viſible tranſgreſſion, are yet but *unprofitable ſervants:*—What then are *we*, whoſe crimes are haſtening us to the grave before our time?—Let us *work with fear and trembling*, but ſtill let us endeavour to *work out our ſalvation*. Let us hope without preſumption; let us fear without deſperation; and let our faith animate us to that which we were to conſider,

Secondly, "Sincere *Obedience* to the laws of God." Our obedience, for the ſhort time yet remaining, is re-
ſtrained

strained to a narrow circle. Those duties which are called social and relative, are for the most part out of our power. We can contribute very little to the general happiness of mankind, while on those whom kindred and friendship have allied to us, we have brought disgrace and sorrow. We can only benefit the publick by an example of contrition, and fortify our friends against temptation by warning and admonition.

The obedience left us now to practise is " submission to the will of God, and calm acquiescence in his wisdom and his justice." We must not allow ourselves to repine at those miseries which have followed our offences, but suffer, with silent humility and resigned patience, the punishment which we deserve; remembering that, according to the Apostle's decision, no praise is due to them who bear with *patience to be buffeted for their faults.*

When we consider the wickedness of our past lives, and the danger of having been summoned to the final judgment without preparation, we shall, I hope, gradually rise so much above the conceptions of human nature, as to return thanks to God for what once seemed the most dreadful of all evils—our detection and conviction!—We shrink back, by immediate and instinctive terror from the publick eye, turned as it is upon us with indignation and contempt. Imprisonment is afflictive, and ignominious death is fearful! But let us compare our condition with that which our actions might reasonably have incurred. The robber might have died in the act of violence, by lawful resistance. The man of fraud might have sunk into the grave, while he was enjoying the gain of his artifice:—and *where then had been our hope?* We have now leisure for thought; we have opportunities of instruction, and whatever we suffer from offended laws, may yet reconcile ourselves to God, who, if we sincerely *seek* him, will assuredly be fund.

But how are we to *seek the Lord?* By the way which he himself hath appointed; by humble, fervent, and frequent prayer. Some hours of worship are appointed us; let us duly observe them. Some assistance to our devotion

tion is supplied; let us thankfully accept it. But let us not rest in formality and prescription: let us call upon God night and day. When, in the review of the times which we have past, any offence arises to our thoughts, let us humbly implore forgiveness; and for those faults (and many there are and must be) which we cannot recollect, let us solicit mercy in general petitions. But it must be our constant care, that we pray not merely with our lips; but that when we lament our sins, we are really humbled in self-abhorrence;* and that, when we call for mercy, we raise our thoughts to hope and trust in the goodness of God, and merits of our blessed Saviour, Jesus Christ.

The reception of the *holy sacrament*, to which we shall be called in the most solemn manner, perhaps a few hours before we die, is the highest act of Christian worship. At that awful moment it will become us to drop for ever all worldly thoughts, to fix our hopes solely upon Christ, whose death is represented; and to consider ourselves as no longer connected with mortality.—And possibly, it may please God to afford *us* some consolation, some secret intimations of acceptance and forgiveness. But these radiations of favour are not always felt by the sincerest penitents. To the greater part of those whom angels stand ready to receive, nothing is granted in this world beyond rational *hope*; and with *hope*, founded on *promise*, we may well be satisfied.

But such promises of salvation are made only to the *penitent*. It is requisite then that we consider,

Thirdly, "How *Repentance* is to be exercised." Repentance, in the general state of Christian life, is such a sorrow for sin as produces a change of manners, and an amendment of life. It is that disposition of mind, by which he *who stole, steals no more*; by which the *wicked man turneth away from his wickedness, and doeth that which is lawful and right.* And to the man thus reformed, it is expressly promised, that *he shall save his*

See *Job*, chap. xlii. verse 6,

soul

soul alive.* Of this repentance the proofs are visible, and the reality certain, always to the penitent, and commonly to the church with whom he communicates; because the state of the mind is discovered by the outward actions.—But of the repentance which *our* condition requires and admits, no such evidence can appear; for to us many crimes and many virtues are made impossible by confinement; and the shortness of the time which is before us, gives little power, even to ourselves, of distinguishing the effects of terror from those of conviction; of deciding, whether our present sorrow for sin proceeds from abhorrence of guilt or dread of punishment, whether the violence of our inordinate passions be totally subdued by the fear of God, or only crushed and restrained by the temporary force of present calamity.

Our repentance is like that of other sinners on their death-bed; but with this advantage, that our danger is not greater, and our strength is more. Our faculties are not impaired by weakness of body. We come to the great work not withered by pains, nor clouded by the fumes of disease, but with minds capable of continued attention, and with bodies of which *we* need have no care! We may therefore better discharge this tremendous duty, and better judge of our performance.

Of the efficacy of a death-bed repentance many have disputed; but we have no leisure for controversy. Fix in your minds this decision, "Repentance is a change of the heart, of an evil to a good disposition." When that change is made, repentance is complete. God will consider that life as amended, which would have been amended if he had spared it. Repentance in the sight of man, even of the penitent, is not known but by its *fruits*; but our Creator sees the fruit, in the blossom or the seed. He knows those resolutions which are fixed, those conversions which would be permanent; and will

---

* There cannot be a stronger exemplification of this idea than the conduct of the *Goaler*, who uttered the question, with which we commenced our enquiry—*What shall I do to be saved?* - What a change of mind and manners was wrought in him by the power of God! Read Acts, chap. xvi.

receive them who are qualified by holy desires for works of righteousness, without exacting from them those outward duties which the shortness of their lives hindered them from performing.

Nothing therefore remains, but that we apply with all our speed, and with all our strength, to rectify our desires, and purify our thoughts; that we set God before us in all his goodness and terrors; that we consider him as the Father and the Judge of all the earth; as a Father desirous to save; as a Judge, who cannot pardon unrepented iniquity: that we fall down before him self-condemned, and excite in our hearts an intense detestation of those crimes which have provoked him; with vehement and steady resolutions, that if life were granted us, it should be spent hereafter in the practice of our duty:* that we pray the Giver of *grace* to strengthen and impress these holy thoughts, and to accept our repentance, though late, and in its beginnings violent: that we improve every good motion by diligent prayer: and having *declared* and *confirmed* † our *faith* by the holy communion, we deliver ourselves into his hands, in firm hope, that he who created and redeemed us will not suffer us to perish. *Rom.* v. viii. 32.

The condition, without which forgiveness is not to be obtained, is, that we forgive others. There is always a danger lest men, fresh from a trial in which life has been lost, should remember with resentment and malignity the prosecutor, the witnesses, or the judges. It is, indeed, scarcely possible, that with all the prejudices of an interest so weighty, and so affecting, the convict should

---

* See 2 Cor. chap. v. verse 14, 15.

† I would have this expression to be particularly attended to—While as a dying man, and with all possible sincerity of soul, I add, that if I could wish to *declare* my faith I know not of any words in which I could do it so well, and so perfectly to my satisfaction, as in the *Communion* service of our Church: and if I would wish to *confirm* that faith, I know not of any appointed method so thoroughly adapted to that end as *participation* in that communion itself.—See particularly in this service, the *Exhortation, Confession*, prayer beginning *We do not presume*, &c.—*Consecration*—and prayer after receiving, *O Lord and heavenly Father*, &c.——Convicts should diligently and repeatedly read over this service before they communicate.

f   think

think otherwise, than that he has been
part of the process with unnecessary se
opinion he is perhaps singular, and th
mistaken. But there is no time for c
must try to find the shortest way to pea
to forgive than to reason right. He t
juriously or unnecessarily harrassed, ha
ty more of proving his sincerity, by forgi
and praying for his enemy.

It is the duty of a penitent to repair,
the power, the injury which he has c
can do, is commonly nothing more th
world an example of contrition. On t
when the sentence of the law has its l
will be found to have affected a shame
negligent intrepidity. Such is not the
of a convicted criminal. To rejoice i
privilege of a martyr; to meet death w
the right only of innocence, if in any h
nocence could be found. Of him, wh
ened by his crimes, the last duties are h
abasement. We owe to God sincere
owe to man the appearance of repentai
not to propagate an opinion, that he w
edness can die with courage. If the f
with which some men have ended a lit
unfeigned, they can be imputed only
stupidity, or, what is more horrid, to v
cation: if they were artificial and hy
were acts of deception, the useless a
crimes of pride unmortified, and obstii

There is yet another crime possible,
reason to believe, sometimes committe
ment, on the margin of eternity.—Me
a stedfast denial of crimes, of which it
to suppose them innocent. By what eq
serve they may have reconciled their con
hood, if their consciences were at all co
possible to know. But if they thought,
were to die, they paid their legal forfeit, a
had no further demand upon them; th

might, by keeping their own secrets, try to leave behind them a disputable reputation; and that the falsehood was harmless, because none were injured;—they had very little considered the nature of society. One of the principal parts of national felicity, arises from a wise and impartial administration of justice. Every man reposes upon the tribunal of his country the stability of possession, and the serenity of life. He therefore who unjustly exposes the courts of judicature to suspicion, either of partiality or error, not only does an injury to those who dispense the laws, but diminishes the public confidence in the laws themselves, and shakes the foundation of public tranquillity.

For my own part, I confess, with deepest compunction, the crime which has brought me to this place: and admit the justice of my sentence, while I am sinking under its severity. And I earnestly exhort you, my fellow-prisoners, to acknowledge the offences which have been already proved; and to bequeath to our country that confidence in public justice, without which there can be neither peace nor safety.

As few men suffer for their first offences, and most convicts are conscious of more crimes than have been brought within judicial cognizance, it is necessary to enquire how far confession ought to be extended. Peace of mind, or desire of instruction, may sometimes demand, that to the minister, whose council is requested, a long course of evil life should be discovered:—but of this every man must determine for himself.—To the public, every man, before he departs from life, is obliged to confess those acts which have brought, or may bring unjust suspicion upon others; and to convey such information, as may enable those who have suffered losses to obtain restitution.

Whatever good remains in our power we must diligently perform.—We must prevent, to the utmost of our power, all the evil consequences of our crimes.—We must forgive all who have injured us.—We must, by fervency of prayer, and constancy in meditation, endeavour to repress all worldly passions, and generate in our minds that love of goodness, and hatred of sin, which

may

may fit us for the society of heavenly minds —And, finally, we must commend and entrust our souls to HIM who died for the sins of men; with earnest wishes and humble hopes that he will admit us with the labourers who entered the vineyard at the *last hour*, and associate us with the *thief* whom he pardoned on the cross!

To this great end, you will not refuse to unite with me, on bended knees, and with humbled hearts, in fervent prayer to the throne of grace! May the Father of mercy hear our supplications, and have compassion upon us!

" O almighty Lord God, the righteous JUDGE of all the earth, who in thy providential justice dost frequently inflict severe vengeance upon sinners in this life, that thou mayest by their sad examples effectually deter others from committing the like heinous offences; and that they themselves, truly repenting of their faults, may escape the condemnation of hell — look down in mercy upon us, *thy sorrowful servants*, whom thou hast suffered to become the unhappy objects of offended justice in this world!

" Give us a thorough sense of all those evil *thoughts*, *words*, and *works*, which have so provoked thy patience that thou hast been pleased to permit this public and shameful judgment to fall upon us; and grant us such a portion of grace and godly sincerity, that we may heartily confess, and unfeignedly repent of every breach of those most *holy laws and ordinances, which if a man do, he shall even live in them.*

" Let no root of bitterness and malice, no habitual and deadly sin, either of *omission* or *commission*, remain undisturbed in our hearts! But enable us to make our repentance universal, without the least flattering or deceitful reserve, that so we may clear our consciences before we close our eyes.

" And now that thou hast brought us within the view of our long home, and made us sensible that the time of our dissolution draweth near; endue us, we humbly pray thee, O gracious Father, with such Christian fortitude, that neither the terrors of thy present dispensa-
tions,

tions, nor the remembrance of our former sins, may have power to sink our spirits into a despondency of thy everlasting mercies in the adorable Son of thy love.

"Wean our thoughts and affections good Lord, from all the vain and delusive enjoyments of this transitory world; that we may not only with patient resignation submit to the appointed stroke of death, but that our faith and hope may be so elevated, that we may conceive a longing desire to be dissolved from these our earthly tabernacles, and to be with Christ, which is far better than all the happiness we can wish for besides!

"And in a due sense of our own extraordinary want of forgiveness at thy hands, and of our utter unworthiness of the very least of all thy favours, of the meanest crumbs which fall from thy table—Oh! blessed Lord Jesus! make us so truly and universally charitable, that in an undissembled compliance with thy own aweful command, and most endearing example, we may both freely forgive, and cordially pray for our most inveterate *enemies, persecutors,* and *slanderers!*—Forgive them. O Lord, we beseech thee,- turn their hearts, and fill them with thy love!

"Thus, may we humbly trust, our sorrowful prayers and tears will be acceptable in thy sight. Thus shall we be qualified, through Christ, to exchange this dismal bodily confinement [and these uneasy fetters] for the glorious liberty of the sons of God.—And thus shall our legal doom upon earth be changed into a comfortable declaration of mercy in the highest heavens: and all through thy most precious and all sufficient merits, O blessed Saviour of mankind!—who, with the Father, and the Holy Ghost, livest and reignest ever, *One God,* world without end. AMEN.

Of C. and G. KEARSLEY, FLEET-STREET, may be had the following ENTERTAINING WORKS.

THE BEAUTIES OF SHAKSPEARE,

Selected from his Works.

To which are added the principal Scenes in the same Author, and an Account of his Life.

The FIFTH EDITION, corrected, revised, enlarged, and ornamented with Copper Plates.

Price 3s. 6d. sewed.

THE BEAUTIES OF STERNE,

Including many of his Letters and Sermons, all his pathetic Tales, humourous Descriptions, and most distinguished Observations on Life; selected for the Heart of Sensibility.—To which are added, MEMOIRS OF HIS LIFE.

THE ELEVENTH EDITION, enlarged and ornamented with several Plates, from original Drawings.

Price 3s. 6d. sewed.

THE BEAUTIES OF THE RAMBLER, ADVENTURER, CONNOISSEUR, WORLD, AND IDLER,

In two Volumes, Price 6s. sewed.

BEAUTIES, &c.

ACTIONS.

THINGS may be feen differently, and differently fhewn; but *actions* are vifible, though motives are fecret.

Life of Cowley.

AUTHORS.

Thofe writers who lie on the watch for *novelty*, can have little hope of *greatnefs*; for *great things* cannot have efcaped former obfervation.

Ibid.

It is the fault of fome writers, that they purfue their thoughts to their *laft ramifications*; by which they lofe the *grandeur of generality*.

Ibid.

There are thofe who condemn authors for a want of *novelty*, which they are only *fuppofed to want*, from their accufers having already found fimilar thoughts in later books; not knowing, or enquiring, who produced them firft. This treatment is unjuft. Let not the original author lofe by his imitators.

Life of Waller.

The skilful writer *irritat*, *mulcet*; makes a due distribution of the style and animated parts.

It is for want of this artful intertexture, and those necessary changes, that the *whole* of a book may be tedious though all the *parts* are praised.

Life of Butler.

He who purposes to be an *author*, should first be a *student*.

Life of Dryden.

The writer who thinks his works formed for duration, mistakes his interest when he mentions his enemies. He degrades his own dignity by shewing that he was affected by their censures, and gives lasting importance to names, which, left to themselves, would vanish from remembrance.

Ibid.

To judge rightly of an author, we must transport ourselves to his time, and examine what were the wants of his contemporaries, and what were his means of supplying them. That which is easy at one time, was difficult at another.

Ibid.

It is not easy for any man to write upon literature, or common life, so as not to make himself known to those with whom he familiarly converses, and who are acquainted with his track of study, his favourite topics, his peculiar notions, and his habitual phrases.

Life of Addison.

The two most engaging powers of an author, are to make *new* things *familiar*, and *familiar* things *new*.

Life of Pope.

Next

Next to the crime of writing contrary to what a man thinks, is that of writing without thinking.
Life of Savage.

Making any material alterations in the works of a writer, after his death, is a liberty which, as it has a manifest tendency to lessen the confidence of society, and to confound the characters of authors by making one man write by the judgment of another, cannot be justified by any supposed propriety of the alteration or kindness of the friend.
Life of Thompson.

There is nothing more dreadful to an author than *neglect*;—compared with which, reproach, hatred, and opposition, are names of happiness: yet this worst, this meanest fate, every one who dares to write has reason to fear.
Rambler, vol. 1, p. 11.

A successful author is equally in danger of the diminution of his fame, whether he continues or ceases to write. The regard of the public is not to be kept but by tribute; and the remembrance of past service will quickly languish, unless successive performances frequently revive it. Yet in every new attempt there is new hazard; and there are few who do not at some unlucky time, injure their own characters by attempting to enlarge them.
Ibid. p. 130.

It ought to be the first endeavour of a writer, to distinguish nature from custom; or that which is established because it is right, from that which is right only because it is established; that he may neither violate essential principles by a desire of novelty,

novelty, nor debar himself from the attainment of beauties within his view, by a needless fear of breaking rules which no literary dictator had authority to enact.

Ibid. vol. 3, p. 304.

He that lays out his labours upon temporary subjects, easily finds readers, and quickly loses them: for what should make the book valued, when its subject is no more?

Idler, vol. 2, p. 37.

Let honest credulity beware of receiving characters from contemporary writers.

Life of Dryden.

The task of an author is either to teach what is not known, or to recommend known truths by his manner of adorning them; either to let new light upon the mind, and open new scenes to the prospect, or vary the dress and situation of common objects, so as to give them fresh grace and more powerful attractions. To spread such flowers over the regions through which the intellect has already made its progress, as may tempt it to return, and take a second view of things hastily passed over, or negligently regarded.

Rambler, vol. 1, p. 13.

Whilst an author is yet living, we estimate his powers by the worst performance. When he is dead, we rate them by his best.

Preface to Shakespeare, p. 1.

An author who sacrifices virtue to convenience, and seems to write without any moral purpose, even the barbarity of his age cannot extenuate;

for

for it is always a writer's duty to make the world better, and justice is a virtue independent on time and place.

Ibid. p. 19 & 20.

It is seldom that authors rise much above the standard of their own age. To add a little to what is best will always be sufficient for present praise; and those who find themselves exalted into fame, are willing to credit their encomiasts, and to spare the labour of contending with themselves.

Ibid. p. 44.

He that misses his end, will never be as much pleased as he that attains it, even when he can impute no part of his failure to himself; and when the end is to please the multitude, no man, perhaps, has a right, in things admitting of gradation and comparison, to throw the whole blame upon his judges, and totally to exclude diffidence and shame by a haughty consciousness of his own excellence.

Life of Cowley.

Many causes may vitiate a writer's judgment of his own works. On that which has cost him much labour he sets a high value, because he is unwilling to think he has been diligent in vain; what has been produced without toilsome effort is considered with delight, as a proof of vigorous faculties and fertile invention; and the last work, whatever it be, has necessarily most of the grace of novelty.

Life of Milton.

A writer who obtains his full purpose loses himself in his own lustre. Of an opinion which is no longer doubted, the evidence ceases to be examined.

examined. Of an art univerfally practifed the teacher is forgotten. Learning once made popular is no longer learning; it has the appearance of fomething which we have beftowed upon ourfelves, as the dew appears to rife from the field which it refreshes.

Life of Dryden.

There is a fpecies of writers, who, without much labour have attained high reputation, and who are mentioned with reverence, rather for the poffeffion than the exertion of uncommon abilities.

Life of Smith.

Tedioufnefs, in an author, is the moft fatal of all faults. Negligence or errors are fingle and local, but tedioufnefs pervades the whole; other faults are cenfured and forgotten, but the power of tedioufnefs propagates itfelf. He that is weary the firft hour is more weary the fecond, as bodies formed into motion, contrary to their tendency, pafs more and more flowly through every fucceffive interval of fpace.

Life of Prior.

An author who afks a fubfcription foon finds that he has enemies. All who do not encourage him, defame him. He that wants money will rather be thought angry than poor, and he that wifhes to fave his money, conceals his avarice by his malice.

Life of Pope.

An author buftling in the world, fhewing himfelf in public, and emerging occafionally from time to time into notice, might keep his works alive by his perfonal influence; but that which
conveys

conveys little information, and gives no great pleasure, must soon give way, as the succession of things produces new topics of conversation, and other modes of amusement.

Life of Mallet.

He that expects flights of wit, and sallies of pleasantry, from a successful writer, will be often disappointed. A man of letters, for the most part, spends in the privacies of study, that season of life in which the manners are to be softened into ease, and polished into elegance; and when he has gained knowledge enough to be respected, has neglected the minuter arts by which he might have pleased.

Rambler, vol. 1, p. 83.

He by whose writings the heart is rectified, the appetites counteracted, and the passions repressed, may be considered as not unprofitable to the great republic of humanity, even though his own behaviour should not always exemplify his rules. His instructions may diffuse their influence to regions in which it will not be inquired, whether the author be good or bad; to times when all his faults, and all his follies shall be lost in forgetfulness, among things of no concern or importance to the world; and he may kindle in thousands, and ten thousands, that flame which burnt but dimly in himself, through the fumes of passion, or the damps of cowardice. The vicious moralist may be considered as a taper by which we are lighted through the labyrinth of complicated passions; he extends his radiance further than his heart, and guides all that are within view, but burns only those who make too near approaches.

Ibid. vol. 2, p. 133.

But the wickedneſs of a looſe or profane author, in his writings, is more atrocious than that of the giddy libertine, or drunken raviſher; not only becauſe it extends its effects wider (as a peſtilence that taints the air is more deſtructive than poiſon infuſed in a draught) but becauſe it is committed with cool deliberation. By the inſtantaneous violence of deſire, a good man may ſometimes be ſurpriſed before reflection can come to his reſcue: when the appetites have ſtrengthened their influence by habit they are not eaſily reſiſted or ſuppreſſed; but for the frigid villainy of ſtudious lewdneſs, for the calm malignity of laboured impiety, what apology can be invented? what puniſhment can be adequate to the crime of him who retires to ſolitude for the refinement of debauchery; who tortures his fancy, and ranſacks his memory, only that he may leave the world leſs virtuous than he found it; that he may intercept the hopes of the riſing generation, and ſpread ſnares for the ſoul with more dexterity.

Ibid. p. 134.

He that commences a writer may be conſidered as a kind of general challenger, whom every one has a right to attack, ſince he quits the common rank of life, ſteps forward beyond the liſts, and offers his merit to the public judgment. To commence author, is to claim praiſe; and no man can juſtly aſpire to honour but at the hazard of diſgrace.

Ibid. p. 231.

Authors and lovers always ſuffer ſome infatuation through the fondneſs for their ſeparate objects, which only abſence can ſet them free; and every man ought to reſtore himſelf to the full exerciſe ercife of his judgment, before he does that which he cannot do improperly without injuring his honour and his quiet.

Ibid. vol. 4, p. 54.

That of conniving at another man printing his works, and then denying that he gave any authority, is a ftratagem by which an author, panting for fame, and yet afraid of feeming to challenge it, may (at once to gratify his vanity and preferve the appearance of modefty) enter the lifts and fecure a retreat; and this candour might fuffer to pafs undetected as an innocent fraud, but that, indeed, no fraud is innocent; for the confidence which makes the happinefs of fociety is, in fome degree, diminifhed by every man whofe practice is at variance with his words.

Life of Sir T. Browne, p. 257.

He that teaches us any thing which we knew not before, is undoubtedly to be reverenced as a mafter; he that conveys knowledge, by more pleafing ways, may very properly be loved as a benefactor; and he that fupplies life with innocent amufement will be certainly careffed as a pleafing companion.

Idler, vol. 2, p. 184.

That Shakefpeare once defigned to have brought Falftaff on the fcene again, we know from himfelf; but whether he could contrive no train of adventures fuitable to his character, or could match him with no companions likely to quicken his humour, or could open no new vein of pleafantry, and was afraid to continue the fame ftrain, left it fhould not find the fame reception; he has, in the play of Henry V. for ever difcarded him, and made haste to dispatch him; perhaps for the same reason for which Addison killed Sir Roger de Coverly, that no other hand might attempt to exhibit him.

Let meaner authors learn from this example, that it is dangerous to *sell the bear which is not yet hunted*——to promise to the public what they have not written.

Notes upon Shakespeare, vol. 6, p. 55.

It is in vain for the most skilful author to cultivate barrenness, or to paint on vacuity. Even Shakespeare could not write well without a proper subject.

Ibid. p. 161.

Neither genius nor practice will always supply a hasty writer with the most proper diction.

Ibid. vol. 10, p. 383.

It is the nature of personal invective to be soon unintelligible, and the *author* that gratifies private malice *animam vulnere ponit*, destroys the efficacy of his own writings, and sacrifices the esteem of succeeding times to the laughter of a day.

Ibid. vol. 2, p. 434.

AFFECTION.

As for Affection, those that know how to operate upon the passions of men, rule it by making it operate in obedience to the notes which please or disgust it.

Ibid. vol. 3, p. 215.

AFFECTATION.

Affectation naturally counterfeits those excellences which are placed at the greatest distance from

from possibility of attainment, because, knowing our own defects, we eagerly endeavour to supply them with artificial excellence.

Rambler, vol. 4, p. 104.

Affectation is to be always distinguished from *hypocrisy*, as being the art of counterfeiting those qualities which we might with innocence and safety be known to want. Hypocrisy is the necessary burthen of villainy—Affectation part of the chosen trappings of folly.

Ibid. vol. 1, p. 124 & 125.

Every man speaks and writes with an intent to be understood; and it can seldom happen, but he that understands himself might convey his notions to another, if content to be understood, he did not seek to be admired; but when once he begins to contrive how his sentiments may be received, not with most ease to his reader, but with most advantage to himself, he then transfers his consideration from words to sounds, from sentences to periods, and as he grows more elegant, becomes less intelligible.

Idler, vol. 1, p. 202.

AGRICULTURE.

Nothing can more fully prove the ingratitude of mankind (a crime often charged upon them, and often denied) than the little regard which the disposers of honorary rewards have paid to *Agriculture*; which is treated as a subject so remote from common life by all those who do not immediately hold the plough, or give fodder to the ox, that there is room to question, whether a great part of mankind has yet been informed that life is sustained by the fruits of the earth.

Universal Visiter, p. 111.

Agriculture not only gives riches to a nation, but the only riches we can call our own, and of which we need not fear either deprivation or diminution.

Ibid. p. 112.

Of nations, as of individuals, the first blessing is independence. Neither the man nor the people can be happy to whom any human power can deny the necessaries or conveniencies of life. There is no way of living without foreign assistance *but by the product of our own land improved by our own labour.* Every other source of plenty is perishable or casual.

Ibid.

AGRICULTURE OF ENGLAND.

Our country is, perhaps, beyond all others, productive of things necessary to life. The pine-apple thrives better between the tropics, and better furs are found in the Northern regions. But let us not envy those unnecessary privileges; mankind cannot subsist upon the indulgencies of nature, but must be supported by her common gifts; they must feed upon bread and be clothed with wool, and the nation that can furnish these universal commodities, may have her ships welcomed at a thousand ports, or sit at home, and receive the tribute of foreign countries, enjoy their arts, or treasure up their gold.

Ibid. p. 114.

ACADEMY.

ACADEMY.

IN this country an *academy for reforming and establishing the English Language* could be expected to do but little. If an academician's place were profitable, it would be given by *interest*; if attendance were gratuitous, it would be rarely paid; and no man would endure the least disgust. Unanimity is impossible, and debate would separate the assembly.

But suppose the philological decree made and promulgated; what would be its authority? In absolute governments, there is sometimes a general reverence paid to all that has the sanction of power and the countenance of greatness. How little this is the state of our country, needs not be told. We live in an age in which it is a kind of public sport to refuse all respect that cannot be enforced. The edicts of an English academy would probably be read by many, only that they might be sure to disobey them.

That our language is in perpetual danger of corruption cannot be denied; but what prevention can be found? The present manners of the nation would deride authority, and therefore nothing is left but that every writer should criticise himself.

Life of Roscommon.

AGE.

It has been found by the experience of mankind, that not even the best seasons of life are able to supply sufficient gratifications without anticipating uncertain felicities: it cannot, surely, be supposed that old age, worn with labours, harrassed with anxieties, and tortured with diseases, should have any gladness of its own, or feel any satisfaction from

from the contemplation of the present—All the comfort that now can be expected must be recalled from the past, or borrowed from the future: the past is very soon exhausted; all the events or actions of which the memory can afford pleasure, are quickly recollected; and the future lies beyond the grave, where it can be reached only by virtue and devotion.

Piety is the only proper and adequate relief of decaying man. He that grows old without religious hope, as he declines into imbecility, and feels pains and sorrows incessantly crowding upon him, falls into a gulph of bottomless misery, in which every reflection must plunge him deeper, and where he finds only new gradations of anguish, and precipices of horror.

Rambler, vol. 2, p. 91.

Custom so far regulates the sentiments, at least of common minds, that I believe men may be generally observed to grow less tender as they advance in age.

Ibid. p. 140.

To the long catalogue of the inconveniencies of old age, which moral and satirical writers have so copiously displayed, may be often added the loss of fame.

Ibid. vol. 3, p. 130.

Length of life is distributed impartially to very different modes of life in very different climates. A cottager grows old over his oaten cakes, like a citizen at a turtle feast. He is indeed seldom incommoded by corpulence: Poverty preserves him from sinking under the *burthen of himself*, but he escapes no other injury of time.

Western Islands, p. 193.

He that would pass the latter part of his life with honour and decency, must, when he is *young*, consider that he shall one day be *old*, and remember, when he is *old*, that he has once been *young*.

Rambler, vol. 1, p. 304.

Age seldom fails to change the conduct of youth. We grow negligent of time in proportion as we have less remaining, and suffer the last part of life to steal from us in languid preparations for future undertakings, or slow approaches to remote advantages, in weak hopes of some fortuitous occurrence, or drowsy equilibrations of undetermined counsel. Whether it be that the aged having tasted the pleasures of man's condition, and found them delusive, become less anxious for their attainment, or that frequent miscarriages have depressed them to despair, and frozen them to inactivity; or that death shocks them more as it advances upon them, and they are afraid to remind themselves of their decay, or discover to their own hearts that the time of trifling is past.

Ibid. vol. 3, p. 32.

The truth of many maxims of age gives too little pleasure to be allowed till it is felt, and the miseries of life would be increased beyond all human power of endurance, if we were to enter the world with the same opinions we carry from it.

Ibid. vol. 4, p. 195.

It is one of the melancholy pleasures of an old man to recollect the kindness of friends, whose kindness he shall experience no more.

Treatise on the Longitude, p. 14.

An old age unsupported with matter for discourse and meditation, is much to be dreaded. No state can be more destitute than that of him, who, when the delights of sense forsake him, has no pleasures of the mind.

Notes upon Shakespeare, vol. 9, p. 249.

There is sometimes a dotage encroaching upon wisdom, that produces contradictions. Such a man is positive and confident, because he knows that his mind was once strong, and knows not that it is become weak. Such a man fails not in general principles, but fails in the particular application. He is knowing in retrospect, and ignorant in foresight. While he depends upon his memory, and can draw from his repositories of knowledge, he utters weighty sentences, and gives useful counsel; but, as the mind gets enfeebled, he loses the order of his ideas, and entangles himself in his own thoughts, till he recovers the leading principle, and falls again into its former train.

Ibid. vol. 10, p. 241.

THE VANITY OF WISHING FOR OLD AGE.

Enlarge my life with multitude of days,
In health and sickness, thus the suppliant prays;
Hides from himself his state, and shuns to know
That life protracted—is protracted woe.
Time hovers o'er, impatient to destroy,
And shuts up all the passages of joy:
In vain the gifts their bounteous seasons pour,
The fruit autumnal and the vernal flower;
With listless eyes the dotard views the store,
He views and wonders that they please no more.
Now pall the tasteless meats and joyless wines,
And luxury with sighs her slave resigns.

Approach

Approach ye minstrels, try the soothing strain,
And yield the tuneful lenitives of pain,
No found, alas! would touch th' impervious ear,
Tho' dancing mountains witness Orpheus near.
No lute nor lyre his feeble power attend,
Nor sweeter music of a virtuous friend;
But everlasting dictates crowd his tongue,
Perversely grave or positively wrong.
The still returning tale, and ling'ring jest,
Perplex the fawning niece and pamper'd guest;
While growing hopes scarce awe the gath'ring sneer,
And scarce a legacy can bribe to hear;
The watchful guests still hint the last offence,
The daughter's petulance—the son's expence,
Improve his heady rage with treach'rous skill,
And mould his passions till they make his will.

 Unnumber'd maladies his joints invade,
Lay siege to life, and press the dire blockade;
But unextinguish'd av'rice still remains,
And dreaded losses aggravate his pains;
He turns, with anxious heart and crippled hands,
His bonds of debts and mortgages of lands;
Or views his coffers with suspicious eyes,
Unlocks his gold and counts it till he dies.

 But grant the virtues of a temp'rate prime
Bless with an age exempt from scorn or crime,
An age that melts in unperceiv'd decay,
And glides in modest innocence away;
Whose peaceful day benevolence endears,
Whose night congratulating conscience cheers,
The gen'ral fav'rite as the gen'ral friend,
Such age there is, and who would wish its end?

 Yet ev'n on this her load misfortune flings,
To press the weary minutes' flagging wings;
New sorrow rises as the day returns,
A sister sickens, or a daughter mourns.
Now kindred merit fills the sable bier,
Now lacerated friendship claims a tear;

Year chafes year, decay purfues decay,
Still drops fome joy from with'ring life away;
New forms arife, and diff'rent views engage,
Superfluous lags the vet'ran on the ftage,
Till pitying Nature figns the laft releafe,
And bids afflicted worth retire to peace.

Vanity of Human Wifhes.

AGE AND YOUTH.

The notions of the old and young are like liquors of different gravity and texture, which never can unite.

Rambler, vol. 2, p. 89.

In youth it is common to meafure right and wrong by the opinion of the world, and in age to act without any meafure but intereft, and to ofe fhame without fubftituting virtue.

Ibid. vol. 4, p. 198.

Such is the condition of life that fomething is always wanting to happinefs. In youth we have warm hopes, which are foon blafted by rafhnefs and negligence, and great defigns, which are defeated by inexperience. In age we have knowledge and prudence, without fpirit to exert, or motives to prompt them: we are able to plan fchemes and regulate meafures, but have not time remaining to bring them to completion.

Ibid.

ARTS.

An art cannot be taught but by its proper terms; but it is not always neceffary to teach the art.

Idler, vol. 2, p. 99.

Every

Every art is improved by the emulation of competitors. Those who make no advances towards excellence, may stand as warnings against faults.

Preliminary Discourse to the London Chronicle, p. 156.

ANGER.

Men of a *passionate temper* are sometimes not without understanding or virtue, and are therefore not always treated with the severity which their neglect of the ease of all about them might justly provoke. They have obtained a kind of prescription for their folly, and are considered by their companions as under a predominant influence that leaves them not master of their conduct or language, as acting without consciousness, and rushing into mischief with a mist before their eyes. They are therefore pitied rather than censured; and their sallies are passed over as the involuntary blows of a man agitated by the spasms of a convulsion.

It is surely not to be observed without indignation, that men may be found of minds mean enough to be satisfied with this treatment; wretches who are proud to obtain *the privilege of madmen*, and can, without shame, and without regret, consider themselves as receiving hourly pardons from their companions, and giving them continual opportunities of exercising their patience and boasting their clemency.

Rambler, vol. 1, p. 62.

It is told by Prior, in a panegyric on the Duke of Dorset, that his servants used to put themselves in his way when he was angry, because he was sure to recompense them for any indignities which he made them suffer. This is the round of a

passionate

passionate man's life—he contracts debts when he is furious, which his virtue (if he has virtue) obliges him to discharge at the return of his reason. He spends his time in outrage and acknowledgment, injury and reparation.

Ibid. p. 65.

Nothing is more despicable, or more miserable, than the old age of a passionate man. When the vigour of youth fails him, and his amusements pall with frequent repetition, his occasional rage sinks, by decay of strength, into peevishness; that peevishness, for want of novelty and variety, becomes habitual; the world falls off from around him; and he is left, as Homer expresses it, to *devour his own heart* in solitude and contempt.

Ibid. p. 66.

The maxim which Periander of Corinth, one of the seven sages of Greece, left as a memorial of his knowledge and benevolence, was, " Be master of your anger." He considered anger as the great disturber of human life; the chief enemy both of public happiness and private tranquillity, and thought he could not lay on posterity a stronger obligation to reverence his memory, than by leaving them a salutary caution against this outrageous passion. Pride is undoubtedly the origin of anger; but pride, like every other passion, if it once breaks loose from reason, counteracts its own purposes. A passionate man, upon the review of his day, will have very few gratifications to offer to his pride, when he has considered how his outrages were caused, why they were borne, and in what they are likely to end at last.

Rambler, vol. 1, p. 60 & 62.

There is an inconsistency in Anger, very common in life; which is, That those who are vexed to impatience, are angry to see others less disturbed than themselves; but, when others begin to rave, they immediately see in them what they could not find in themselves, the deformity and folly of useless rage.

Notes upon Shakespeare, vol. 6, p. 372.

AVARICE.

It is no defence of a covetous man, to instance his inattention to his own affairs—as if he might not at once be corrupted by avarice and idleness.

Life of Sheffield.

Few listen without a desire of conviction to those who advise them to spare their money.

Idler, vol. 1, p. 144.

Avarice is always poor, but poor by her own fault.

Ibid. vol. 2, p. 126.

Avarice is an uniform and tractable vice; other intellectual distempers are different in different constitutions of mind. That which soothes the pride of one, will offend the pride of another; but to the favour of the covetous bring money and nothing is denied.

Prince of Abyssinia, p. 232.

THE ANCIENTS.

Such is the general conspiracy of human nature against contemporary merit, that if we had inherited from antiquity enough to afford employment for the laborious, and amusement for the idle, what room would have been left for modern genius or modern industry? Almost every subject would have been pre-occupied, and every style would have been fixed by a preeedent from which few would have ventured to depart: every writer would have had a rival whose superiority was already acknowledged, and to whose fame his work would, even before it was seen, be marked out for a sacrifice.

Idler, vol. 2, p. 77.

Antiquity, like every other quality that attracts the notice of mankind, has votaries that reverence it, not from reason, but from prejudice. Some seem to admire indiscriminately whatever has been long preserved, without considering that time has sometimes co-operated with chance. All, perhaps, are more willing to honour past than present excellence; and the mind contemplates genius through the shades of age as the eye surveys the sun through artificial opacity.

Preface to Shakespeare, p. 95.

ADVERSITY.

Adversity has ever been considered as the state in which a man most easily becomes acquainted with himself; and this effect it must produce, by withdrawing flatterers, whose business it is to hide our weaknesses from us; or by giving loose to malice, and licence to reproach; or, at least, by cutting off those pleasures which called us away from meditation on our own conduct, and repressing that pride which too easily persuades us that we merit whatever we enjoy.

Rambler, vol. 1, p. 172.

ADVICE.

ADVICE.

The chief rule to be observed in the exercise of this dangerous office of giving ADVICE, is to preserve it pure from all mixture of *interest* or *vanity*; to forbear admonition or reproof when our consciences tell us that they are incited, not by the hopes of reforming faults, but the desire of shewing our discernment, or gratifying our own pride by the mortification of another. It is not indeed certain that the most refined caution will find a proper time for bringing a man to the knowledge of his own failings, or the most zealous benevolence reconcile him to that judgment by which they are detected. But he who endeavours only the happiness of him whom he reproves, will always have either the satisfaction of obtaining or deserving kindness: if he succeeds, he benefits his friend; and if he fails, he has at least the consciousness that he suffers for only doing well.

Rambler, vol. 1, p. 246.

It was the maxim, I think, of Alphonsus of Arragon, that *dead counsellors are safest*. The grave puts an end to flattery and artifice, and the information we receive from books is pure from interest, fear, and ambition. Dead counsellors are likewise most instructive, because they are heard with patience and with reverence. We are not unwilling to believe that man wiser than ourselves, from whose abilities we may receive advantage, without any danger of rivalry or opposition, and who affords us the light of his experience without hurting our eyes by flashes of insolence.

Ibid. vol. 2, p. 192.

If we consider the manner in which those who assume the office of directing the conduct of others execute their undertaking, it will not be very wonderful that their labours, however zealous, or affectionate, are frequently useless. For, what is the advice that is commonly given? A few general maxims, enforced with vehemence and inculcated with importunity; but failing for want of particular reference and immediate application.

Ibid. vol. 2, p. 19.

It is not often that a man can have so much knowledge of another as is necessary to make instruction useful. We are sometimes not ourselves conscious of the original motives of our actions, and when we know them, our first care is to hide them from the sight of others, and often from those most diligently whose superiority either of power or understanding, may intitle them to inspect our lives. It is therefore very probable that he, who endeavours the cure of our intellectual maladies, mistakes their cause, and that his prescriptions avail nothing, because he knows not which of the passions, or desires, is vitiated.

Ibid.

Advice, as it always gives a temporary appearance of superiority, can never be very grateful, even when it is most necessary, or most judicious; but, for the same reason, every one is eager to instruct his neighbours. To be wise or to be virtuous, is to buy dignity and importance at a high price: but when nothing is necessary to elevation but detection of the follies or the faults of others, no man is so insensible to the voice of fame as to linger on the ground.

Ibid.

Advice is offensive, not because it lays us open to unexpected regret, or convicts us of any fault which has escaped our notice, but because it shews that we are known to others as well as ourselves; and the officious monitor is persecuted with hatred, not because his accusation is false, but because he assumes the superiority which we are not willing to grant him, and has dared to detect what we desire to conceal.

Ibid. vol. 3, p. 295.

AMBITION.

Ambition is generally proportioned to men's capacities: Providence seldom sends any into the world with an inclination to attempt great things, who have not abilities likewise to perform them.

Life of Dr. Boerhave, p. 213.

—— Ambition, scornful of restraint,
Ev'n from the birth, affects supreme command,
Swells in the breast, and with resistless force
O'erbears each gentler motion of the mind;
As when a deluge o'erspreads the plains,
The wand'ring rivulets and silver lakes
Mix undistinguish'd in the general roar.

Irene, p. 32.

A Picture of Ambition in the Fate of Cardinal Wolsey.

In full-blown dignity see Wolsey stand,
Law in his voice, and Fortune in his hand,
To him the church, the realm, their powers consign,
Through him the rays of regal bounty shine.
Still to new heights his restless wishes tow'r,
Claim leads to claim, and power advances pow'r;
Till conquest unresisted cease to please,
And rights submitted, left him none to seize.

At length his Sov'reign frowns—the train of state
Mark the keen glance, and *watch the sign to hate*;
Where'er he turns he meets a stranger's eye,
His suppliants scorn him, and his followers fly;
At once is lost the pride of awful state,
The golden canopy, the glit'ring plate,
The regal palace, the luxurious board,
The liv'ried army, and the menial lord;
With age, with cares—with maladies oppress'd,
He seeks the refuge of monastic rest.
Grief adds disease, remember'd folly stings,
And his last sighs, reproach the fate of kings.
Vanity of Human Wishes.

ADVERSARY.

Candour and tenderness are in any relation, and on all occasions, eminently amiable, but when they are found in an adversary, and found so prevalent as to overpower that zeal which his cause excites, and that heat which naturally increases in the prosecution of argument, and which may be, in a great measure, justified by the love of truth, they certainly appear with particular advantages; and it is impossible not to envy those who possess the friendship of him whom it is even some degree of good fortune to have known as an enemy.
Letter to Dr. Douglas, p. 3.

ADMIRATION.

Admiration must be continued by that novelty which first produced it; and how much soever is given, there must always be reason to imagine that more remains.
Rambler, vol. 4, p. 257.

A man once distinguished, soon gains admirers.
Life of Roger Ascham, p. 244.

ADDRESS.

ADDRESS.

The strictest moralists allow *forms* of *address* to be used, without much regard to their literal acceptation, when either respect or tenderness requires them; because they are universally known to denote, not the degree, but the species of our sentiments.

Idler, vol. 1, p. 283.

ASSURANCE.

He whose stupidity has armed him against the shafts of ridicule, will always act and speak with greater audacity than they whose sensibility represses their ardour, and who dare never let their confidence outgrow their abilities.

Rambler, vol. 3, p. 252.

ADVERTISEMENT.

Promise—large promise,—is the soul of an advertisement.

Idler, vol. 1, p. 225.

ABSTINENCE.

To set the mind above the appetites is the end of abstinence; which one of the fathers observes to be, not a virtue, but the *ground-work of a virtue*. By forbearing to do what may innocently be done, we may add hourly new vigour to resolution, and secure the power of resistance when pleasure or interest shall lend their charms to guilt.

Ibid. p. 294.

AUCTION.

He that has lived without knowing to what height desire may be raised by vanity, with what rapture

rapture baubles are snatched out of the hands of rival collectors: how the eagerness of one raises eagerness in another, and one worthless purchase makes another necessary, may, by passing a few hours at an *auction*, learn more than can be shewn by many volumes of maxims or essays.

Ibid, vol. 2, p. 21.

ATHEIST.

It has been long observed that an Atheist has no just reason for endeavouring conversions, and yet none harrass those minds, which they can influence, with more importunity of solicitation to adopt their opinions. In proportion as they doubt the truth of their own doctrines, they are desirous to gain the attestation of another understanding, and industriously labour to win a proselyte; and eagerly catch at the slightest pretence to dignify their sect with a celebrated name.

Life of Sir T. Brown, p. 283.

ABILITY.

It was well observed by Pythagoras, that ability and necessity dwell near each other.

Idler, vol. 2, p. 154.

ACCIDENT.

In every performance, perhaps in every great character, part is the gift of nature, part the contribution of accident, and part, very often not the greatest part, the effect of voluntary election and regular design.

Memoirs of the King of Prussia, p. 100.

ANTICIPATION.

Whatever advantage we fnatch beyond a certain portion allotted us by nature, is like money fpent before it is due, which at the time of regular payment, will be miffed and regretted.

Idler, vol. 2, p. 35.

APPLAUSE.

It frequently happens that applaufe abates diligence. Whoever finds himfelf to have performed more than was demanded, will be contented to fpare the labour of unneceffary performances, and fit down to enjoy at eafe his fuperfluities of honour. But long intervals of pleafure diffipate attention and weaken conftancy; nor is it eafy for him that has funk from diligence into floth, to roufe out of his lethargy, to recollect his notions, re-kindle his curiofity, and engage with his former ardour in the toils of ftudy.

Rambler, vol. 3, p. 34.

ART.

The nobleft beauties of art are thofe of which the effect is extended with rational nature, or at leaft, with the whole circle of polifhed life: What is lefs than this can only be pretty, the plaything of fafhion, and the amufement of a day.

Life of Weft.

APPEARANCES. *(often deceitful)*

In the condition of men, it frequently happens that grief and anxiety lie hid under the golden robes of profperity, and the gloom of calamity is cheered by fecret radiations of hope and comfort;

as in the works of nature the bog is sometimes covered with flowers, and the mine concealed in the barren crags.

Rambler, vol. 3, p. 135.

ARMY.

An army, especially a defensive army, multiplies itself. The contagion of enterprize spreads from one heart to another; zeal for a native, or detestation for a foreign sovereign, hope of sudden greatness or riches, friendship or emulation between particular men, or what are perhaps more general and powerful, desire of novelty, and impatience of inactivity, fill a camp with adventurers, add rank to rank, and squadron to squadron.

Memoirs of the King of Prussia, p. 118.

APHORISMS.

We frequently fall into error and folly, not because the true principles of action are not known, but because, for a time, they are not remembered: he may therefore justly be numbered among the benefactors of mankind, who contracts the great rules of life into short sentences that may be easily impressed on the memory, and taught by frequent recollection to recur habitually to the mind.

Rambler, vol. 4, p. 84.

AXIOMS.

Pointed axioms, and acute replies, fly loose about the world, and are assigned successively to those whom it may be the fashion to celebrate.

Life of Waller.

BOOKS.

B.

BOOKS.

Such books as make *little things too important*, may be confidered as fhewing the world under a falfe appearance, and fo far as they obtain credit from the young and inexperienced, as mifleading expectation, and mifguiding practice.

Life of Waller.

He that merely makes a *book from books*, may be ufeful, but can fcarcely be great.

Life of Butler.

That *book* is good in vain which the reader throws away. He only is the mafter who keeps the mind in pleafing captivity; whofe pages are perufed with eagernefs, and in hope of new pleafure are perufed again; and whofe conclufion is perceived with an eye of forrow, fuch as the traveller cafts upon departing day.

Life of Dryden.

" *Books*" fays Bacon, " *can never teach the ufe of books*". The ftudent muft learn by commerce with mankind to reduce his fpeculations to practice, and accommodate his knowledge to the purpofes of life.

Rambler, vol. 3, p. 189.

No man fhould think fo highly of himfelf as to imagine he could receive no lights from books, nor fo meanly, as to believe he can difcover nothing but what is to be learned from them.

Life of Dr. Boerhave, p. 229.

Books are faithful repositories, which may be a while neglected or forgotten, but when they are opened again, will again impart their instruction. Memory once interrupted is not to be recalled. Written learning is a fixed luminary, which, after the cloud that had hidden it is past away, is again bright in its proper station. Tradition is but a meteor, which, if it once falls, cannot be rekindled.

Western Islands, p. 259.

When a language begins to teem with books, it is tending to refinement, as those who undertake to teach others must have undergone some labour in improving themselves; they set a proportionate value on their own thoughts, and wish to enforce them by efficacious expressions. Speech becomes embodied and permanent; different modes and phrases are compared, and the best obtain an establishment. By degrees one age improves upon another; exactness is first obtained and afterwards elegance. But diction merely vocal is always in its childhood: as no man leaves his eloquence behind him, the new generations have all to learn. There may possibly be books without a polished language, but there can be no polished language without books.

Ibid. p. 268.

There are books only known to antiquaries and collectors, which are sought because they are *scarce*; but they would not have been *scarce* had they been much esteemed.

Preface to Shakspeare, p. 126.

BENEFITS.

It is not necessary to refuse benefits from a bad man, when the acceptance implies no approbation of his crimes: nor has the subordinate officer any obligation to examine the opinions or conduct of those under whom he acts, except that he may not be made the instrument of wickedness.

Life of Addison.

BURLESQUE.

Burlesque consists in a disproportion between the style and the sentiments, or between the adventitious sentiments and the fundamental subject. It therefore, like all bodies compounded of heterogeneous parts, contains in it a principle of corruption. All disproportion is unnatural, and from what is unnatural we can derive only the pleasure which novelty produces. We admire it a while as a strange thing; but when it is no longer strange, we perceive its deformity. It is a kind of artifice, which, by frequent repetition, detects itself; and the reader, learning in time what he is to expect, lays down his book; as the spectator turns away from a second exhibition of those tricks, of which the only use is, to shew that they can be played.

Life of Butler.

BEAUTY.

If the opinion of *Bacon* be thought to deserve much regard, very few sighs would be vented for eminent and superlative elegance of form. "For beautiful women (says he) are seldom of any great accomplishments, because they, for the most part, study behaviour rather than virtue."

Rambler, vol. 1, p. 230.

We recommend the care of their nobler part to women, and tell them how little addition is made, by all their arts, to the graces of the mind. But when was it known that female goodness or knowledge was able to attract that officiousness, or inspire that ardour, which beauty produces whenever it appears?.

Ibid. vol. 2, p. 74.

The bloom and softness of the female sex are not to be expected among the lower classes of life, whose faces are exposed to the rudeness of the climate, and whose features are sometimes contracted by want, and sometimes hardened by blasts. Supreme beauty is seldom found in cottages, or workshops, even where no real hardships are suffered. To expand the human face to its full perfection, it seems necessary that the mind should co-operate by placidness of content, or consciousness of superiority.

Western Islands, p. 190.

Beauty is so little subject to the examination of reason, that Paschal supposes it to end where demonstration begins, and maintains that, without incongruity and absurdity, we cannot speak of geometrical beauty.

Rambler, vol. 2, p. 219.

Beauty is well known to draw after it the persecutions of impertinence; to incite the artifices of envy, and to raise the flames of unlawful love; yet among ladies whom prudence or modesty have made most eminent, who has ever complained of the inconveniences of an amiable form, or would have purchased safety by the loss of charms?

Ibid. vol. 3, p. 35.

It

It requires but little acquaintance with the heart, to know that woman's firſt wiſh is to be handſome; and that conſequently the readieſt method of obtaining her kindneſs is to praiſe her beauty.

Ibid. vol. 4, p. 159.

As we are more accuſtomed to beauty than deformity, we may conclude that to be the reaſon why we approve and admire it, as we approve and admire cuſtoms and faſhions of dreſs, for no other reaſon than that we are uſed to them: ſo that though habit and cuſtom cannot be ſaid to be the cauſe of beauty, it is certainly the cauſe of our liking it.

Idler, vol. 2, p. 167.

In the works of nature, if we compare one ſpecies with another, all are equally beautiful, and preference is given from cuſtom, or ſome aſſociation of ideas; and in creatures of the ſame ſpecies, beauty is the medium, or centre, of all its various forms.

Ibid. p. 172.

Beauty without kindneſs dies unenjoyed, and undelighting.

Notes upon Shakeſpeare, vol. 1, p. 191.

Neither man nor woman will have much difficulty to tell how *beauty makes riches pleaſant*, except by declaring ignorance of what every one knows, and confeſſing inſenſibility of what every one feels.

Ibid. vol. 2, p. 76.

It is an obſervation countenanced by Shakeſpeare, and ſome of our beſt writers, that no woman

man can ever be offended with the mention of her beauty.

Ibid. vol. 7, p. 13.

THE DANGER OF BEAUTY.

The teeming mother, anxious for her race,
Begs for each birth the fortune of a face;
Yet *Vane* could tell what ills from *Beauty* spring,
And *Sedley* curs'd the form that pleas'd a king.
 Ye nymphs of rosy lips and radiant eyes,
Whom pleasure keeps too busy to be wise;
Whom joys with soft varieties invite,
By day the frolic, and the dance by night;
Who frown with vanity, who smile with art,
And ask the latest fashion of the heart;
What care, what rules, your heedless charms shall save,
Each nymph your rival, and each youth your slave?
Against your fame with fondness, hate combines,
The rival batters, and the lover pines.
With distant voice neglected Virtue calls,
Less heard and less, the faint remonstrance falls:
Tir'd with contempt she quits the slipp'ry reign,
And Pride and Prudence take her seat in vain;
In crowds at once, where none the pass defend,
The harmless freedom and the private friend.
The guardians yield by force superior pli'd,
By int'rest, Prudence; and by flatt'ry, Pride:
Now Beauty falls betray'd, despis'd, distrest,
And hissing infamy proclaims the rest.

Vanity of Human Wishes.

BIOGRAPHY.

 There has, perhaps, rarely passed a life, of which a judicious and faithful narrative would not be useful. For not only every man has, in the mighty mass of the world, great numbers in the same condition

condition with himself, to whom his mistakes and miscarriages, escapes and expedients, would be of immediate and apparent use; but there is such an uniformity in the state of man, considered apart from adventitious and separable decorations and disguises, that there is scarce any possibility of good or ill but is common to human kind.

Rambler, vol. 1, p. 37.

The necessity of complying with times, and of sparing persons, is the great impediment of biography. History may be formed from permanent monuments and records, but lives can only be written from personal knowledge, which is growing every day less, and in a short time is lost for ever. What is known can seldom be immediately told, and when it might be told, is no longer known.

Life of Addison.

The writer of his own life has at least the first qualification of an historian, the knowledge of the truth; and though it may plausibly be objected, that his temptations to disguise it, are equal to his opportunities of knowing it, yet it cannot but be thought, that impartiality may be expected with equal confidence from him that relates the passages of his own life, as from him that delivers the transactions of another. What is collected by conjecture (and by conjecture only can one man judge of another's motives or sentiments) is easily modified by fancy or desire; as objects imperfectly discerned take forms from the hope or fear of the beholder. But that which is fully known cannot be falsified but with reluctance of understanding, and alarm of conscience;—of understanding, the

lover

lover of truth;—of conscience, the sentinel of virtue.

Idler, vol. 2, p. 281.

BUSTLERS.

There is a kind of men who may be classed under the name of *bustlers*, whose *business* keeps them in perpetual motion, yet whose motion *always eludes their business*; who are always to do what they never do; who cannot stand still because they are wanted in another place, and who are wanted in many places because they can stay in none.

Ibid. vol. 1, p. 104.

BENEVOLENCE.

That benevolence is always strongest which arises from participation of the same pleasures, since we are naturally most willing to revive in our minds the memory of persons with whom the idea of enjoyment is connected.

Rambler, vol. 2, p. 267.

Men have been known to rise to favour and to fortune only by being skilful in the sports with which their patron happened to be delighted, by concurring with his taste for some particular species of curiosities, by relishing the same wine, or applauding the same cookery.

Ibid. p. 268.

Even those whom wisdom and virtue have placed above regard to such petty recommendations, must nevertheless be gained by similitude of manners. The highest and noblest enjoyment of familiar life, the communication of knowledge and reciprocation of sentiments, must always presuppose

suppose a disposition to the same enquiry, and delight in the same discoveries.

Ibid.

BUSINESS.

Whoever is engaged in a multiplicity of business, must transact much by substitution, and leave something to hazard; and he that attempts to do all, will waste his life in doing little.

Idler, vol. 1, p. 107.

It very seldom happens to a man that his business is his pleasure. What is done from necessity, is so often to be done when against the present inclination, and so often fills the mind with anxiety, that an habitual dislike steals upon us, and we shrink involuntarily from the remembrance of our task. This is the reason why almost every one wishes to quit his employment: he does not like another state, but is disgusted with his own.

Ibid. vol. 2, p. 275.

NATURAL BOUNTIES.

If the extent of the human view could comprehend the whole frame of the universe, perhaps it would be found invariably true, that Providence has given that in greatest plenty, which the condition in life makes of greatest use; and that nothing is penuriously imparted, or placed from the reach of man, of which a more liberal distribution, or a more easy acquisition, would encrease real and rational felicity.

Ibid. vol. 1, p. 206.

C.

CONFIDENCE.

Confidence is the common consequence of success. They whose excellence of any kind has been loudly celebrated, are ready to conclude that their powers are universal.

Preface to Shakespeare, p. 49.

Self-confidence is the first requisite to great undertakings, yet he who forms his opinion of himself, without knowing the powers of other men, is very liable to error.

Life of Pope.

It may be no less dangerous to claim, on certain occasions, too little than too much. There is something captivating in spirit and intrepidity, to which we often yield as to a resistless power; nor can he reasonably expect the confidence of others, who too apparently distrusts himself.

Rambler, vol. 1, p. 3.

There would be few enterprizes of great labour or hazard undertaken, if we had not the power of magnifying the advantages which we persuade ourselves to expect from them.

Ibid. p. 9.

Men who have great confidence in their own penetration, are often, by that confidence deceived; they imagine they can pierce through all the involutions of intrigue without the diligence necessary to weaker minds, and therefore sit idle and secure. They

They believe that none can hope to deceive them, and therefore that none will try.

Memoirs of the King of Pruffia, p. 122.

Nothing is more fatal to happiness or virtue than that confidence which flatters us with an opinion of our own strength, and, by assuring us of the power of retreat, precipitates us into hazard.

Idler, vol. 1, p. 292.

Whatever might be a man's confidence in his dependants or followers, on general occasions, there are some of such particular importance, he ought to trust to none but himself, as the same credulity that might prevail upon him to trust another, might induce another to commit the same office to a third, and at length, that some of them may be deceived.

Life of Drake, p. 198.

Men overpowered with distress eagerly listen to the first offers of relief, close with every scheme, and believe every promise. He that has no longer any confidence in himself, is glad to repose his trust in any other that will undertake to guide him.

Ibid. p. 340.

COMMERCE.

Commerce, however we may please ourselves with the contrary opinion, is one of the daughters of fortune, inconstant and deceitful as her mother. She chooses her residence where she is least expected,

pected, and shifts her abode when her continuance is, in appearance, most firmly settled.

Universal Visiter, p. 112.

Where there is no commerce nor manufacture, he that is born poor can scarcely become rich; and if none are able to buy estates, he that is born to land, cannot annihilate his family by selling it.

Western Islands, p. 194.

It may deserve to be enquired, Whether a great nation ought to be totally commercial? Whether, amidst the uncertainty of human affairs, too much attention to one mode of happiness may not endanger others? Whether the pride of riches must not sometimes have recourse to the protection of courage? And whether, if it be necessary to preserve in some part of the empire the military spirit, it can subsist more commodiously in any place than in remote and unprofitable provinces, where it can commonly do little harm, and whence it may be called forth at any sudden exigence?

It must however be confessed, that a man who places honour only in successful violence, is a very troublesome and pernicious animal in time of peace, and that the martial character cannot prevail in a whole people, but by the diminution of all other virtues. He that is accustomed to resolve all right into conquest, will have very little tenderness or equity. All the friendship in such a life can be only a confederacy of invasion, or alliance of defence. The strong must flourish by force, and the weak subsist by stratagem.

Ibid. p. 210 & 211.

COMPLAISANCE.

There are many arts of graciousness and conciliation which are to be practised without expence, and by which those may be made our friends, who have never received from us any real benefit. Such arts, when they include neither guilt nor meanness, it is surely reasonable to learn; for who would want that love which is so easily to be gained?

Rambler, vol. 2, p. 16.

The universal axiom in which all complaisance is included, and from which flow all the formalities which custom has established in civilized nations, is, " That no man should give any preference to himself," a rule so comprehensive and certain, that perhaps it is not easy for the mind to imagine an incivility without supposing it to be broken.

Ibid. p. 262.

There are, indeed, in every place, some particular modes of the ceremonial part of good breeding, which being arbitrary and accidental, can be learned only by habitude and conversation. Such are the forms of salutation, the different gradations of reverence, and all the adjustments of place and precedence. These, however, may be often violated without offence, if it be sufficiently evident that neither malice nor pride contributed to the failure, but will not atone, however rigidly observed, for the tumour of insolence, or petulance of contempt.

Ibid. p. 262.

Wisdom and virtue are by no means sufficient, without the supplemental laws of good breeding, to secure freedom from degenerating into rudeness, or self-esteem from swelling into insolence. A thousand incivilities may be committed, and a thousand offices neglected, without any remorse of conscience, or reproach from reason.

Ibid. p. 261.

If we would have the kindness of others, we must endure their follies. He who cannot persuade himself to withdraw from society, must be content to pay a tribute of his time to a multitude of tyrants. To the loiterer, who makes appointments which he never keeps; to the consulter, who asks advice which he never takes; to the boaster, who blusters only to be praised; to the complainer, who whines only to be pitied; to the projector, whose happiness is to entertain his friends with expectations, which all but himself know to be vain; to the œconomist, who tells of bargains and settlements; to the politician, who predicts the fate of battles and breach of alliances; to the usurer, who compares the different funds; and to the talker, who talks only because he loves to be talking.

Idler, vol. 1, p. 80.

SELF-COMPLACENCY.

He that is pleased with himself, easily imagines he shall please others.

Life of Pope.

CHARITY.

Charity would lose its name were it influenced by so mean a motive as human praise.

Introduction to the Proceedings of the Committee for Clothing French Prisoners, p. 158.

To do the best can seldom be the lot of man; it is sufficient if, when opportunities are presented, he is ready to do good. How little virtue could be practised if beneficence were to wait always for the most proper objects, and the noblest occasions;—occasions that may never happen, and objects that may never be found?

Ibid. p. 159.

That Charity is best of which the consequences are most extensive.

Ibid.

Of Charity it is superfluous to observe, that it could have no place if there were no want; for of a virtue which could not be practised, the omission could not be culpable. Evil is not only the occasional, but the efficient, cause of charity. We are incited to the relief of misery, by the consciousness that we have the same nature with the sufferer; that we are in danger of the same distresses; and may sometime implore the same assistance.

Idler, vol. 2, p. 209.

CHARITY TO CAPTIVES.

The relief of enemies has a tendency to unite mankind in fraternal affection, to soften the acrimony of adverse nations, and dispose them to peace and amity. In the mean time it alleviates captivity, and takes away something from the miseries of war. The rage of war, however mitigated, will always fill the world with calamity and horror. Let it not then be unnecessarily extended: let animosity and hostility cease together, and no man be

be longer deemed an enemy than while his sword is drawn against us.
Introduction to the Proceedings of the Committee for Clothing French Prisoners, p. 159.

CENSURE.

Censure is willingly indulged, because it always implies some superiority. Men please themselves with imagining that they have made a deeper search, or wider survey than others, and detected faults and follies which escape vulgar observation.
Rambler, vol. 1, p. 7.

Those who raise envy will easily incur censure.
Idler, vol. 1, p. 78.

CUSTOM.

Established custom is not easily broken, till some great event shakes the whole system of things, and life seems to re-commence upon new principles.
Western Islands, p. 18.

Custom is commonly too strong for the most resolute resolver, though furnished for the assault with all the weapons of philosophy. "He that endeavours to free himself from an ill habit (says Bacon) must not change too much at a time, lest he should be discouraged by difficulty; nor too little, for then he will make but slow advances."
Idler, vol. 1, p. 152.

To advise a man unaccustomed to the eyes of the multitude, to mount a tribunal without perturbation; to tell him, whose life has passed in the shades of contemplation, that he must not be disconcerted or perplexed in receiving and returning the

the compliments of a splendid assembly, is to advise an inhabitant of Brazil or Sumatra not to shiver at an English winter, or him who has always lived upon a plain, to look from a precipice without emotion. It is to suppose custom instantaneously controllable by reason, and to endeavour to communicate by precept, that which only time and habit can bestow.

Rambler, vol. 3, p. 317.

CHEATS.

Cheats can seldom stand long against laughter.

Life of Butler.

CHARACTERS.

In cities, and yet more in courts, the minute discriminations of character, which distinguish one man from another, are, for the most part, effaced. The peculiarities of temper and opinion are gradually worn away by promiscuous converse, as angular bodies and uneven surfaces lose their points and asperities, by frequent attrition against one another, and approach by degrees to uniform rotundity.

Rambler, vol. 3, p. 192.

The opinions of every man must be learned from himself. Concerning his practice it is safest to trust the evidence of others. Where those testimonies concur, no higher degree of certainty can be obtained of his character.

Life of Sir Thomas Browne, p. 286.

To get a name can happen but to few. A name, even in the most commercial nation, is one of the few things which cannot be bought; it is the

the free gift of mankind, which must be deserved before it will be granted, and is at last unwillingly bestowed.
Idler, vol. 1, p. 66.

The exhibition of *character* is the first requisite in dramatic fable.
Universal Visiter, p. 118.

CHANCE.

There are few minds sufficiently firm to be trusted in the hands of chance. Whoever finds himself to anticipate futurity, and exalt possibility to certainty, should avoid every kind of casual adventure, since his grief must be always proportionate to his hope.
Rambler, vol. 4, p. 118.

The most timorous prudence will not always exempt a man from the dominion of chance; a subtle and insidious power, who will sometimes intrude upon the greatest privacy, and embarrass the strictest caution.
Ibid. p. 132.

Whatever is left in the hands of chance must be subject to vicissitude, and when any establishment is found to be useful, it ought to be the next care to make it permanent.
Idler, vol. 1, p. 21.

COMPLAINT.

What cannot be repaired is not to be regretted.
Prince of Abyssinia, p. 29.

The usual fortune of complaint, is to excite contempt more than pity.
Life of Cowley.

To hear complaints with patience, even when complaints are vain, is one of the duties of friendship: and though it must be allowed, that he suffers most like a hero who hides his grief in silence, yet it cannot be denied, that he who complains, acts like a man—like a social being, who looks for help from his fellow-creatures.

Rambler, vol. 2, p. 35.

Though seldom any good is gotten by complaint, yet we find few forbear to complain but those who are afraid of being reproached as the authors of their own miseries.

Idler, vol. 2, p. 137.

CALAMITY.

The state of the mind oppressed with a sudden calamity is like that of the fabulous inhabitants of the new created earth, who, when the first night came upon them, supposed that day would never return.

Prince of Abyssinia, p. 211.

Differences are never so effectually laid asleep, as by some common calamity. An enemy unites all to whom he threatens danger.

Rambler, vol. 2, p. 150.

He that never was acquainted with adversity, (says Seneca) has seen the world but *on one side*, and is ignorant of half the scenes of nature. As no man can enjoy happiness without thinking that he enjoys it, the experience of calamity is necessary to a just sense of better fortune; for the good of our present state is merely comparative; and the evil which every man feels will be sufficient to disturb and harrafs him, if he does not know how much he efcapes. The luftre of diamonds is invigorated by the interpofition of darker bodies; the lights of a picture are created by the fhades.

Ibid. vol. 3, p. 265 & 267.

Notwithftanding the warnings of philofophers, and the daily examples of loffes and misfortunes which life forces upon our obfervation, fuch is the abforption of our thoughts in the bufinefs of the prefent day, fuch the refignation of our reafon to empty hopes of future felicity, or fuch our unwillingnefs to forefee what we dread, that every calamity comes fuddenly upon us, and not only preffes us as a burden, but crufhes as a blow.

Idler, vol. 1, p. 229.

The diftance of a calamity from the prefent time feems to preclude the mind from contact, or fympathy. Events long paft, are barely known; they are not confidered.

Weftern Iflands, p. 15.

CARE.

Care will fometimes betray to the appearance of negligence. He that is catching opportunities which feldom occur, will fuffer thofe to pafs by unregarded which he expects hourly to return; and he that is fearching for remote things will neglect thofe that are obvious.

Preface to Dictionary, fol. p. 8.

CHOICE.

The caufes of good and evil are fo various and uncertain, fo often entangled with each other, fo diverfified by various relations, and fo much fubject to accidents which cannot be forefeen, that he who would fix his condition upon inconteftible
reafons

reasons of preference, must live and die enquiring and deliberating.

Prince of Abyssinia, p. 109.

CLEANLINESS.

There is a kind of anxious cleanliness, which is always a characteristic of a slattern; it is the superfluous scrupulosity of guilt, dreading discovery and shunning suspicion. It is the violence of an effort against habit, which being impelled by external motives, cannot stop at the middle point.

Rambler, vol. 3, p. 58.

CHANGE.

All change is of itself an evil, which ought not to be hazarded but for evident advantage.

Plan of an English Dictionary, p. 37.

All change, not evidently for the better, alarms a mind taught by experience to distrust itself.

Vision of Theodore, p. 81.

CONSCIENCE.

Tranquillity and guilt, disjoin'd by Heav'n,
Still stretch in vain their longing arms afar,
Nor dare to pass th' insuperable bound.

Irene, p. 43.

CAPTIVITY.

The man whose miscarriage in a just cause has put him in the power of his enemy, may, without any violation of his integrity, regain his liberty or preserve his life, by a promise of neutrality; for the stipulation gives the enemy nothing which he had not before. The neutrality of a captive may be always secured by his imprisonment or death.

He that is at the disposal of another, may not promise to aid him in any injurious act, because no power can compel active obedience. He may engage to do nothing, but not to do ill.
Life of Cowley.

COMPETENCY.

A competency ought to secure a man from poverty; or, if he wastes it, make him ashamed of publishing his necessities.
Life of Dryden.

CONTEMPT.

Contempt is a kind of gangrene, which, if it seizes one part of a character, corrupts all the rest by degrees.
Life of Blackmore.

CIVILITY.

The civilities of the great are never thrown away.
Memoirs of the K. of Prussia, p. 107.

CONTENT.

The foundation of content must spring up in a man's own mind; and he who has so little knowledge of human nature as to seek happiness by changing any thing but his own disposition, will waste his life in fruitless efforts, and multiply the griefs which he purposes to remove.
Rambler, vol. 1, p. 35.

The necessity of erecting ourselves to some degree of intellectual dignity, and of preserving resources of pleasure which may not be wholly at the mercy of accident, is never more apparent than when

when we turn our eyes upon those whom fortune has let loose to their own conduct; who, not being chained down by their condition to a regular and stated allotment of their hours, are obliged to find themselves business or diversion, and, having nothing *within* that can entertain or employ them, are compelled to try all the arts of destroying time.

The general remedy of those who are uneasy without knowing the cause, is CHANGE OF PLACE. They are willing to imagine that their pain is the consequence of some local inconvenience, and endeavour to fly from it as children from their shadows, always hoping for some more satisfactory delight from *every new scene*, and always returning home with disappointment and complaint. Such resemble the expedition of cowards, who, for want of venturing to look behind them, think the enemy perpetually at their heels.

Rambler, vol. 1, p. 31, 32, & 34.

CONSOLATION.

No one ought to remind another of misfortunes of which the sufferer does not complain, and which there are no means proposed of alleviating. We have no right to excite thoughts which necessarily give pain, whenever they return, and which perhaps might not have revived but by absurd and unseasonable compassion.

Rambler, vol. 2, p. 122.

Nothing is more offensive to a mind convinced that its distress is without a remedy, and preparing to submit quietly to irresistible calamity, than those petty and conjectured comforts which unskilful officiousness thinks it virtue to administer.

Notes upon Shakespeare, vol. 5, p. 197.

CURIOSITY.

Curiosity, like all other desires, produces pain as well as pleasure.

Rambler, vol. 4, p. 8.

Curiosity is one of the permanent and certain characteristics of a vigorous intellect. Every advance into knowledge opens new prospects, and produces new incitements to further progress.

Rambler, vol. 2, p. 287.

Curiosity is the thirst of the soul; it inflames and torments us, and makes us taste every thing with joy, however otherwise insipid, by which it may be quenched.

Ibid. p. 289.

There is no snare more dangerous to busy and excursive minds than the *cobwebs of petty inquisitiveness*, which entangle them in trivial employments and minute studies, and detain them in a middle state between the tediousness of total inactivity and the fatigue of laborious efforts, enchant them at once with ease and novelty, and vitiate them with the luxury of learning. The necessity of doing something, and the fear of undertaking much, sinks the historian to a genealogist; the philosopher to a journalist of the weather; and the mathematician to a constructor of dials.

Ibid. p. 290.

Favours of every kind are doubled when they are speedily conferred. This is particularly true of the gratification of CURIOSITY. He that long delays a ſtory, and ſuffers his auditor to torment himſelf with expectation, will ſeldom be able to recompenſe the uneaſineſs, or equal the hope which he ſuffers to be raiſed.

Ibid. vol. 4, p. 188.

CRITICISM.

The eye of the intellect, like that of the body, is not equally perfect in all, nor equally adapted in any to all objects. The end of Criticiſm is to ſupply its defects. Rules are the inſtruments of mental viſion, which may, indeed, aſſiſt our faculties when properly uſed, but produce confuſion and obſcurity by unſkilful application.

Ibid. p. 91.

In Criticiſm, as in every other art, we fail ſometimes by our weakneſs, but more frequently by our fault. We are ſometimes bewildered by ignorance, and ſometimes by prejudice, but we ſeldom deviate far from the right, but when we deliver ourſelves up to the direction of vanity.

Ibid. p. 92.

Whatever is much read will be much criticiſed.
Life of Sir T. Browne, p. 257.

An account of the labours and productions of the learned was for a long time among the deficiencies of Engliſh literature; but as the caprice of man is always ſtarting from too little to too much, we have now, among other diſturbers of human quiet, a numerous body of *reviewers* and *remarkers*.

Preliminary Diſcourſe to the London Chronicle, p. 156.

He who is taught by a critic to dislike that which pleased him in his natural state, has the same reason to complain of his instructor, as the madman to rail at his Doctor, who, when he thought himself master of *Peru*, physicked him to poverty.

Idler, vol. 1, p. 16.

No genius was ever blasted by the breath of critics; the poison, which, if confined, would have burst the heart, fumes away in empty hisses, and malice is set at ease with very little danger to merit.

Ibid. vol. 2, p. 40.

The critic will be led but a little way towards the just estimation of the sublime beauties in works of genius, who judges merely by rules; for whatever part of an art that can be executed or criticised thus, that part is no longer the work of genius, which implies excellence out of the reach of rules.

Ibid. p. 130.

That reading may generally be suspected to be *right*, which requires many words to prove it *wrong*; and the emendation wrong, which cannot without so much labour appear to be right.

Preface to Shakespeare, p. 66.

Every man acquainted with critical emendations, must see how much easier they are destroyed than made, and how willingly every man would be changing the text, if his imagination would furnish alterations.

Notes upon Shakespeare, vol. 1, p. 20.

When there are *two* ways of setting a passage in an author right, it gives reason to suspect that there may be a *third* way better than either.

Ibid. vol. 2, p. 381.

The coinage of new words in emendatory criticism is a violent remedy, not to be used but in the last necessity.

Ibid. vol. 3, p. 40.

In the chasms of old writings, which cannot be filled up with authority, attempting to restore the words is impossible; all that can be done without copies, is to note the fault.

Ibid. p. 387.

There is no reason for critics to persecute their predecessors with such implacable anger as they sometimes do. The dead, it is true, can make no resistance; they may be attacked with great security; but, since they can neither feel, nor mend, the safety of mauling them seems greater than the pleasure. Nor, perhaps, would it much misbeseem them to remember, that amidst all our triumphs over the *nonsensical* and the *senseless*, that we likewise are men, and as Swift observed to Burnet, " shall soon be among the dead ourselves."

Ibid. vol. 10, p. 293.

To choose the *best* among *many good*, is one of the most hazardous attempts of criticism.

Life of Cowley.

What Baudius says of Erasmus seems applicable to many *(critics)*: *Magis habuit quod fugeret, quam quod*

quod sequeretur. They determine rather what to condemn than what to approve.

Life of Milton.

In trusting to the sentence of a critic, we are in danger, not only from that vanity which exalts writers too often to the dignity of teaching what they are yet to learn, but from that negligence which sometimes steals upon the most vigilant caution, and that fallibility to which the condition of nature has subjected every human understanding, but from a thousand extrinsic and accidental causes, from every thing which can excite kindness or malevolence, veneration or contempt.

Rambler, vol. 2, p. 228.

Critics, like all the rest of mankind, are very frequently misled by interest. The bigotry with which editors regard the authors whom they illustrate or correct, has been generally remarked. Dryden was known to have written most of his critical dissertations only to recommend the work upon which he then happened to be employed; and Addison is suspected to have denied the expediency of poetical justice, because his own Cato was condemned to perish in a good cause.

Ibid. p. 229.

There are prejudices which authors, not otherwise weak or corrupt, have indulged without scruple; and perhaps some of them are so complicated with our natural affections, that they cannot easily be disentangled from the heart. Scarce any can hear with impartiality, *a comparison between the writers of his own and another country*; and though it cannot, I think, be charged equally on all nations,

tions, that they are blinded with this *literary patriotism*, yet there are none that do not look upon their authors with the fondness of affinity, and esteem them as well for the place of their *birth*, as for their knowledge or their wit.

Ibid.

The works of a writer whose genius can embellish impropriety, and whose authority can make error venerable, are proper objects of critical inquisition. To expunge faults where there are no excellences, is a task equally useless with that of the chemist, who employs the arts of separation and refinement upon ore in which no precious metal is contained, to reward his operations.

Ibid. vol. 3, p. 198.

Criticism, though dignified from the earliest ages by the labours of men eminent for knowledge and sagacity, and, since the revival of polite literature, the favourite study of European scholars, has not yet attained the *certainty* and *stability* of science. The rules hitherto received, are seldom drawn from any settled principle, or self-evident postulate, or adapted to the natural and invariable constitution of things, but will be found, upon examination, the arbitrary edicts of legislators authorised only by themselves, who, out of various means by which the same end may be attained, selected such as happened to occur to their own reflection, and then by a law, which idleness and timidity were too willing to obey, prohibited new experiments of wit, restrained fancy from the indulgence of her innate inclination to hazard and adventure,

adventure, and condemned all future flights of genius, to pursue the path of the Meonian eagle.

Ibid. vol. 3, p. 310.

For this reason the laws of every species of writing have been settled by the ideas of him who first raised it to reputation, without enquiry whether his performances were not yet susceptible of improvement.

Ibid. p. 311.

The care of the *theatrical critic* should be, to distinguish error from inability, faults of inexperience from defects of nature. Action irregular and turbulent may be reclaimed; vociferation vehement and confused may be restrained and modulated; the stalk of the tyrant may become the gait of a man; the yell of inarticulate distress may be reduced to human lamentation. All these faults should be, for a time, overlooked, and afterwards censured with gentleness and candour. But if in an actor there appears an utter vacancy of meaning, a frigid equality, a stupid languor, a torpid apathy, the greatest kindness that can be shewn him, is a speedy sentence of expulsion.

Idler, vol. 1, p. 139.

That a proper respect should be paid to the rules of criticism, will be very readily allowed; but there is always an appeal from *criticism* to *nature*.

Preface to Shakespeare, p. 102.

This moral precept may be well applied to criticism, *quod dubitas, ne feceris.*

Ibid. p. 145.

CONVICT.

Imprisonment is afflictive, and ignominious death is fearful, but let the convict compare his condition with that which his actions might reasonably have incurred. The robber might have died in the act of violence by lawful resistance. The man of fraud might have sunk into the grave, whilst he was enjoying the gain of his artifice, and where then had been their hope? By imprisoment, even with the certainty of death before their eyes, they have leisure for thought; opportunities for instruction; and whatever they suffer from offended laws, they may yet reconcile themselves to God, who, if he is sincerely sought for, will most assuredly be found.

Convicts Address, p. 12.———Generally attributed to the late Dr. Dodd, but written for him, whilst under Sentence of Death, by Dr. Johnson.

CHILDREN.

It cannot be hoped that out of any progeny, more than *one* shall deserve to be mentioned.

Life of Roger Ascham, p. 235.

CREDULITY.

We are inclined to believe those whom we do not know, because they never have deceived us.

Idler, vol. 2, p. 157.

Of all kinds of credulity, the most obstinate and wonderful is that of political zealots; of men who being numbered they know not how, or why, in any of the parties that divide a state, resign the use of their own eyes and ears, and resolve to believe

lieve nothing that does not favour thofe whom they profefs to follow.
Idler, vol. 1, p. 53.

Credulity on one part is a ftrong temptation to deceit on the other.
Weftern Iflands, p. 276.

COMPILATION.

Particles of fcience are often very widely fcattered. Writers of extenfive comprehenfion have incidental remarks upon topics very remote from the principal fubject, which are often more valuable than formal treatifes, and which yet, are not known becaufe they are not promifed in the title. He that collects thofe under proper heads, is very laudably employed; for, though he exerts no great abilities in the work, he facilitates the progrefs of others, and by making that eafy of attainment which is already written, may give fome mind more vigorous, or more adventurous than his own, leifure for new thoughts and original defigns.
Ibid. p. 185.

COURT.

It has been always obferved of thofe that frequent a court, that they foon, by a kind of contagion, catch the regal fpirit of neglecting futurity. The minifter forms an expedient to fufpend or perplex an enquiry into his meafures for a few months, and applauds and triumphs in his own dexterity. The peer puts off his creditor for the prefent day, and forgets that he is ever to fee him more.
Marmor Norfolcienfe, p. 20.

CUNNING.

CUNNING.

Cunning differs from wisdom as twilight from open day. He that walks in the sun-shine, goes boldly forward by the nearest way; he sees that when the path is strait and even, he may proceed in security, and when it is rough and crooked, he easily complies with the turns, and avoids the obstructions. But the traveller in the dusk, fears more as he sees less; he knows there may be danger, and therefore suspects that he is never safe, tries every step before he fixes his foot, and shrinks at every noise, lest violence should approach him. Cunning discovers little at a time, and has no other means of certainty than multiplication of stratagems, and superfluity of suspicion. Yet men thus narrow by nature and mean by art, are sometimes able to rise by the miscarriages of bravery and the openness of integrity; and by watching failures and snatching opportunities, obtain advantages which belong properly to higher characters.

Idler, vol. 2, p. 223 & 227.

COURAGE.

The courage of the English vulgar proceeds from that dissolution of dependence, which obliges every man to regard his own character. While every man is fed by his own hand, he has no need of any servile arts; he may always have wages for his labour, and is no less necessary for his employer, than his employer is to him; while he looks for no protection from others, he is naturally roused to be his own protector, and having nothing to abate his esteem of himself, he consequently aspires to the esteem of others. Thus every man that crowds our streets is a man of honour,

nour, disdainful of obligation, impatient of reproach, and desirous of extending his reputation among those of his own rank; and as courage is in most frequent use, the fame of courage is most eagerly pursued. From this neglect of subordination, it is not to be denied that some inconveniences may, from time to time, proceed. The power of the law does not always sufficiently supply the want of reverence, or maintain the proper distinction, between different ranks; but good and evil will grow up in this world together; and they who complain in peace, of the insolence of the populace, must remember, that their insolence in peace is bravery in war.
Bravery of English Common Soldiers, p. 329.

Personal courage is the quality of highest esteem among a warlike and uncivilized people; and with the ostentatious display of courage, are closely connected promptitude of offence, and quickness of resentment.
Western Islands, p. 99.

We may as easily make wrong estimates of our own courage as our own humility, by mistaking a sudden effervescence of imagination for settled resolution.
Life of Sir T. Browne, p. 280.

COMPANION.

There is no man more dangerous than he that, with a will to corrupt, hath the power to please; for neither wit nor honesty ought to think themselves safe with such a companion, when they frequently see the best minds corrupted by them.
Notes upon Shakespeare, vol. 5, p. 612.

There

There are times in which the wife and the knowing are willing to receive praise, without the labour of deserving it, in which the most elevated mind is willing to descend, and the most active to be at rest. All therefore are, at some hour or another, fond of *companions* whom they can entertain upon easy terms, and who will relieve them from solitude, without condemning them to vigilance and caution. We are most inclined to love when we have nothing to fear; and he that encourages us to please ourselves, will not be long without preference in our affection, to those whose learning holds us at the distance of pupils, or whose wit calls all attention from us, and leaves us without importance, and without regard.

Rambler, vol. 2, p. 104.

He that amuses himself among well-chosen companions, can scarcely fail to receive, from the most careless and obstreperous merriment which virtue can allow, some useful hints; nor can converse on the most familiar topics, without some casual information. The loose sparkles of thoughtless wit may give new light to the mind, and the gay contention for paradoxical positions rectify the opinions.

This is the time in which those friendships that give happiness or consolation, relief or security, are generally formed. A wise and good man is never so amiable, as in his unbended and familiar intervals. Heroic generosity, or philosophical discoveries, may compel veneration and respect; but love always implies some kind of natural or voluntary equality, and is only to be excited by that levity and chearfulness which disencumbers all minds

minds from awe and solicitude, invites the modest to freedom, and exalts the timorous to confidence.

Ibid. p. 205.

It is discovered by a very few experiments, that no man is much pleased with a companion who does not increase, in some respect, his fondness of himself.

Ibid. p. 295.

CRIMES.

The crime which has been once committed, is committed again with less reluctance.

Notes upon Shakespeare, vol. 2, p. 497.

COPIES COMPARED WITH ORIGINALS.

Copies are known from originals even when the painter copies his own picture; so if an author should literally translate his he would lose the manner of an original. But though copies are easily known, good imitations are not detected with equal certainty, and are by the best judges often mistaken. Nor is it true that the writer has always peculiarities equally distinguishable with those of the painter. The peculiar manner of each arises from the desire natural to every performer of facilitating his subsequent works by recurrence to his former ideas; this recurrence produces that repetition which is called *habit*. The painter, whose work is partly intellectual, and partly manual, has habits of the mind, the eye, and the hand: the writer has only habits of the mind. Yet some painters have differed as much from themselves as from any other; and it is said there is little resemblance between the first works of Raphael and the last.

The

The same variation may be expected in writers, and if it be true, as it seems, that they are less subject to habit, the difference between their works may be yet greater.

Ibid. vol. 1, p. 123.

COMPLIMENT.

Compliment is, as *Armado* well expresses it, the varnish of a complete man.

Ibid. vol. 2, p. 385.

No rank in life precludes the efficacy of a well-timed compliment. When Queen Elizabeth asked an ambassador how he liked her ladies, he replied, " It was hard to judge of stars in the presence of the sun."

Ibid. p. 484.

COMPARISON.

Very little of the pain or pleasure which does not begin and end in ourselves, is otherwise than relative. We are rich or poor, great or little, in proportion to the number that excel us, or fall beneath us in any of these respects; and therefore a man whose uneasiness arises from reflection on any misfortune that throws him below those with whom he was once equal, is comforted by finding that he is not yet lowest. Again, when we look abroad, and behold the multitudes that are groaning under evils heavier than those which we have experienced, we shrink back to our own state, and, instead of repining that so much must be felt, learn to rejoice that we have not more to feel.

By this observation of the miseries of others, fortitude is strengthened, and the mind brought to a more extensive knowledge of her own powers.

Rambler, vol. 1, p. 315.

CITY.

There is such a difference between the pursuits of men in great cities, that one part of the inhabitants lives to little other purpose than to wonder at the rest. Some have hopes and fears, wishes and aversions, which never enter into the thoughts of others; and enquiry is labouriously exerted, to gain that which those who possess it are ready to throw away.

Idler, vol. 2, p. 20.

COMMUNITY.

There will always be a part, and always a very large part of every community, that have no care but for themselves, and whose care for themselves reaches little farther than impatience of immediate pain, and eagerness for the nearest good.

Taxation no Tyranny, p. 9.

CONVENIENCIES.

Conveniencies are never missed, where they were never enjoyed.

Western Islands, p. 237.

CONTROVERSY.

Through the mist of controversy, it can raise no wonder that the truth is not easily discovered. When a quarrel has been long carried on between individuals, it is often very hard to tell by whom it was begun. Every fact is darkened by distance, by interest, and by multitudes. Information is not easily procured from far; those whom the truth will not favour, will not step voluntarily forth

forth to tell it; and where there are many agents, it is easy for every single action to be concealed.

Observations on the State of Affairs, 1756, p. 20.

CALUMNY.

As there are to be found in the service of envy, men of every diversity of temper, and degree of understanding, calumny is diffused by all arts and methods of propagation. Nothing is too gross or too refined, too cruel or too trifling, to be practised; very little regard is had to the rules of honourable hostility, but every weapon is accounted lawful; and those who cannot make a thrust at life, are content to keep themselves in play with petty malevolence, to teize with feeble blows and impotent disturbance.

Rambler, vol. 3, p. 233.

Those who cannot strike with force, can however poison their weapon, and weak as they are, give mortal wounds, and bring a hero to the grave. So true is that observation, " that many are able to do hurt, but few to do good."

Life of Dr. Boerhave, p. 215.

CAUTION.

There is always a point at which caution, however solicitous, must limit its preservatives, because one terror often counteracts another.

Rambler, vol. 3, p. 126.

EUROPEAN CONQUESTS.

What mankind has lost and gained by European conquests, it would be long to compare, and very difficult to estimate. Much knowledge has been acquired, and much cruelty committed: the belief of religion has been very little propagated, and its laws have been outrageously and enormously violated. The Europeans have scarcely visited any coast, but to gratify avarice and extend corruption, to arrogate dominion without right, and practise cruelty without incentive. Happy had it then been for the oppressed, if the designs of the original invader had slept in his bosom; and, surely, more happy for the oppressors! But there is reason to hope, that out of much evil good may be sometimes produced, and that the light of the gospel will at last illuminate the sands of Africa, and the deserts of America; though its progress cannot but be slow, when it is so much obstructed by the lives of Christians.

Introduction to the World Displayed, p. 178.

D.

DESIRE.

Some desire is necessary to keep life in motion; and he whose real wants are supplied, must admit those of fancy.

Prince of Abyssinia, p. 52.

The desires of man increase with his acquisitions; every step which he advances brings something within his view, which he did not see before, and which, as soon as he sees it, he begins to want. Where necessity ends, curiosity begins; and no sooner are we supplied with every thing that

that nature can demand, than we sit down to contrive artificial appetites.

Idler, vol. 1, p. 165.

DEATH.

Reflect that life and death, affecting sounds!
Are only varied modes of endless being:
Reflect that life, like ev'ry other blessing,
Derives its value from its use alone:
Not for itself,—but for a nobler end,
Th' Eternal gave it, and that end is virtue!
When inconsistent with a greater good,
Reason commands to cast the less away:
Thus life, with loss of wealth, is well preserv'd,
And virtue cheaply sav'd with loss of life.

Irene, p. 41.

The death of great men is not always proportioned to their lives. Hannibal, says Juvenal, did not perish by a javelin, or a sword; the slaughters of Cannæ were revenged by a ring.

Life of Pope.

It was perhaps ordained by Providence, to hinder us from tyrannising over one another, that no individual should be of such importance, as to cause, by his retirement or death, any chasm in the world.

Rambler, vol. 1, p. 34.

The great disturbers of our happiness in this world, are our desires, our griefs, and our fears; and to all these the *consideration of mortality* is a certain and adequate remedy. " Think (says Epictetus) frequently on poverty, banishment, and death,

death, and thou wilt never indulge violent defires, or give up thy heart to mean fentiments."
Ibid. p. 101.

It is remarkable that death increafes our veneration for the good, and extenuates our hatred of the bad.
Ibid. vol. 2, p. 5.

To neglect at any time preparation for death, is to fleep on our poft at a fiege; but to omit it in old age, is to fleep at an attack.
Ibid. p. 141.

To die is the fate of man; but to die with lingering anguifh, is generally his folly.
Ibid. p. 178.

To rejoice in tortures is the privilege of a martyr; to meet death with intrepidity is the right only of innocence (if in any human being innocence can be found); but of him whofe life is fhortened by his crimes, the laft duties are humility and felf-abafement.
Convicts Addrefs, p. 18.

Death is no more than every being muft fuffer, though the dread of it is peculiar to man.
Notes upon Shakefpeare, vol. 2, p. 79.

If all the bleffings of our condition are enjoyed with a conftant fenfe of the uncertainty of life; if we remember that whatever we poffefs is to be in our hands but a very little time, and that the little which our moft lively hopes can promife us, may be made lefs by ten thoufand accidents; we fhall not much repine at a lofs, of which we cannot eftimate estimate the value, but of which, though we are not able to tell the least amount, we know, with sufficient certainty, the greatest, and are convinced that the greatest is not much to be regretted.

Rambler, vol. 1, p. 103.

What are our views of all worldly things (and the same appearances they would always have, if the same thoughts were always predominant) when a sharp or tedious sickness has set death before our eyes, and the last hour seems to be approaching? The extensive influence of greatness, the glitter of wealth, the praises of admirers, and the attendance of supplicants, have all appeared vain and empty things. We then find the absurdity of stretching out our arms incessantly to grasp that which we cannot keep, and wearing out our lives in endeavours to add new turrets to the fabric of ambition, when the foundation itself is shaking, and the ground on which it stands is mouldering away.

Ibid. p. 102.

Death, says *Seneca*, falls heavy upon him, who is too much known to others, and too little to himself.

Ibid. p. 174.

DEPENDENCE.

There is no state more contrary to the dignity of wisdom, than perpetual and unlimited dependence, in which the understanding lies useless, and every motion is received from external impulse. Reason is the great distinction of human nature, the faculty by which we approach to some degree of association with celestial intelligences; but as the excellence of every power appears only in its operations,

operations, not to have reason, and to have it useless and unemployed, is nearly the same.

Rambler, vol. 4, p. 12.

Wherever there is wealth, there is dependence and expectation; and wherever there will be dependence, there will be an emulation of servility.

Ibid. p. 158.

If it be unhappy to have one patron, what is his misery who has many?

Ibid. vol. 1, p. 161.

The dependant who consults delicacy in himself, very little consults his own tranquillity.

Ibid. vol. 3, p. 262.

DIFFIDENCE.

The pain of miscarriage is naturally proportionate to the desire of excellence; and therefore till men are hardened by long familiarity with reproach, or have attained, by frequent struggles, the art of suppressing their emotions, Diffidence is found the insuperable associate of understanding.

Ibid. vol. 4, p. 186.

Diffidence may check resolution and obstruct performance, but compensates its embarrassments by more important advantages: it conciliates the proud, and softens the severe; averts envy from excellence, and censure from miscarriage.

Ibid. vol. 3, p. 317.

A request made with diffidence and timidity is easily

easily denied, because the petitioner himself seems to doubt its fitness.

Ibid. vol. 4, p. 36.

DELICACY.

He that too much refines his delicacy, will always endanger his quiet.

Ibid. p. 221.

Many pains are incident to a man of delicacy, which the unfeeling world cannot be persuaded to pity; and which, when they are separated from their peculiar and personal circumstances, will never be considered as important enough to claim attention or deserve redress.

Ibid. p. 217.

DISAPPOINTMENT.

We do not so often disappoint others as ourselves, as we do not only think more highly than others of our own abilities, but allow ourselves to form hopes which we never communicate, and please our thoughts with employments which none ever will allot us, and with elevations to which we are never expected to rise.

Idler, vol. 2, p. 203.

DISEASE.

It may be said that disease generally begins that equality which death completes. The distinctions which set one man so much above another, are very little perceived in the gloom of a sick chamber, where it will be vain to expect entertainment from the gay or instruction from the wise, where all human glory is obliterated: the wit is clouded, the reasoner perplexed, and the hero subdued; where the highest and brightest of mortal beings finds

finds nothing left him but the confcioufnefs of innocence.

Rambler, vol. 1, p. 290.

DISTRUST.

It is impoffible to fee the long fcrolls in which every contract is included, with all their appendages of feals and atteftation, without wondering at the depravity of thofe beings who muft be reftrained from violation of promife by fuch formal and public evidences, and precluded from equivocation and fubterfuge by fuch punctilious minutenefs. Among all the fatires to which folly and wickednefs have given occafion, none is equally fevere with a bond or a fettlement.

Ibid. vol. 3, p. 155.

DELAY.

The folly of allowing ourfelves to delay what we know cannot be finally efcaped, is one of the general weakneffes which, in fpite of the inftruction of moralifts, and the remonftrances of reafon, prevail to a greater or lefs degree in every mind: even they who moft fteadily withftand it, find it, if not the moft violent, the moft pertinacious, of their paffions, always renewing its attacks, and though often vanquifhed, never deftroyed.

Ibid. vol. 3, p. 170.

The certainty that life connot be long, and the probability that it will be much fhorter than nature allows, ought to awaken every man to the active profecution of whatever he is defirous to perform. It is true, that no diligence can afcertain fuccefs; death may intercept the fwifteft career,

reer, but he who is cut off in the execution of an honest undertaking, has at least the honour of falling in his rank, and has fought the battle, though he missed the victory.
Ibid. p. 134.

Timorous thoughts, and cautious disquisitions, are the dull attendance of delay.
Notes upon Shakespeare, vol. 6, p. 116.

DECEPTION.

Deceit and falsehood, whatever conveniencies they may for a time promise or produce, are, in the sum of life, obstacles to happiness. Those who profit by the cheat distrust the deceiver, and the act by which kindness was sought puts an end to confidence.
Ibid. vol. 10, p. 530.

SELF-DECEPTION.

There is an art of sophistry by which men have deluded their own consciences, by persuading themselves, that what would be criminal in others, is virtuous in them; as if the obligations which are laid upon us by a higher power, can be over-ruled by obligations which we lay upon ourselves.
Ibid. vol. 4, p. 487.

DEVOTION.

Some men's minds are so divided between heaven and earth, that they pray for the prosperity of guilt, while they deprecate its punishment.
Ibid. vol. 5, p. 579.

Poetical devotion cannot often please. The doctrines of religion may, indeed, be defended in a Didactic poem; and he who has the power of arguing in verse, will not lose it because his subject is sacred. A poet may describe the beauty and grandeur of nature; the flowers of the spring, and the harvests of autumn; the vicissitudes of the tide, and the revolutions of the sky; and praise the Maker for his works in lines which no reader shall lay aside. The subject of the disputation is not piety, but the motives to piety; that of the description is not God, but the works of God.

Contemplative piety, or the intercourse between God and the human soul, cannot be poetical. Man admitted to implore the mercy of his Creator, and plead the merits of his Redeemer, is already in a higher state than poetry can confer.

The essence of poetry is invention; such invention as, by producing something unexpected, surprises and delights. The topics of devotion are few, and being few, are universally known; but few as they are, they can be made no more; they can receive no grace from novelty of sentiment, and very little from novelty of expression.

Poetry pleases by exhibiting an idea more grateful to the mind than the things themselves afford. This effect proceeds from the display of those parts of nature which attract, and the concealment of those which repel the imagination: but religion must be shewn as it is; suppression and addition equally corrupt it; and such as it is, it is known already: from poetry the reader justly expects, and from good poetry always obtains, the enlargement of his comprehension, and elevation of his fancy; but this is rarely to be hoped by Christians from metrical devotion. Whatever is great, desirable, or tremendous, is comprised in the name of the Supreme Being. Omnipotence cannot be exalted;

ed; infinity cannot be amplified; perfection cannot be improved.

The employments of pious meditation are faith, thankfgiving, repentance, and fupplication. Faith, invariably uniform, cannot be invefted by fancy with decorations. Thankfgiving, the moft joyful of all holy effufions, yet addreffed to a Being without paffions, is confined to a few modes, and is to be felt rather than expreffed. Repentance, trembling in the prefence of the judge, is not at leifure for cadence and epithets. Supplication of man to man may diffufe itfelf through many topics of perfuafion; but fupplication to God can only cry for mercy.

Of fentiments purely religious, it will be found that the moft fimple expreffion is the moft fublime. Poetry lofes its luftre and its power, becaufe it is applied to the decorations of fomething more excellent than itfelf. All that verfe can do is to help the memory, and delight the ear; and for thefe purpofes it may be very ufeful: but it fupplies nothing to the mind. The ideas of Chriftian theology are too fimple for eloquence, too facred for fiction, and too majeftic for ornament; to recommend them by tropes and figures, is to magnify by a concave mirror the fideral hemifphere.

Life of Waller.

DUTY.

When we act according to our duty, we commit the event to him by whofe laws our actions are governed, and who will fuffer none to be finally punifhed for obedience. But, when in profpect of fome good, whether natural or moral, we break the rules prefcribed to us, we withdraw from the direction of superior wisdom, and take all consequences upon ourselves.

Prince of Abyssinia, p. 203.

DUTIES.

Much of the prosperity of a trading nation depends upon duties properly apportioned; so that what is necessary may continue cheap, and what is of use only to luxury, may in some measure atone to the public for the mischief done to individuals. Duties may often be so regulated, as to become useful, even to those that pay them; and they may be likewise so unequally imposed, as to discourage honesty, depress industry, and give temptation to fraud and unlawful practices.

Preface to Dictionary of Commerce, p. 289.

DILIGENCE.

Diligence in employments of less consequence is the most successful introduction to greater enterprizes.

Life of Drake, p. 160.

Diligence is never wholly lost.

Life of Collins.

DUPLICITY.

It is generally the fate of a *double dealer*, to *lose* his power, and *keep* his enemies.

Life of Swift.

DISGUISE.

Disguise can gratify no longer than it deceives.

Life of Somerville.

DULNESS.

Dulness or deformity are not culpable in themselves, but may be very justly reproached when they pretend to the honour of *wit* or the influence of *beauty*.

Life of Pope.

DELUSION.

If delusion be once admitted, it has no certain limitation.

Preface to Shakespeare, p. 113.

DIFFICULTY.

Nothing is difficult, when gain and honour unite their influence.

Falkland Islands, p. 4.

E.

ENVY.

He that knows himself despised, will always be envious; and still more envious and malevolent if he is condemned to live in the presence of those who despise him.

Prince of Abyssinia, p. 86.

To see the highest minds levelled with the meanest, may produce some solace to the consciousness of weakness, and some mortification to the pride of wisdom; but let it be remembered, that minds are not levelled in their powers, but when they are first levelled in their desires.

Life of Dryden.

It is not only to many more pleasing to recollect those faults which place others below them, than those virtues by which they are themselves comparatively depressed, but it is likewise more easy to neglect than to recompense; and though there are few who will practise a laborious virtue, there never will be wanting multitudes that will indulge an easy vice.

Life of Savage.

The great law of mutual benevolence is, perhaps oftener violated by envy than by interest. Interest can diffuse itself but to a narrow compass. Interest requires some qualities not universally bestowed. Interest is seldom pursued but at some hazard; but to spread suspicion, to invent calumnies, to propagate scandal, requires neither talents, nor labour, nor courage.

Rambler, vol. 4, p. 125 & 126.

EXAMPLE.

Every man, in whatever station, has, or endeavours to have, his followers, admirers, and imitators; and has therefore the influence of his example to watch with care; he ought to avoid not only crimes, but the appearance of crimes, and not only to practise virtue, but to applaud, countenance, and support it; for it is possible, for want of attention, we may teach others faults from which ourselves our free, or, by a cowardly desertion of a cause, which we ourselves approve, may pervert those who fix their eyes upon us, and having no rule of their own to guide their course, are easily misled by the aberrations of that example which they choose for their directions.

Ibid. vol. 2, p. 95.

Every art is best taught by example. Nothing contributes more to the cultivation of propriety, than remarks on the works of those who have most excelled.
Dissertation upon the Epitaphs of Pope, p. 302.

EMULATION.

Where there is emulation, there will be vanity; and where there is vanity, there will be folly.
Life of Shenstone.

Every man ought to endeavour at eminence, not by pulling others down, but by raising himself, and enjoy the pleasure of his own superiority, whether imaginary or real, without interrupting others in the same felicity. The philosopher may very justly be delighted with the extent of his views, and the artificer with the readiness of his hands; but let the one remember, that without mechanical performances, refined speculation is an empty dream; and the other, that without theoretical reasoning, dexterity is little more than a brute instinct.
Rambler, vol. 1, p. 52.

Whatever is done skilfully, appears to be done with ease; and art, when it is once matured to habit, vanishes from observation. We are therefore more powerfully excited to *emulation* by those who have attained the highest degree of excellence, and whom we can therefore with least reason hope to equal.
Ibid. vol. 3, p. 101.

EDUCATION.

The knowledge of external nature, and of the sciences which that knowledge requires or includes,

cludes, is not the great, or the frequent business of the human mind. Whether we provide for action or conversation, whether we wish to be useful or pleasing, the first requisite is the religious and moral knowledge of right and wrong. The next is an acquaintance with the history of mankind, and with those examples, which may be said to embody truth, and prove by events the reasonableness of opinions. Prudence and justice are virtues and excellences of all times and all places. We are perpetually moralists, but we are geometricians by chance. Our intercourse with intellectual nature is necessary; our speculations upon matter are voluntary, and at leisure.

Life of Milton.

Pysical knowledge is of such rare emergence, that one man may know another half his life without being able to estimate his skill in hydrostatics or astronomy; but his moral and prudential character immediately appears. Those authors therefore, are to be read at school, that supply most axioms of prudence, most principles of moral truth, and most materials for conversation; and these purposes are best served by poets, orators, and historians.

Ibid.

It ought always to be steadily inculcated, that virtue is the highest proof of understanding, and the only solid basis of greatness; and that vice is the natural consequence of narrow thoughts; that it begins in mistake, and ends in ignominy.

Rambler, vol. 1, p. 24.

The general rule of consulting the genius for particular offices in life is of little use, unless we are

are told how the genius can be known. If it is to be discovered only by experiment, life will be lost before the resolution can be fixed; if any other indications are to be found, they may perhaps be very easily discerned. At least, if to miscarry in the attempt be a proof of having mistaken the direction of the genius, men appear not less frequently deceived with regard to themselves, than to others; and therefore no one has much reason to complain that his life was planned out by his friends, or to be confident that he should have had either more honour or happiness by being abandoned to the chance of his own fancy.

Ibid. p. 120.

Many wonders are told of the Art of Educaton, and the very early ages at which boys are conversant in the Greek and Latin tongues, under some preceptors. But those who tell, or receive, those stories, should consider, that nobody can be taught faster than he can learn. The speed of the best horseman must be limited by the power of his horse. Every man that has undertaken to instruct others, can tell what slow advances he has been able to make, and how much patience it requires to recal vagrant inattention, to stimulate sluggish indifference, and to rectify absurd misapprehension.

Life of Milton.

It was the labour of Socrates, to turn philosophy from the study of nature to speculations upon life; but there have been, and are, other preceptors, who are turning off attention from *life* to *nature*. They seem to think, that we are placed here to watch the growth of plants, or the motion of the stars; but Socrates was rather of opinion,

that

that what we had to learn, was how to *do good*, and *avoid evil*.

Ibid.

The bulk of mankind muft, without the affiftance of education and inftruction, be informed only with the underftanding of a child.

Rambler, vol. 3, p. 270.

Neither a capital city, nor a town of commerce, are adapted for the purpofes of a college: the firft expofes the ftudents too much to levity and diffolutenefs, the other to grofs luxury. In one the defire of knowledge eafily gives way to the love of pleafure, and in the other there is danger in yielding to the love of money.

Weftern Iflands, p. 11.

EMPLOYMENT.

Employment is the great inftrument of intellectual dominion. The mind cannot retire from its enemy into total vacancy, or turn afide from one object, but by paffing to another. The gloomy and the refentful are always found among thofe who have *nothing to do*, or who *do nothing*. We muft be bufy about good, or evil, and he to whom the *prefent* offers nothing, will often be looking backward on the *paft*.

Idler, vol. 2, p. 113.

It is the fate of thofe who toil at the lower employments of life, to be rather driven by the fear of evil, than attracted by the profpect of good; to be expofed to cenfure, without hope of praife; to be difgraced by mifcarriage, or punifhed for neglect,

lect, where fuccefs would have been without applaufe, and diligence without reward.

Preface to Johnfon's Dictionary, p. 55.

EVIL.

No evil is infupportable, but that which is accompanied with confcioufnefs of wrong.

Prince of Abyffinia, p. 296.

Eftimable and ufeful qualities joined with an evil difpofition, give that evil difpofition power over others, who, by admiring the virtue, are betrayed to the malevolence. The Tatler, mentioning the fharpers of his time, obferves, " that fome of them are men of fuch elegance and knowledge, that a young man, who falls in their way, is betrayed as much by his judgement as his paffions."

Notes upon Shakefpeare, vol. 4, p. 7.

It is the nature of man to imagine no evil fo great, as that which is near him.

Ibid. vol. 5, p. 86.

EMPIRE.

Extended empire, like expanded gold, exchanges folid ftrength for feeble fplendour.

Irene, p. 16.

EXCELLENCE.

Thofe who attain any excellence, commonly fpend life in one purfuit; for excellence is not often gained upon eafier terms.

Life of Pope.

There is a vigilance of observation, and accuracy of distinction, which books and precepts cannot confer; and from this almost all original and native excellence proceeds.

Preface to Shakespeare, p. 123.

They whose excellence of any kind has been loudly celebrated, are ready to conclude that their powers are universal.

Ibid. p. 131.

ENQUIRY.

In the zeal of enquiry we do not always reflect on the silent encroachments of time, or remember that no man is in more danger of doing little, than he who flatters himself with abilities to do all.

Treatise on the Longitude, p. 14.

EQUANIMITY.

Evil is uncertain, in the same degree, as good; and for the reason we ought not to hope too securely, we ought not to fear with too much dejection. The state of the world is continually changing, and none can tell the result of the next vicissitude. Whatever is afloat in the stream of time, may, when it is very near us, be driven away by an accidental blast, which shall happen to cross the general course of the current. The sudden accidents by which the powerful are depressed, may fall upon those whose malice we fear, and the greatness by which we expect to be overborne, may become another proof of the false flatteries of fortune. Our enemies may become weak, or we grow strong, before our encounter; or we may advance against each other without ever meeting.

ing. There are indeed natural evils, which we can flatter ourselves with no hopes of escaping, and with little of delaying; but of the ills which are apprehended from human malignity, or the opposition of rival interests, we may always alleviate the terror, by considering that our persecutors are weak, ignorant, and mortal, like ourselves.

Rambler, vol. 1, p. 178.

ERROR.

"Errors," says Dryden, flow upon the surface"; but there are some who will fetch them from the bottom.

Notes upon Shakspeare, vol. 4, p. 393.

It is incumbent on every man who consults his own dignity, to retract his error as soon as he discovers it, without fearing any censure so much as that of his own mind. As justice requires that all injuries should be repaired, it is the duty of him who has seduced others by bad practices, or false notions, to endeavour that such as have adopted his errors should know his retraction, and that those who have learned vice by his example, should, by his example, be taught amendment.

Rambler, vol. 1, p. 192.

The men who can be charged with fewest failings, either with respect to abilities, or virtue, are generally most ready to allow them. *Cæsar* wrote an account of the errors committed by him in his wars of Gaul; and Hippocrates, whose name is, perhaps, in rational estimation, greater than Cæsar's, warned posterity against a mistake into which he he had fallen. "*So much (says* CELSUS) *does the open and artless confession of an error become a man conscious that he has enough remaining to support his character.*"

Ibid. p. 191.

That which is strange, is delightful; and a pleasing error is not willingly detected.

Western Islands, p. 63.

EPITAPH.

To define an epitaph is useless; every one knows it is an inscription on a tomb; an epitaph, therefore, implies no particular character of writing, but may be composed in verse or prose. It is, indeed, commonly panegyrical, because we are seldom distinguished with a stone, but by our friends; but it has no rule to restrain, or modify it, except this, that it ought not to be longer than common beholders may be expected to have leisure and patience to peruse.

Dissertation on the Epitaphs of Pope, p. 303.

The name of the deceased should never be omitted in an epitaph, whose end is to convey some account of the dead, and to what purpose is any thing told of him whose name is concealed? An epitaph, and a history of a nameless hero, are equally absurd, since the virtues and qualities so recounted, in either are scattered, at the mercy of fortune, to be appropriated by guess. The name, it is true, may be read upon the stone, but what obligation has it to the poet, whose verses wander over the earth, and leave their subject behind them; and who is forced, like an unskilful painter,

painter, to make his purpose known by adventitious help?

Ibid. p. 307.

The difficulty of writing epitaphs, is to give a particular and appropriate praise.

Ibid. p. 314.

ESTEEM.

To raise esteem we must benefit others; to procure love, we must please them.

Rambler, vol. 4, p. 5.

ELECTION.

Perhaps no election, by a plurality of suffrages, was ever made among human beings, to which it might not be objected, that voices were not procured by illicit influence.

Memoirs of the King of Prussia, p. 125.

EXPECTATION.

Expectation, when once her wings are expanded, easily reaches heights which performance never will attain; and when she has mounted the summit of perfection, derides her follower, who dies in the pursuit.

Plan of an English Dictionary, p. 32.

EFFECTS.

(Not always proportioned to their Causes.)

It seems to be almost the universal error of historians, to suppose it politically, as it is physically, true, that every effect has a proportionate cause.

In

In the inanimate action of matter upon matter, the motion produced can be but equal to the force of the moving power; but the operations of life, whether public, or private, admit no such laws. The caprices of voluntary agents, laugh at calculation. It is not always there is a strong reason for a great event; obstinacy and flexibility, malignity and kindness, give place alternately to each other; and the reason of those vicissitudes, however important may be the consequences, often escapes the mind in which the change is made.

Falkland Islands, p. 55.

ELEGANCE.

Elegance is surely to be desired, if it be not gained at the expence of dignity. A hero would wish to be loved, as well as to be reverenced.

Life of Pope.

Honesty is not greater where elegance is less.

Western Islands.

ENGLAND.

In all ages foreigners have affected to call England their country; even when, like the Saxons of old, they came to conquer it.

Marmor Norfolciense, p. 10.

ESTIMATION.

Little things are not valued, but when they are done by those who can do greater.

Life of Philips.

ELEGY.

ELEGY.

Elegy is the effusion of a contemplative mind, sometimes plaintive, and always serious, and therercfore superior to the glitter of flight ornaments.

Life of Shenstone.

ESSAY-WRITING.

He that questions his abilities to arrange the dissimilar parts of an extensive plan, or fears to be lost in a complicated system, may yet hope to adjust a few pages without perplexity; and if, when he turns over the repositories of his memory, he finds his collection too small for a volume, he may yet have enough to furnish an essay.

Rambler, vol. 1, p. 6.

EXERCISE.

Such is the constitution of man, that *labour* may be styled *its own reward:* nor will any external incitements be requisite, if it be considered how much happiness is gained, and how much misery escaped, by frequent and violent agitation of the body.

Ibid. vol. 2, p. 177.

Exercise cannot secure us from that dissolution to which we are decreed; but, while the soul and body continue united, it can make the association pleasing, and give probable hopes that they shall be disjoined by an easy separation. It was a principle among the ancients, that acute diseases are from heaven, and chronicle, from ourselves: the dart

dart of death, indeed, falls from heaven; but we poison it by our own misconduct.

Ibid. p. 178.

EATING.

It is not very easy to fix the principle upon which mankind have agreed to eat some animals, and reject others; and as the principle is not evident, it is not uniform. That which is selected as delicate in one country, is, by its neighbours, abhorred as loathsome. The Neapolitans lately refused to eat potatoes, in a famine: an Englishman is not easily persuaded to dine on snails with an Italian, on Frogs with a Frenchman, or on horse-flesh with a Tartar. The vulgar inhabitants of Sky, one of the Western islands of Scotland, have not only eels, but pork and bacon, in abhorrence.

Western Islands. p. 136.

F.

FAME.

He that is loudly praised, will be clamorously censured. He that rises hastily into fame, will be in danger of sinking suddenly into oblivion.

Idler, vol. 2, p. 25.

The memory of mischief is no desirable fame.

Prince of Abyssinia, p. 257.

The true satisfaction which is to be drawn from the consciousness that we shall share the attention of

of future times, muſt ariſe from the hope, that with our names, our virtues ſhall be propagated, and that thoſe whom we cannot benefit in our lives, may receive inſtruction from our example, and incitemennt from our renown.
Rambler, vol. 1, p. 298.

Fame cannot ſpread wide, or endure long, that is not rooted in nature, and manured by art. That which hopes to reſiſt the blaſts of malignity, and ſtand firm againſt the attacks of time, muſt contain in itſelf ſome original principle of growth.
Ibid. vol. 3, p. 292.

He that purſues fame with juſt claims, truſts his happineſs to the winds; but he that endeavours after it by falſe merit, has to fear, not only the *violence of the ſtorm*, but the *leaks of his veſſel*.
Ibid. vol. 1, p. 126.

Every period of time has produced thoſe bubbles of artificial fame, which are kept up a while by the breath of faſhion, and then break at once, and are annihilated.
Ibid. vol. 3, p. 3.

FATHER.

A Father above the common rate of men, has commonly a ſon below it. Heroum filii noxæ.
Notes upon Shakeſpeare, vol. 1, p. 14.

FRIENDSHIP.

Few love their Friends ſo well as not to deſire ſuperiority by unexpenſive benefaction.
Falſe Alarm, p. 47.

Friendship in letter-writing has no tendency to secure veracity; for by whom can a man so much wish to be thought better than he is, as by him whose kindness he desires to gain or keep? Even in writing to the world there is less constraint; the author is not confronted with his reader, and takes his chance of approbation amongst the different dispositions of mankind. But a letter is addressed to a single mind, of which the prejudices and partialities are known, and must therefore please, if not by favouring them, by forbearing to oppose them.

Life of Pope.

Friendship is not always the sequel of obligation.

Life of Thompson.

Unequal friendships are easily dissolved.—This is often the fault of the superior; yet if we look without prejudice on the world, we shall often find that men, whose consciousness of their own merit, sets them above the compliances of servility, are apt enough, in their association with superiors, to watch their own dignity with troublesome and punctilious jealousy, and in the fervour of independence, to exact that attention which they refuse to pay.

Life of Grey.

So many qualities are necessary to the possibility of friendship, and so many accidents must concur to its rise and its continuance, that the greatest part of mankind content themselves without it, and supply its place as they can with interest and dependence.

Rambler, vol. 2, p. 59.

That

That friendship may be at once fond and lasting, there must not only be equal virtue on each part, but virtue of the same kind; not only the same end must be proposed, but the same means must be approved by both.

Ibid. vol. 2, p. 61.

Among the uncertainties of the human state, we are doomed to number the instability of friendship.

Life of Addison.

It were happy if, in forming friendships, virtue could concur with pleasure; but the greatest part of human gratifications approach so nearly to vice, that few who make the delight of others their rule of conduct, can avoid disingenuous compliances; yet certainly he that suffers himself to be driven or allured from virtue, mistakes his own interest, since he gains succour by means for which his friend, if ever he becomes wise, must scorn him; and for which, at last, he must scorn himself.

Rambler, vol. 4, p. 5.

Many have talked in very exalted language of the perpetuity of friendship: of invincible constancy and unalienable kindness; and some examples have been seen of men who have continued faithful to their earliest choice, and whose affections have predominated over changes of fortune and contrariety of opinion. But these instances are memorable, because they are rare. The friendship which is to be practised or expected by common mortals, must take its rise from mutual pleasure, and must end when the power ceases of delighting each other.

Idler, vol. 1, p. 126.

The most fatal disease of friendship is gradual decay, or dislike hourly increased by causes too slender for complaint, and too numerous for removal. Those who are angry may be reconciled. Those who have been injured may receive a recompense; but when the desire of pleasing, and willingness to be pleased, is silently diminished, the renovation of friendship is hopeless; as when the vital powers sink into languor, there is no longer any use of the physician.

Ibid. vol. 1, p. 130.

Men only become friends by community of pleasures. He who cannot be softened into gaiety cannot easily be melted into kindness. Upon this principle Falstaff despairs of gaining the love of Prince John of Lancaster, for "he could not make him laugh."

Notes upon Shakespeare, vol. 5, p. 560.

The kindnesses which are first experienced, are seldom forgotten.

Life of Walsh.

When Mr. Addison was made Secretary to the Marquis of Wharton, then Lord Lieutenant of Ireland, he made a law to himself, never to remit his regular fees *in civility to his friends*. "For," said he, "I may have an hundred friends; and, if my fee be two guineas, I shall, by relinquishing my right, lose *two hundred guineas*, and no friend gain more than *two*; there is, therefore, no proportion between the good imparted and the evil suffered.

Life of Addison.

Men sometimes suffer by injudicious kindness

and become ridiculous without their own faults, by the abfurd admiration of their friends.

Life of Phillips.

There are few who, in the wantonnefs of thoughtlefs mirth, or heat of tranfient refentment, do not fometimes fpeak of their friends and benefactors with levity and contempt, though, in their cooler moments, they want neither fenfe of their kindnefs nor reverence for their virtues. This weaknefs is very common, and often proceeds rather from negligence than ingratitude.

Life of Savage.

He cannot be properly chofen for a friend, whofe kindnefs is exhaled by its own warmth or frozen by the firft blaft of flander; he cannot be a ufeful counfeller, who will hear no opinion but his own; he will not much invite confidence, whofe principal maxim is to fufpect; nor can the candour and franknefs of that man be much efteemed, who fpreads his arms to human kind, and makes every man, without diftinction, a denizen of his bofom.

Rambler, vol. 2, p. 61.

One of the Golden Precepts of *Pythagoras* direct us, " That a friend fhould not be hated for little faults."

Ibid. vol. 4, p. 220.

Friendfhip, like love, is deftroyed by long abfence, though it may be increafed by fhort intermiffions. What we have miffed long enough to want it, we value more when it is regained; but that which has been loft till it is forgotten, will be found

found at last with little gladness, and with still less if a substitute has supplied the place.

Idler, vol. 1, p. 127.

Among the many enemies of friendship may be reckoned *suspicion* and *disgust*. The former is always hardening the cautious, and the latter repelling the delicate.

Ibid. p. 130.

Among the pleasing incidents of life may be numbered the unexpected renewals of old acquaintances.

Western Islands, p 24.

All feel the benefits of private friendship, but few can discern the advantages of a well constituted government; hence the greater part of mankind will be naturally prejudiced against *Brutus*.

Review of the Memoirs of the Court of Augustus, p. 5.

FLATTERY.

In every instance of vanity it will be found that the blame ought to be shared among more than it generally reaches. All who exalt trifles by immoderate praise, or instigate needless emulation by invidious incitements, are to be considered as perverters of reason, and corrupters of the world; and since every man is obliged to promote happiness and virtue, he should be careful not to mislead unwary minds, by appearing to set too high a value upon things, by which no real excellence is conferred.

Rambler, vol. 4, p. 84.

To be flattered is grateful, even when we know that our praises are not believed by those who pronounce them; for they prove at least our power, and shew that our favour is valued, since it is purchased by the meanness of falsehood.

Ibid. p. 120.

In order that all men may be taught to speak truth, it is necessary that all likewise should learn to hear it; for no species of falsehood is more frequent than flattery, to which the coward is betrayed by fear, the dependent by interest, and the friend by tenderness. Those who are neither servile, or timorous, are yet desirous to bestow pleasure; and while unjust demands of praise continue to be made, there will always be some whom hope, fear, or kindness, will dispose to pay them.

Ibid. p. 247.

He that is much flattered, soon learns to flatter himself. We are commonly taught our duty by fear or shame; and how can they act upon the man who hears nothing but his own praises?

Life of Swift.

Just praise is only a debt, but flattery is a present.

Rambler, vol. 3, p. 294.

Neither our virtues or vices are all our own. If there were no cowardice, there would be little insolence. Pride cannot rise to any great degree, but by the concurrence of blandishment, or the sufferance of tameness. The wretch who would shrink and crouch before one who should dart his eyes upon him with the spirit of natural equality, becomes capricious and tyrannical when he sees himself approached with a downcast look, and hears

hears the soft addresses of awe and servility. To those who are willing to purchase favour by cringes and compliance, is to be imputed the haughtiness that leaves nothing to hoped by firmness and integrity.

Ibid. vol. 4, p. 3.

The flatterer is not often detected; for an honest mind is not apt to suspect, and no one exerts the power of discernment with much vigour when self-love favours the deceit.

Rambler, vol. 2, p. 120.

It is necessary to the success of flattery, that it be accommodated to particular circumstances or characters, and enter the heart on that side where the passions stand ready to receive it.

Ibid. vol. 3, p. 1.

FOLLY.

No man will be found in whose mind airy notions do not sometimes tyrannise, and force him to hope or fear beyond the limits of sober probability.

Prince of Abyssinia, p. 259.

The folly which is adapted to persons and times, has its propriety, and therefore produces no censure; but the folly of wise men, when it happens, taints their wit, and destroys the reputation of their judgment.

Notes upon Shakespeare, vol. 4, p. 225.

As with folly no man is willing to confess himself very intimately acquainted, therefore its pains and pleasures are kept secret.

Review of the Origin of Evil, p. 10.

FORTUNE.

FORTUNE.

Fortune often delights to dignify what nature has neglected, and that renown, which cannot be claimed by intrinsic excellence or greatness, is sometimes derived from unexpected accidents.

Falkland Iflands, p. 2.

When fortune strikes her hardest blows, to be wounded and yet continue calm, requires a generous policy. Perhaps the first emotions of nature are nearly uniform, and one man differs from another in the power of endurance, as he is better regulated by precept and instruction.

Notes upon Shakefpeare, vol. 6, p. 128.

Examples need not be sought at any great distance, to prove that *superiority of fortune* has a natural tendency to kindle pride, and that pride seldom fails to exert itself in contempt and insult. This is often the effect of hereditary wealth, and of honours only enjoyed by the merit of others.

Life of Savage.

FOREIGNER.

To be a foreigner was always in England a reason of dislike.

Notes upon Shakefpeare, vol. 1, p. 265.

FEAR.

All fear is in itself painful: and when it conduces not to safety, is painful without use.

Rambler, vol. 1, p. 180.

Fear is implanted in us as a preservative from evil; but its duty, like that of other passions, is not to overbear reason, but to assist it; nor should it be suffered to tyrannise in the imagination, to raise phantoms of horror, or beset life with supernumerary distresses.

Ibid. vol. 3, p. 125.

FORGIVENESS.

Whoever considers the weakness both of himself and others, will not long want persuasives to forgiveness. We know not to what degree of malignity any injury is to be imputed, or how much its guilt, if we were to inspect the mind of him that committed it, would be extenuated by mistake, precipitance, or negligence. We cannot be certain how much more we feel than was intended, or how much we increase the mischief to ourselves by voluntary aggravations. We may charge to design the effects of accident. We may think the blow violent, only because we have made ourselves delicate and tender; we are, on every side, in danger of error and guilt, which we are certain to avoid only by speedy forgiveness.

Rambler, vol. 4, p. 137.

A constant and unfailing obedience is above the reach of terrestrial diligence; and therefore the progress of life could only have been the natural descent of negligent despair from crime to crime, had not the universal persuasion of *forgiveness*, to be obtained by proper means of reconciliation, recalled those to the paths of virtue whom their passions had solicited aside, and animated to new attempts and firmer perseverance those whom difficulty had discouraged, or negligence surprised.

Ibid. vol. 3, p. 26.

FRUGALITY.

FRUGALITY.

Frugality may be termed the daughter of prudence, the sister of temperance, and the parent of liberty. He that is extravagant, will quickly become poor, and poverty will enforce dependence, and invite corruption. It will almost always produce a passive compliance with the wickedness of others, and there are few who do not learn by degrees to practise those crimes which they cease to censure.

Ibid. vol. 2, p. 21.

Without frugality none can be rich, and with it, very few would be poor.

Ibid.

Though in every age there are some who, by bold adventures or by favourable accidents, rise suddenly into riches, the bulk of mankind must owe their affluence to small and gradual profits, below which their expence must be resolutely reduced.

Ibid. p. 23.

The mercantile wisdom of " a penny saved is two-pence got," may be accommodated to all conditions, by observing, that not only they who pursue any lucrative employment will save time when they forbear expence, and that time may be employed to the increase of profit; but that they, who are above such minute considerations, will find by every victory over appetite or passion, new strength added to the mind, will gain the power of refusing those solicitations by which the young and vivacious are hourly assaulted, and, in time,

set

set themselves above the reach of extravagance and folly.

Ibid. p. 24.

It may, perhaps, be enquired, by those who are willing rather to cavil than to learn, what is the just measure of frugality? To such no general answer can be given, since the liberty of spending, or necessity of parsimony, may be varied without end by different circumstances. These three rules, however, may be laid down as not to be departed from:

"A man's voluntary expences should not exceed his income."

"Let no man anticipate uncertain profits."

"Let no man squander against his inclination."

Ibid.

It appears evident that *frugality* is necessary even to complete the pleasure of expence; for it may be generally remarked of those who squander what they know their fortune not sufficient to allow, that, in their most jovial expence, there always breaks out some proof of discontent and impatience: they either scatter with a kind of wild desperation and affected lavishness, as criminals brave the gallows when they cannot escape it, or pay their money with a peevish anxiety, and endeavor at once to *spend idly*, and to *save meanly:* having neither firmness to deny their passions, nor courage to gratify them, they murmur at their own enjoyments, and poison the bowl of pleasure by reflections on the cost.

Rambler, vol. 3, p. 135.

FAVOUR.

FAVOUR.

Favours of every kind are doubled when they are speedily conferred.
Rambler, vol. 4, p. 183.

FANCY.

The fanciful sports of great minds, are never without some advantage to knowledge.
Life of Sir Thomas Browne, p. 267.

FAULTS.

Many seeming faults are to be imputed rather to the nature of the undertaking, than the negligence of the performer.
Preface to Johnson's Dictionary, p. 71.

FABLE.

A fable, to be well adapted to the stage, should be sufficiently removed from the present age to admit properly the fictions necessary to complete the plan; for the mind, which naturally loves truth, is always most offended with the violation of those truths of which we are most certain; and we, of course, conceive those facts most certain, which approach nearest to our own time.
Life of Savage.

To select a singular event, and swell it to a giant's bulk by *fabulous appendages*, has little difficulty; for he that forsakes the probable, may always find the marvellous; and it has little use. We are affected only as we believe; we are improved only as we find something to be imitated or declined.
Life of Gray.

FASHION.

There are few enterprises so hopeless as contests with the *fashion*, in which the opponents are not only made confident by their numbers, and strong by their union, but are hardened by contempt of their antagonist, whom they always look upon as a wretch of low notions, contracted views, mean conversation, and narrow fortune; who envies the elevations which he cannot reach; who would gladly embitter the happiness which his inelegance or indigence deny him to partake, and who has no other end in his advice than to revenge his own mortification, by hindering those whom their birth and taste have set above him, from the enjoyment of their superiority, and bringing them down to a level with himself.

Rambler, vol. 1, p. 88.

FALSEHOOD.

Though many artifices may be used to maintain falsehood by fraud, they generally lose their force by counteracting one another.

Taxation no Tyranny, p. 4.

FORTITUDE.

Nil mortalibus arduum est. There is nothing which human courage will not undertake, and little that human patience will not endure.

Falkland Islands, p. 17.

FACTION.

In the general censure thrown upon *faction*, it perhaps never happens that every single man should be included. In all lead, says the chemist, there is silver, and in all copper there is gold. But mingled masses are justly denominated by the greater

greater quantity; and when the precious particles are not worth extraction, a *faction*, and a *pig*, muſt be melted down together, to the forms and offices that chance allots them.

Falſe Alarm, p. 52.

G.

GENIUS.

True genius is a mind of large general powers accidentally determined to ſome particular direction.

Life of Cowley.

Genius is powerful when inveſted with the glitter of affluence. Men willingly pay to fortune that regard which they owe to merit, and are pleaſed when they have an opportunity at once of gratifying their vanity, and practiſing their duty.

Life of Savage.

Whoever is apt to hope good from others, is diligent to pleaſe them; but he that believes his powers ſtrong enough to force their own way, commonly tries only to pleaſe himſelf.

Life of Gay.

Men have ſometimes appeared of ſuch tranſcendant abilities, that their ſlighteſt and moſt curſory performances, excel all that labour and ſtudy can enable meaner intellects to compoſe. As there are regions of which the ſpontaneous products cannot be equalled in other ſoils, by care and culture. But it is no leſs dangerous for any man to

place

place himself in this rank of understanding, and fancy that he is born to be illustrious without labour, than to omit the care of husbandry, and expect from his ground the blossoms of Arabia.

Rambler, vol. 4, p. 50.

Misapplied genius most commonly proves ridiculous.

Idler, vol. 2, p. 231.

There are men who seem to think nothing so much characteristic of genius, as to do common things in an uncommon way; like Hudribras, *to tell the clock by Algebra*, or like the lady in Dr. Young's Satire, " to drink tea by stratagem."

Ibid. vol. 1, p. 202.

Great powers cannot be exerted but when great exigencies make them necessary. Great exigencies can happen but seldom, and therefore those qualities which have a claim to the veneration of mankind, lie hid, for the most part, like subterranean treasures, over which the foot passes as on common ground, till necessity breaks open the golden cavern.

Ibid. p. 287.

It seems to have been in all ages, the pride of wit to shew how it could exalt the low, and amplify the little. To speak not inadequately of things really, and naturally, great, is a task not only difficult but disagreeable, because the writer is degraded in his own eyes by standing in comparison with his subject, to which he can hope to add nothing from his imagination. But it is a perpetual triumph of fancy to expand a scanty theme, to raise glittering ideas from obscure properties, and

to

to produce to the world an object of wonder, to which nature had contributed little. To this ambition, perhaps, we owe the Frogs of Homer, the Gnat and the Bees of Virgil, the Butterfly of Spencer, the Shadow of Woverus, and the Quincunx of Brown.

Life of Sir Thomas Browne, p. 266.

Genius now and then produces a lucky trifle. We still read the *Dove* of Anacreon, and *Sparrow* of Catullus; and a writer naturally pleases himself with a performance which owes nothing to the subject.

Life of Waller.

By the general consent of critics, the first praise of GENIUS is due to the writer of an epic poem, as it requires an assemblage of all the powers which are singly sufficient for other compositions. Poetry is the art of uniting pleasure with truth, by calling imagination to the help of reason. Epic poetry undertakes to teach the most important truths by the most pleasing precept, and therefore relates some great event in the most affecting manner. History must supply the writer with the rudiments of narration, which he must improve and exalt by a nobler art, animate by dramatic energy, and diversify by retrospection and anticipation; morality must teach him the exact bounds, and different shades, of vice and virtue; from policy and the practice of life he has to learn the discriminations of character, and the tendency of the passions, either single or combined, and physiology must supply him with illustrations and images. To put these materials to poetical use, is required an imagination capable of painting nature, and realizing fiction; nor is he yet a poet till he has attained

attained the whole extenfion of his language, diftinguifhed all the delicacies of phrafe, and all the colours of words, and learned to adjuft the different founds to all the varieties of metrical modulation.
Life of Milton.

It is certain that no eftimate is more in danger of erroneous calculations, than thofe by which a man computes the force of his genius.
Rambler, vol. 3, p. 288.

It is not fafe to judge of the works of genius merely by the event.
Ibid, p. 303.

The genius of the Englifh nation is faid to appear rather in *improvement* than *invention*.
Idler, vol. 1, p. 218.

Thofe who are willing to attribute every thing to genius, or natural fagacity, independent of a previous education, are encouraged to this opinion by lazinefs or pride, being willing to forego the labour of accurate reading and tedious enquiry, and to fatisfy themfelves and others with illuftrious examples.
Life of Dr. Sydenham.

There are many forcible expreffions which would never have been found, but by venturing to the utmoft verge of propriety, and flights which would never have been reached, but by thofe who have had very little fear of the fhame of falling.
Life of Sir T. Brown, p. 283.

As among the works of nature no man can properly call a river deep, or a mountain high, without

without the knowledge of many mountains and many rivers; so, in the productions of genius, nothing can be styled excellent till it has been compared with other works of the same kind.
Preface to Shakspeare, p. 126.

Many works of genius and learning have been performed in states of life, that appear very little favourable to thought or to enquiry; so many, that he who considers them, is inclined to think that he sees enterprise and perseverance predominating over all external agency, and bidding help and hindrance vanish before them.
Ibid. p. 125.

GOVERNMENT.

Governments formed by chance, and gradually improved by such expedients as the successive discovery of their defects happened to suggest, are never to be tried by a regular theory. They are fabrics of dissimilar materials, raised by different architects upon different plans. We must be content with them as they are; should we attempt to mend their disproportions, we might easily demolish, and with difficulty rebuild them.
False Alarm, p. 24.

In all political regulations, good cannot be complete, it can only be predominant.
Western Islands, p. 208.

No scheme of policy has, in any country, yet brought the rich on equal terms into courts of judicature. Perhaps experience, improving on experience, may in time effect it.
Ibid. p. 215.

To hinder infurrection by driving away the people, and to govern peaceably, by having no subjects, is an expedient that argues no great profundity of politics. To soften the obdurate, to convince the miftaken, to mollify the refentful, are worthy of a ftatefman; but it affords a legiflator little felf-applaufe to confider, that where there was formerly an infurrection, there is now a wildernefs.

Ibid. p. 224.

The general ftory of mankind will evince, that lawful and fettled authority is very feldom refifted when it is well employed. Grofs corruption or evident imbecility, is neceffary to the fuppreffion of that reverence, with which the majority of mankind look upon their governors, or thofe whom they fee furrounded by fplendour, and fortified by power.

Rambler, vol. 1, p. 301.

No government could fubfift for a day, if fingle errors could juftify defection.

Taxation no Tyranny, p. 62.

Government is neceffary to man; and when obedience is not compelled, there is no government.

Ibid. p. 77.

To prevent evil is the great end of government, the end for which vigilance and feverity are properly employed.

Rambler, vol. 3, p. 12.

Forms of government are feldom the refult of much deliberation; they are framed by chance in popular

popular assemblies, or in conquered countries by despotic authority.

Idler, vol. 1, p. 60.

In sovereignty there are no gradations. There may be limited royalty; there may be limited consulship; but there can be *no limited government*. There must in every society be some power or other from whence there is no appeal, which admits no restrictions, which pervades the whole mass of the community, regulates and adjusts all subordination, enacts laws or repeals them, erects or annuls judicatures, extends or contracts privileges, exempts itself from question or control, and bounded only by physical necessity.

Taxation no Tyranny, p. 24.

Few errors and few faults of government can justify an appeal to the rabble, who ought not to judge of what they cannot understand, and whose opinions are not propagated by reason, but caught by contagion.

Patriot, p. 7.

As government advances towards perfection, *provincial judicature* is, perhaps, in every empire, gradually abolished.

Western Islands, p. 100.

In all changes of government, there will be many that suffer real or imaginary grievances; and therefore many will be dissatisfied.

Political State of Great-Britain in 1756, p. 44.

GUILT.

Guilt is generally afraid of light; it considers darkness as a natural shelter, and makes night the confidante

confidante of those actions, which cannot be trusted to the tell-tale day.

Notes upon Shakefpeare, vol. 6, p. 377.

It may be observed, perhaps, without exception, that none are so industrious to detect wickedness, or so ready to impute it, as they whose crimes are apparent and confessed. They envy an unblemished reputation, and what they envy they are busy to destroy: they are unwilling to suppose themselves meaner and more corrupt than others, and therefore willingly pull down from their elevations those with whom they cannot rise to an equality.

Rambler, vol. 2, p. 126.

Men are willing to try all methods of reconciling guilt and quiet, and, when their understandings are stubborn and uncomplying, raise their passions against them, and hope to overpower their own knowledge.

Ibid.

SELF-GOVERNMENT.

No man, whose appetites are his masters, can perform the duties of his nature with strictness and regularity. He that would be superior to external influences, must first become superior to his own passions.

Idler, vol. 1, p. 293.

UNIVERSAL GOOD.

All skill ought to be exerted for universal good. Every man has owed much to others, and ought to pay the kindness that he has received.

Prince of Abyssinia, p. 41.

GREATNESS.

GREATNESS.

He that becomes acquainted and is invested with authority and influence, will in a short time be convinced, that, in proportion as the power of doing well is enlarged, the temptations to do ill are multiplied and enforced.

Rambler, vol. 2, p. 58.

That awe which great actions or abilities impress, will be inevitably diminished by *acquaintance*, though nothing either mean or criminal should be found; because we do not easily consider him as great whom in our own eyes we see to be little; nor labour to keep present to our thoughts the latent excellences of him who shares with us all our weaknesses and many of our follies; who, like us, is delighted with light amusements, busied with trifling employments, and disturbed by little vexations.

Idler, vol. 1, p. 285 & 287.

GRATITUDE.

There are minds so impatient of inferiority, that their gratitude is a species of revenge; and they return benefits, not because recompense is a pleasure, but because obligation is a pain.

Rambler, vol. 2, p. 192.

The charge against ingratitude is very general. Almost every man can tell what favours he has conferred upon insensibility, and how much happiness he has bestowed without return; but, perhaps, if these patrons and protectors were confronted with any whom they boast of having befriended, it would often appear that they consulted only their own pleasure or vanity, and repaid themselves

selves their petty donatives by gratifications of in-solence, and indulgence of contempt.

Ibid. vol. 3, p. 259.

H.

HAPPINESS.

We are long before we are convinced that happiness is never to be found; and each believes it possessed by others, to keep alive the hope of obtaining it for himself.

Prince of Abyssinia, p. 108.

Whether perfect happiness can be procured by perfect goodness, this world will never afford an opportunity of deciding. But this, at least, may be maintained, that we do not always find visible happiness in proportion to visible virtue.

Ibid. p. 163.

All natural, and almost all political evils, are incident alike to the bad or good. They are confounded in the misery of a famine, and not much distinguished in the fury of a faction. They sink together in a tempest, and are driven together from their country by invaders. All that virtue can afford is *quietness of conscience*, a steady prospect of a happier state, which will enable us to endure every calamity with patience.

Ibid.

He that has no one to love or to confide in, has little to hope. He wants the radical principle of happiness.

Ibid. p. 210.

It is, perhaps, a juſt obſervation, that with regard to outward circumſtances, happineſs and miſery are equally diffuſed through all ſtates of human life. In civilized countries, where regular policies have ſecured the neceſſaries of life, ambition, avarice, and luxury, find the mind at leiſure for their reception, and ſoon engage it in new purſuits; purſuits that are to be carried only by inceſſant labour, and whether vain or ſucceſsful, produce anxiety and contention. Among ſavage nations imaginary wants find, indeed, no place; but their ſtrength is exhauſted by neceſſary toils, and their paſſions agitated, not by conteſts about ſuperiority, affluence, or precedence, but by perpetual care for the preſent day, and by fear of periſhing for want of common food.

Life of Drake, p. 211.

Whatever be the cauſe of happineſs, may be made likewiſe the cauſe of miſery. The medicine which, rightly applied, has power to cure, has, when raſhneſs or ignorance preſcribes it, the ſame power to deſtroy.

Diſſertation on Authors, p. 21.

The happineſs of the generality of people is nothing, if it is not known, and very little if it is not envied.

Idler, vol. 2, p. 155.

It has been obſerved in all ages, that the advantages of nature or of fortune, have contributed very little to the promotion of happineſs; and that thoſe whom the ſplendour of their rank or the extent of their capacity, have placed upon the ſummits of human life, have not often given any juſt occaſion to envy in thoſe who look up to them from a lower station. Whether it be, that apparent superiority incites great designs, and great designs are naturally liable to fatal miscarriages, or that the general lot of mankind is misery, and the misfortunes of those whose eminence drew upon them an universal attention, have been more faitfully recorded, because they were more generally observed, and have, in reality, been only more conspicuous than those of others, more frequent or more severe.

Life of Savage.

It seldom happens that all circumstances concur to happiness or fame.

Rambler, vol. 3, p. 106.

Happiness is not found in self-contemplation; it is perceived only when it is reflected from another.

Idler, vol. 1, p. 232.

DOMESTIC HAPPINESS.

The great end of prudence is to give chearfulness to those hours which splendour cannot gild, and acclamation cannot exhilirate. Those soft intervals of unbended amusement, in which a man shrinks to his natural dimensions, and throws aside the ornaments or disguises which he feels, in privacy, to be useful incumbrances, and to lose all effect when they become familiar. *To be happy at home* is the ultimate result of all ambition; the end to which every enterprise and labour tends, and of which every desire prompts the prosecution. It is indeed at home that every man must be known, by those who would make a just estimate either of his virtue or felicity; for smiles and embroidery are alike occasional, and the mind is often

often dreſſed for ſhow in painted honour, and fictitious benevolence.
Rambler, vol. 2, p. 82.

The higheſt panegyric that domeſtic virtue can receive, is the praiſe of ſervants; for however vanity or inſolence may look down with contempt on the ſuffrage of men undignified by wealth, and unenlightened by education, it very ſeldom happens that they commend or blame without juſtice.
Ibid. p. 84.

HABITS.

No man forgets his original trade; the rights of nations and of kings ſink into queſtions of grammar, if grammarians diſcuſs them.
Life of Milton.

The diſproportions of abſurdity grow leſs and leſs viſible, as we are reconciled by degrees to the deformity of a miſtreſs; and falſehood, by long uſe, is aſſimilated to the mind, as poiſon to the body.
Rambler, vol. 2, p. 245.

It is not eaſy, when we converſe much with one whoſe general character excites our veneration, to eſcape all contagion of his peculiarities, even when we do not deliberately think them worthy of our notice, and when they would have excited laughter or diſguſt, had they not been protected by their alliance to nobler qualities, and accidentally conſorted with knowledge or with virtue.
Ibid. vol. 4, p. 26.

It is the peculiar artifice of *habit*, not to suffer her power to be felt at first. Those whom she *leads*, she has the address of only appearing to *attend*.

Vision of Theodore, p. 85.

HOPE.

Our powers owe much of their energy to our hopes; *possunt quia posse videntur*.

Life of Milton.

The understanding of a man, naturally sanguine, may be easily vitiated by the *luxurious indulgence of hope*, however necessary to the production of every thing great or excellent, as some plants are destroyed by too open an exposure to that sun, which gives life and beauty to the vegetable world.

Rambler, vol. 1, p. 10.

Hope is necessary in every condition. The miseries of poverty, of sickness, of captivity, would, without this comfort, be insupportable; nor does it appear that the happiest lot of terrestrial existence, can set us above the want of this general blessing; or that life, when the gifts of nature and fortune are accumulated upon it, would not still be wretched, were it not elevated and delighted by the expectation of some new possession, of some enjoyment yet behind, by which the wish shall be at last satisfied, and the heart filled up to its utmost extent. Yet hope is very fallacious, and promises what it seldom gives; but its promises are more valuable than the gifts of fortune, and it seldom frustrates us without assuring us of recompensing the delay by a great bounty.

Ibid. vol. 2, p. 75.

—Where there is no hope, there can be no endeavour.
Ibid. vol. 3, p. 26.

Hope is the chief blessing of man, and that hope only is rational, of which we are certain that it cannot deceive us.
Ibid. vol. 4, p. 36.

Without hope there can be no caution.
Ibid. vol. 3, p. 81.

It is seldom that we find either men or places such as we expect them. He that has pictured a prospect upon his fancy, will receive little pleasure from his eyes; he that has anticipated the conversation of a wit, will wonder to what prejudice he owes his reputation. Yet it is necessary to *hope*, though hope should always be deluded; for hope itself is happiness, and its frustrations, however frequent, are yet less dreadful than its extinction.
Idler, vol. 2, p. 34.

Whatever enlarges hope, will likewise exalt courage.
Western Islands, p. 383.

HUMANITY.

He does nothing who endeavours to do more than is allowed to humanity.
Prince of Abyssinia, p. 179.

HEALTH.

Such is the power of health, that, without its co-operation, every other comfort is torpid and lifeless as the power of vegetation without the sun.
Rambler, vol. 1, p. 291.

Health is so necessary to all the duties of life, as well as the pleasures of life, that the crime of squandering it is equal to the folly; and he that, for a short gratification, brings weakness and diseases upon himself, and for the pleasure of a few years passed in the tumults of diversion and clamours of merriment, condemns the maturer and more experienced part of his life to the chamber and the couch, may be justly reproached, not only as a spendthrift of his own happiness, but as a robber of the public; as a wretch that has voluntarily disqualified himself for the business of his station, and refused that part which Providence assigns him in the general task of human nature.

Ibid. p. 289.

The valetudinarian race have made the care of health ridiculous, by suffering it to prevail over all other considerations; as the miser has brought frugality into contempt, by permitting the love of money not to share, but to engross his mind.

Ibid.

HISTORY.

He that records transactions in which himself was engaged, has not only an opportunity of knowing innumerable particulars which escape spectators, but has his natural powers exalted by that ardour which always rises at the remembrance of our own importance, and by which every man is enabled to relate his own actions better than another's.

Idler, vol. 2, p. 69.

He that writes the history of his own times, if he adheres strictly to truth, will write that which his own times will not easily endure. He must

be content to repofite his book till all private paffions shall cease, and love and hatred give way to
curiosity.
Ibid. p. 72.

Those familiar histories which draw the portraits of living manners, may perhaps be made of
greater use than the solemnities of professed morality, and convey the knowledge of vice and virtue
with more efficacy than axioms and definitions.
But if the power of example is so great as to take
possession of the memory by a kind of violence,
and produce effects almost without the interven-
tion of the will, care ought to be taken, that when
the choice is unrestrained, the *best examples* only
should be exhibited, and that which is likely to
operate so strongly, should not be mischievous or
uncertain in its effects.
Rambler, vol. 1, p. 21.

It is not a sufficient vindication of a character
in history, that it is drawn as it appears; for many
characters ought never to be drawn: nor of a
narrative, that the train of events is agreeable to
observation and experience; for that observation
which is called *knowledge of the world*, will be found
much more frequently to make men *cunning* than
good.
Ibid. p. 22.

GOOD-HUMOUR.

Good-humour may be defined, a habit of being
pleased; a constant and perennial softness of manner, easiness of approach, and suavity of disposition; like that which every one perceives in himself, when the first transports of new felicity have
subsided,

subsided, and his thoughts are only kept in motion by a slow succession of soft impulses.

Ibid. vol. 2, p. 102.

Good-humour is a state between gaiety and unconcern; the act of a mind at leisure to regard the gratifications of another.

Ibid.

Surely nothing can be more unreasonable than to lose the will to please, when we are conscious of the power, or shew more cruelty than to choose any kind of influence before that of kindness and good-humour. He that regards the welfare of others, should make his virtue approachable, that it may be loved and copied; and he that considers the wants which every man feels, or will feel, of external assistance, must rather wish to be surrounded by those that love him, than by those that admire his excellences or solicit his favours; for admiration ceases with novelty, and interest gains its end and retires. A man whose great qualities want the ornament of superficial attractions, is like a naked mountain with mines of gold, which will be frequented only till the treasure is exhausted.

Ibid. p. 105.

Nothing can more shew the value of *good-humour*, than that it recommends those who are destitute of all other excellences, and procures regard to the trifling, friendship to the worthless, and affection to the dull.

Ibid.

Prince Henry, though well acquainted with the vices and follies of *Falstaff*, and though his conviction compelled him to do justice to superior qualities,

qualities, yet no sooner sees him lying on the ground, but he exclaims, " he could have better spared a better man." His tenderness broke out at the remembrance of the cheerful companion and the loud buffoon, with whom he had passed his time in all the luxury of idleness, who had gladded him with unenvied merriment, and whom he could at once enjoy, and despise.

Ibid.

GOOD-HUMOUR,
(Compared with Gaiety.)

Gaiety is to good-humour as animal perfumes to vegetable fragrance. The one overpowers weak spirits, the other recreates and revives them. Gaiety seldom fails to give some pain; the hearers either strain their faculties to accompany its towerings, or are left behind in envy or despair. Good-humour boasts no faculties, which every one does not believe in his own power, and pleases principally by not offending.

Ibid. p. 102.

HYPOCRISY.

The hypocrite shews the excellency of virtue by the necessity he thinks himself under of *seeming to be virtuous*.

Ibid. vol. 1, p. 125

HONOUR.

Among the *Symerons*, or fugitive Negroes in the South Seas, being a nation that does not set them above continual cares for the immediate necessaries of life, he that can temper iron best, is among them most esteemed: and, perhaps, it would be happy for every nation, if *honours* and *applauses*

applauses were as justly distributed, and he were most distinguished whose abilities were most useful to society. How many chimerical titles to precedence, how many false pretences to respect, would this rule bring to the ground!

Life of Drake, p. 175.

J.

JEALOUSY.

That natural jealousy which makes every man unwilling to allow much excellence in another, always produces a disposition to believe that the mind grows old with the body, and that he whom we are now forced to confess superior, is hastening daily to a level with ourselves. Intellectual decay, doubtless, is not uncommon, but it is not universal. Newton was in his eighty-fifth year improving his chronology, and Waller at eighty-two is thought to have lost none of his poetical powers.

Life of Waller.

Jealousy is a passion compounded of *love* and *suspicion*.

Notes upon Shakespeare, vol. 4, p. 317.

JESTING.

Unless men have the prudence not to appear touched with the sarcasms of a *jester*, they subject themselves to his power, and the wise man will have his folly anatomised by a fool.

Ibid. vol. 3, p. 306.

Jocofe follies and flight offences are only allowed by mankind, in him that overpowers them by great qualities.

Ibid. vol. 4, p. 19.

JOY.

As *briars have sweetness with their prickles*, so are troubles often recompensed with joy.

Ibid. p. 121.

JUDGMENT.

Those who have no power to judge of past times, but by their own, should always doubt their conclusions.

Life of Milton.

As laws operate in civil agency, not to the excitement of virtue, but the repression of wickedness, so judgment, in the operations of intellect, can hinder faults, but not produce excellence.

Life of Prior.

Nothing is more unjust than to judge of a man by too short an acquaintance, and too slight inspection; for it often happens, that in the loose and thoughtless, and dissipated, there is a secret radical worth, which may shoot out by proper cultivation. That the spark of heaven, though dimmed and obstructed, is yet not extinguished, but may, by the breath of counsel and exhortation, be kindled into a flame. To imagine that every one who is not completely good, is irrevocably abandoned, is to suppose that all are capable of the same degree of excellence; it is indeed, to exact from all, that perfection which none ever can attain. And since the purest virtue is consistent with some vice, and the virtue of the greatest number,

number, with almost an equal proportion of contrary qualities, let none too hastily conclude that all goodness is lost, though it may for a time be clouded and overwhelmed; for most minds are the slaves of external circumstances, and conform to any hand that undertakes to mould them, roll down any torrent of custom in which they happen to be caught, or bend to any importunity that bears hard against them.

Rambler, vol. 2, p. 94.

Those that have done nothing in life, are not qualified to judge of those that have done little.

Plan of an English Dictionary, p. 49.

It is impossible for those that have only known affluence and prosperity, to judge rightly of themselves and others. The rich and powerful live in a perpetual masquerade, in which all about them wear borrowed characters; and we only discover in what estimation we are held, when we can no longer give hopes or fears.

Rambler, vol. 2, p. 124.

Judgment is forced upon us by *experience*. He that reads many books, must compare one opinion, or one style, with another; and, when he compares, must necessarily distinguish, reject, and prefer.

Life of Pope.

JUSTICE.

One of the principal parts of national felicity, arises from a wise and impartial administration of justice. Every man reposes upon the tribunals of his country, the stability of profession and the serenity of life. He therefore who unjustly exposes the courts of judicature to suspicion, either of partiality or error, not only does an injury to those who dispense the laws, but diminishes the public confidence in the laws themselves, and shakes the foundation of public tranquillity.

Convicts Address, p. 20.

Of justice, one of the heathen sages have shewn, with great acuteness, that it was impressed upon mankind only by the inconveniencies which *injustice* had produced. " In the first ages, says he, men acted without any rule but the impulse of desire; they practised injustice upon others, and suffered it from others in return; but, in time, it was discovered that the pain of suffering wrong, was greater than the pleasure of doing it, and mankind, by a general compact, submitted to the restraint of laws, and resigned the pleasure to escape the pain."

Idler, vol. 2, p. 208.

What the law does in every nation between individuals, justice ought to do between nations.

Notes upon Shakespeare, vol. 9, p. 58.

INDUSTRY.

Few things are impossible to industry and skill.

Prince of Abyssinia, p. 88.

Many things difficult to design, prove easy to performance.

Ibid. p. 93.

He that shall walk with vigour three hours a day, will pass, in seven years, a space equal to the circumference of the globe.

Ibid.

Whatever bufies the mind without corrupting it, has, at leaft, this ufe, that it refcues the day from idlenefs; and he that is never idle, will not often be vicious.

Rambler, vol. 4, p. 97.

It is below the dignity of a reafonable being, to owe that ftrength to neceffity which ought always to act at the call of choice, or to need any other motive to induftry than the defire of performing his duty.

Ibid. vol. 3. p. 144.

If it be difficult to perfuade the idle to be bufy, it is not eafy to convince the bufy that it is fometimes better to be idle.

Idler, vol. 1, p. 195.

INDISCRETION.

We fometimes fucceed by *indifcretion*, when we fail by *deep laid fchemes*.

Notes upon Shakefpeare, vol. 10, p. 389.

IMITATION.

No man was ever great by imitation.

Prince of Abyffinia, p. 66.

It is juftly confidered as the greateft excellency of art, to imitate nature; but it requires judgment to diftinguifh thofe parts of nature which are moft proper for imitatation.

Rambler, vol. 1, p. 21.

As not every inftance of fimilitude can be confidered as a proof of imitation, fo not every imitation ought to be ftigmatifed as a plagiarifm: the adoption of a noble fentiment, or the infertion

tion of a borrowed ornament, may sometimes display so much judgment, as will almost compensate for invention; and an inferior genius may, without any imputation of servility, pursue the path of the ancients, provided he declines to tread in their footsteps.

Ibid. vol. 3, p. 231.

The reputation which arises from the detail, or transposition of borrowed sentiments, may spread for a while like ivy on the rind of antiquity, but will be torn away by accident, or contempt, and suffered to rot, unheeded, on the ground.

Ibid. p. 292.

When the original is well chosen, and judiciously copied, the imitator often arrives at excellence, which he could never have attained without direction; for few are formed with abilities to discover new possibilities of excellence, and to distinguish themselves by means never tried before.

Ibid. vol. 4, p. 25.

The Macedonian conqueror, when he was once invited to hear a man that sung like a nightingale, replied, with contempt, "That he had heard the nightingale herself:" and the same treatment must every man expect, whose praise is, that he imitates another.

Ibid. vol. 2, p. 182.

Almost all the absurdity of conduct arises from the imitation of those whom we cannot resemble.

Ibid. vol. 3, p. 176.

We are easily flattered by an imitator, when we do not fear ever to be rivalled.

Ibid. p. 249.

Imitations

Imitations produce pain or pleasure, not because they are mistaken for realities, but because they bring realities to the mind. When the imagination is recreated by a landscape, the trees are not supposed capable to give us shade; but we consider how we should be pleased with such fountains playing beside us, and such woods waving over us.

Preface to Shakespeare, p. 114.

INDOLENCE.

It is in vain to put wealth within the reach of him who will not stretch out his hand to take it.

Life of King.

Indolence is one of those vices from which those whom it once infects are seldom reformed.

Rambler, vol. 3, p. 298.

Every other species of luxury operates upon some appetite that is quickly satiated, and requires some concurrence of art, or accident, which every place will not supply; but the *desire of ease* acts equally at all hours, and the longer it is indulged, is the more increased.

Ibid.

He that is himself weary, will soon weary the public. Let him, therefore, lay down his employment, whatever it be, who can no longer exert his former activity, or attention. Let him not endeavour to struggle with censure, or obstinately infest the stage, till a general hiss commands him to depart.

Ibid. vol. 4, p. 258.

IDLENESS.

As pride is sometimes hid under humility, idleness is often covered by turbulence and hurry.

He that neglects his known duty, and real employment, naturally endeavours to croud his mind with something that may bar out the remembrance of his own folly, and does any thing but what he ought to do, with eager diligence, that he may keep himself in his own favour.

Idler, vol. 1, p. 172.

Perhaps every man may date the predominance of those desires that disturb his life, and contaminate his conscience, from some unhappy hour when too much leisure exposed him to their incursions; for he has lived with little observation, either on himself, or others, who does not know that to be idle is to be vicious.

Rambler, vol. 2, p. 181.

There are said to be pleasures in madness, known only to madmen. There are certainly miseries in idleness, which the idler can only conceive.

Idler, vol. 1, p. 15.

Of all the enemies of idleness, want is the most formidable. Fame is soon found to be a sound, and love a dream. Avarice and ambition may be justly suspected of being privy confedrates with idleness; for when they have, for a while, protected their votaries, they often deliver them up, to end their lives under her dominion. Want always struggles against idleness; but want herself is often overcome, and every hour, shews the careful observer those who had rather live in ease than in plenty.

Ibid. p. 51.

No man is so much open to conviction as the *idler*; but there is none on whom it operates so little.

Ibid. p. 175.

The drunkard, for a time, laughs over his wine; the ambitious man triumphs in the miscarriage of his rival; but the *captives of indolence* have neither *superiority* nor *merriment*.

Vision of Theodore, p. 94.

It is not only in the slumber of sloth, but in the dissipation of ill-directed industry, that the shortness of life is generally forgotten. As some men lose their hours in laziness, because they suppose that there is time for the reparation of neglect, others busy themselves in providing that no length of life may want employment; and it often happens, that sluggishness and activity are equally surprised by the last summons, and perish not more differently from each other, than the fowl that received the shot in her flight, from her that is killed upon the bush.

Rambler, vol. 2, p. 99.

Idleness can never secure tranquillity; the call of reason and of conscience will pierce the closest pavilion of the sluggard, and, though it may not have force to drive him from his down, will be loud enough to hinder him from sleep. Those moments which he cannot resolve to make useful, by devoting them to the great business of his being, will still be usurped by powers that will not leave them to his disposal; remorse and vexation will seize upon them, and forbid him to enjoy what he is so desirous to appropriate.

Ibid. vol. 3, p. 172.

Those who attempt nothing themselves, think every thing easily performed, and consider the unsuccessful always as criminal.

Idler, vol. 1, p. 5.

The diligence of an idler is sometimes rapid and impetuous; as ponderous bodies, forced into velocity, move with violence proportionate to their weight.

Ibid.

There are some that profess idleness in its full dignity; who call themselves the *idle*, as Busiris, in the play, calls himself *the proud*; who boast that they do nothing, and thank their stars that they have nothing to do; who sleep every night till they can sleep no longer, and rise only that exercise may enable them to sleep again; who prolong the reign of darkness by double curtains, and never see the sun, but to tell him *how they hate his beams*; whose whole labour is to vary the postures of indulgence; and whose day differs from their night, but as a couch, or chair, differs from a bed.

Ibid. p. 171.

Idleness predominates in many lives where it is not suspected; for, being a vice which terminates in itself, it may be enjoyed without injury to others, and is therefore not watched like fraud, which endangers property, or like pride, which naturally seeks its gratifications in another's inferiority. Idleness is a silent and peaceful quality, that neither raises envy by ostentation, nor hatred by opposition; and therefore nobody is busy to censure or detect it.

Ibid. p. 172.

INTEGRITY.

Integrity without knowledge is weak, and generally useless; and knowledge without integrity is dangerous and dreadful.

Prince of Abyssinia, p. 249.

IGNORANCE.

IGNORANCE.

The man who feels himself ignorant, should, at least, be modest.
Preliminary Discourse to the London Chronicle, p. 156.

Ignorance cannot always be inferred from inaccuracy, knowledge is not always present.
Notes upon Shakespeare, vol. 6, p. 101.

Grofs ignorance every man has found equally dangerous with perverted knowledge. Men left wholly to their appetites and their instincts, with little sense of moral or religious obligation, and with very faint distinctions of right and wrong, can never be safely employed, or confidently trusted. They can be honest only by obstinacy, and diligent only by compulsion or caprice. Some instruction, therefore, is necessary; and much, perhaps, may be dangerous.
Review of the Origin of Evil, p. 11.

Ignorance is most easily kept in subjection by enlightening the mind with truth, fraud and usurpation would be made less practicable, and less secure.
Introduction to the World displayed, p. 180.

IGNORANCE,

(Compared with Knowledge.)

The expectation of ignorance is indefinite, and that of knowledge often tyrannical. It is hard to satisfy those who know not what to demand, or those who demand by design, what they think impossible to be done.
Preface to Shakespeare, p. 68.

IGNORANCE,
(Compared with Confidence.)

In things difficult there is danger from ignorance; in things easy, from confidence.

Preface to Dictionary, fol. p. 9.

IMPRUDENCE.

Those who, in consequence of superior capacities and attainments, disregard the common maxims of life, ought to be reminded, that nothing will supply the want of prudence; and that negligence and irregularity, long continued, will make knowledge useless, wit ridiculous, and genius contemptible.

Life of Savage.

IMPRISONMENT.

Few are mended by imprisonment; and he whose crimes have made confinement necessary, seldom makes any other use of his enlargement, than to do with greater cunning, what he did before with less.

False Alarm, p. 8.

The end of all civil regulations is to secure private happiness from private malignity, to keep individuals from the power of one another. But this end is apparently neglected by *imprisonment for debt*, when a man, irritated with loss, is allowed to be a judge of his own cause, and to assign the punishment of his own pain; when the distinction between guilt and unhappiness, between casualty and design, is entrusted to eyes blind with interest, to understandings depraved by resentment.

Idler, vol. 2, p. 122.

In a prison the awe of the public eye is lost, and the power of the law is spent. There are few fears,

fears, there are no blushes. The lewd inflame the lewd; the audacious harden the audacious. Every one fortifies himself as he can against his own sensibility, and endeavours to practise on others, the arts which are practised on himself, and gains the kindness of his associates by similitude of manners.

Ibid. p. 216.

It is not so dreadful in a high spirit to be imprisoned, as it is desirable in a state of disgrace to be sheltered from the scorn of the gazers.

Notes upon Shakespeare, vol. 6, p. 343.

The confinement of any debtor in the sloth and darkness of a prison, is a loss to the nation, and no gain to the creditor, for, of the multitude who are pining in those cells of misery, a very small part is suspected of any fraudulent act by which they retain what belongs to others. The rest are imprisoned by the wantonness of pride, the malignity of revenge, or the acrimony of disappointed expectation.

Idler, vol. 1, p. 121.

Since poverty is punished among us as a crime, it ought at least to be treated with the same lenity as other crimes: the offender ought not to languish at the will of him whom he has offended, but to be allowed some appeal to the justice of his country. There can be no reason why any debtor should be imprisoned, but that he may be compelled to payment; and a term should therefore be fixed, in which the creditor should exhibit his accusation of concealed property. If such property can be discovered, let it be given to the creditor; if the charge is not offered, or cannot be proved, let the prisoner be dismissed.

Ibid. p. 123.

Those

Those who made the laws of imprisonment for debt, have apparently supposed, that every deficiency of payment is the crime of the debtor. But the truth is, that the creditor always shares the act, and often more than shares the guilt, of improper trust. It seldom happens that any man imprisons another but for debts which he suffered to be contracted in hope of advantage to himself, and for bargains in which he proportioned his profit to his own opinion of the hazard; and there is no reason why one should punish the other for a contract in which both concurred.

Ibid. p. 124.

We see nation trade with nation, where no payment can be compelled: mutual convenience produces mutual confidence; and the merchants continue to satisfy the demands of each other, though they have nothing to dread but the loss of trade.

Ibid. p. 125.

It is in vain, then, to continue an institution, which experience shews to be ineffectual. We have now imprisoned one generation of debtors after another, but we do not find that their numbers lessen. We have now learned that rashness and imprudence will not be deterred from taking credit; let us try whether fraud and avarice may be more easily restrained from giving it.

Ibid.

He whose debtor has perished in prison, though he may acquit himself of deliberate murder, must, at least, have his mind clouded with discontent when he considers how much another has suffered from him; when he thinks of the wife bewailing
her

her husband, or the children begging the bread which their father would have earned.

Ibid. p. 217.

IMPOSITION.

There are those who having got the *cant of the day*, with *a superficial readiness of flight and cursory conversation*, who very often impose themselves as men of understanding, upon wise men.

Notes upon Shakespeare, vol. 10, p. 401.

IMAGINATION.

It is the great failing of a strong imagination to catch greedily at wonders.

Memoirs of the K. of Prussia, p. 118.

A man who once resolves upon ideal discoveries, seldom searches long in vain.

Life of Sir T. Browne, p. 266.

It is a disposition to feel the force of words, and to combine the ideas annexed to them with quickness, that shews one man's imagination to be better than another's, and distinguishes a fine taste from dulness and stupidity.

Review of the Sublime and Beautiful, p. 57.

Imagination is useless without knowledge. Nature gives in vain the power of combination, unless study and observation supply materials to be combined.

Life of Butler.

It is ridiculous to oppose judgment to imagination; for it does not appear, that men have necessarily less of one, as they have more of the other.

Life of Roscommon.

There are some men of such rapid imagination, that, like the Peruvian torrent, when it brings down gold, mingles it with sand.

Plan of an English Dictionary, p. 53.

INTELLIGENCE.

Without intelligence man is not social, he is only gregarious; and little intelligence will there be, where all are constrained to daily labour, and every mind must wait upon the hand.

Western Islands, p. 317.

FOREIGN AND DOMESTIC INTELLIGENCE.

Of remote transactions, the first accounts are always confused, and commonly exaggerated; and in domestic affairs, if the power to conceal is less, the interest to misrepresent is often greater; and what is sufficiently vexatious, truth seems to fly from curiosity; and as many enquiries produce many narratives, whatever engages the public attention, is immediately disguised by the embellishments of fiction.

Preliminary Discourse to the London Chronicle, p. 154.

IRRESOLUTION.

He that knows not whither to go, is in no haste to move.

Life of Swift.

SELF-IMPORTANCE.

Every man is of importance to himself, and therefore, in his own opinion, to others; and supposing the world already acquainted with all his pleasures and his pains, is, perhaps, the first to publish injuries or misfortunes which had never been known unless related by himself, and at which

those

those that hear him will only laugh; for no man sympathises with the sorrows of vanity.

Life of Pope.

The man who threatens the world is always ridiculous; for the world can easily go on without him, and, in a short time, will cease to miss him.

Ibid.

No cause more frequently produces bashfulness than too high an opinion of our *own importance*. He that imagines an assembly filled with his merit, panting with expectation, and hushed with attention, easily terrifies himself with the dread of disappointing them, and strains his imagination in pursuit of something that may vindicate the veracity of fame, and shew that his reputation was not gained by chance.

Rambler, vol. 3, p. 319.

INSULT.

There are innumerable modes of insult, and tokens of contempt, for which it is not easy to find a name, which vanish to nothing in an attempt to describe them, and yet may, by continual repetition, make day pass after day in sorrow and in terror.

Ibid. p. 262.

Whatever be the motive of insult, it is always best to overlook it; for folly scarcely can deserve resentment, and malice is punished by neglect.

Ibid. vol. 4, p. 221.

INCREDULITY.

To refuse credit, confers, for a moment, an appearance of superiority, which every little mind is tempted

tempted to assume, when it may be gained so cheaply, as by withdrawing attention from evidence, and declining the fatigue of comparing probabilities.

Idler, vol. 2, p. 195.

The most pertinacious and vehement demonstrator may be wearied, in time, by continual negation and incredulity, which an old poet, in his address to Raleigh, calls " the wit of fools," obtunds the arguments which it cannot answer, as woolsacks deaden arrows, though they cannot repel them.

Ibid. p. 196.

INDULGENCE.

The man who commits common faults, should not be precluded from common indulgence.

Preliminary Discourse to the London Chronicle, p. 155.

INCLINATION.

It may reasonably be asserted, that he who finds himself strongly attracted to any particular study, though it may happen to be out of his proposed scheme, if it is not trifling or vicious, had better continue his application to it, since it is likely that he will, with much more ease and expedition, attain that which a warm inclination stimulates him to pursue, than that at which a prescribed law compels him to toil.

Idler, vol. 2, p. 85.

RURAL IMPROVEMENTS.

Whether to plant a walk in undulating curves, and to place a bench at every turn where there is an object to catch the view; to make water run

where it will be heard, and to stagnate where it will be seen; to leave intervals where the eye will be pleased, and to thicken the plantation where there is something to be hidden, demands any great powers of mind, we will not enquire. Perhaps a surly and sullen speculator may think such performances rather the sport, than the business of human reason. But it must be at least confessed, that to embellish the form of nature is an innocent amusement, and some praise must be allowed, by the most supercilious observer, to him who does best, what such multitudes are contending to do well.
Life of Shenstone.

INNOCENCE.

There are some reasoners who frequently confound *innocence* with the *mere incapacity of guilt*; but he that never saw, or heard, or thought of strong liquors, cannot be proposed as a pattern of sobriety.
Life of Drake, p. 224.

INCONSTANCY.

Inconstancy is *in* every case a mark of weakness.
Plan of an English Dictionary, p. 37.

INTEREST.

Most men are animated with greater ardour by *interest* than by *fidelity*.
Life of Drake, p. 186.

INTEREST AND PRIDE.

Interest and *pride* harden the heart; and it is vain to dispute against *avarice* and power.
Introduction to the World Displayed, p. 177.

KNOWLEDGE.

K.

KNOWLEDGE.

Man is not weak; knowledge is more than equivalent to force.
Prince of Abyssinia, p. 90.

As knowledge advances, pleasure passes from the eye to the ear; but returns, as it declines, from the ear to the eye.
Preface to Shakespeare, p. 34.

Other things may be seized by might or purchased with money; but knowledge is to be gained only by study, and study to be prosecuted only in retirement.
Rambler, vol. 1, p. 37.

No degree of knowledge, attainable by man, is able to set him above the want of hourly assistance, or to extinguish the desire of fond endearments and tender officiousness; and therefore no one should think it unnecessary to learn those arts by which friendship may be gained. Kindness is preserved by a constant reciprocation of benefits or interchange of pleasures; but such benefits only can be bestowed as others are capable to receive, and such pleasures only imparted as others are qualified to enjoy. By this descent from the pinnacles of art, no honour will be lost; for the condescensions of learning are always overpaid by gratitude. An elevated genius employed in little things, appears, to use the simile of Longinus, "like the sun in its evening declination; he remits his splendor, but retains his magnitude; and pleases more though he dazzles less."
Ibid. vol. 5, p. 190.

Kings, without sometimes passing their time without pomp, and without acquaintance with the various forms of life, and with the genuine passions, interests, desires, and distresses, of mankind, see the world in a mist, and bound their views to a narrow compass. It was, perhaps, to the private condition in which Cromwell first entered the world, that he owed the superiority of understanding, he had over most of our kings. In that state, he learned the art of secret transaction, and the knowledge by which he was able to oppose zeal to zeal, and make one enthusiast destroy another.

Ibid. p. 100.

It is a position long received amongst politicians, that the loss of a king's power is soon followed by the loss of life.

Notes upon Shakespeare, vol. 6, p. 440.

The riches of a king ought not be seen in his own coffers, but in the opulence of his subjects.

Memoirs of the King of Prussia, p. 97.

To enlarge dominions, has been the boast of many princes; to diffuse happiness and security through wide regions has been granted to few.

Ibid. p. 111.

Monarchs are always surrounded with refined spirits, so penetrating, that they frequently discover in their masters great qualities, invisible to vulgar eyes, and which, did not they publish them to mankind, would be unobserved for ever.

Marmor Norfolciense, p. 17.

LIFE.

L.

LIFE.

Life is not to be counted by the ignorance of infancy or the imbecility of age. We are long before we are able to think, and we soon cease from the power of acting.
Prince of Abyssinia, p. 26.

Human life is every where a state in which much is to be endured and little to be enjoyed.
Ibid. p. 78.

Life may be lengthened by care, though death cannot ultimately be defeated.
Preface to Dict. fol. p. 10.

The great art of life is to play for much and stake little.
Dissertation on Authors, p. 29.

It has always been lamented, that of the little time allotted to man, much must be spent upon superfluities. Every prospect has its obstructions, which we must break to enlarge our view. Every step of our progress finds impediments, which, however eager to go forward, we must stop to remove.
Preliminary Discourse to the London Chronicle, p. 153.

An even and unvaried tenor of life always hides from our apprehension the approach of its end. Succession is not perceived but by variation. He that lives to-day as he lived yesterday, and expects that as the present day, such will be to-morrow, easily conceives time as running in a circle, and returning to itself. The uncertainty of our situation is impressed commonly by dissimilitude of condition, and it is only by finding life changeable, that we are reminded of its shortness.

Idler, vol. 2, p. 282.

He that embarks in the voyage of life, will always wish to advance rather by the impulse of the wind, than the strokes of the oar; and many founder in their passage while they lie waiting for the gale.

Ibid. vol. 1, p. 7.

A minute analysis of life at once destroys that splendour which dazzles the imagination. Whatsoever grandeur can display or luxury enjoy, is procured by offices of which the mind shrinks from the contemplation. All the delicacies of the table may be traced back to the shambles and the dunghill; all magnificence of building was hewn from the quarry, and all the pomp of ornament dug from among the damps and darkness of the mine.

Notes upon Shakespeare, vol. 2, p. 73.

In the different degrees of life, there will be often found much *meanness* among the great, and much *greatness* among the mean.

Ibid. vol. 3, p. 181.

Every man has seen the *mean* too often proud of the *humility* of the great, and perhaps the great may sometimes be *humbled in the praises* of the mean; particularly of those who commend them without conviction or discernment.

Ibid. vol. 4, p. 21.

When

When we see, by so many examples, how few are the necessaries of life, we should learn what madness there is in so much superfluity.

Ibid. vol. 8, p. 345.

The main of life is composed of small incidents and petty occurrences, of wishes for objects not remote, and grief for disappointments of no fatal consequence; of insect vexations, which sting us and fly away; and impertinences which buz a while about us, and are heard no more. Thus a few pains and a few pleasures, are all the materials of human life; and of these the proportions are partly allotted by Providence, and partly left to the arrangement of reason and choice.

Rambler, vol. 2, p. 82.

Such is the state of every age, every sex, and every condition in life, that all have their cares either from *nature* or from *folly*; whoever, therefore, that finds himself inclined to envy another, should remember that he knows not the real condition which he desires to obtain, but is certain, that by indulging a vicious passion, he must lessen that happiness which he thinks already too sparingly bestowed.

Ibid. vol. 3, p. 140.

No man past the middle point of life, can sit down to feast upon the pleasures of youth, without finding the banquet embittered by the cup of sorrow.

A few years make such havoc in human generations, that we soon see ourselves deprived of those with whom we entered the world, and whom the participation of pleasures or fatigues had endeared to our remembrance. The man of enterprise recounts his adventures and expedients, but is forced, at the clofe of the relation, to pay a figh to the names of thofe that contributed to his fuccefs. He that paffes his life among the gayer part of mankind, has his remembrance ftored with remarks and repartees of wits, whofe fprightlinefs and merriment are now loft in perpetual filence. The trader, whofe induftry has fupplied the want of inheritance, repines in folitary plenty at the abfence of companions, with whom he had planned out amufements for his latter years; and the fcholar, whofe merit, after a long feries of efforts, raifes him from obfcurity, looks round in vain from his exaltation for his old friends or enemies, whofe applaufe or mortification would heighten his triumph.

Ibid. vol. 4, p. 234.

Life, however fhort, is made ftill fhorter by wafte of time; and its progrefs towards happinefs, though naturally flow, is yet retarded by unneceffary labour.

Idler, vol. 2, p. 217.

Life confifts not of a feries of illuftrious actions or elegant enjoyments; the greater part of our time paffes in compliance with neceffities, in the performance of daily duties, in the removal of fmall inconveniencies, in the procurement of petty pleafures; and we are well or ill at eafe as the main ftream of life glides on fmoothly or is ruffled by fmall obftacles and frequent interruption. In fhort, the true ftate of every nation is the ftate of common life.

Weftern Iflands. p. 44.

If to have all that riches can purchase is to be rich, if to do all that can be done in a long time is to live long, he is equally a benefactor to mankind, who teaches them to protract the duration, or shorten the business of life.

Life of Barretier, p. 141.

LEARNING.

It is not by comparing *line* with *line* that the merit of great works is to be estimated; but by their general effects and ultimate result.

Life of Dryden.

When learning was first rising on the world, in the fifteenth century, ages so long accustomed to darkness, were too much dazzled with its light to see any thing distinctly. The first race of scholars, hence, for the most part, were learning to speak rather than to think, and were therefore more studious of elegance than truth. The contemporaries of Boethius thought it sufficient to know what the ancients had delivered; the examination of tenets and facts was reserved for another generation.

Western Islands, p. 28.

In nations where there is hardly the use of letters, what is once out of sight, is lost for ever. They think but little, and of their few thoughts none are wasted on the part in which they are neither interested by fear nor hope. Their only registers are stated observances and practical representations; for this reason an age of ignorance is an age of ceremony. Pageants and processions, and commemorations, gradually shrink away as better methods come into use, of recording events and preserving rights.

Ibid. p. 145.

False hopes and false terrors are equally to be avoided. Every man who proposes to grow eminent by learning, should carry in his mind at once the difficulty of excellence, and the force of industry; and remember that fame is not conferred but as the recompense of labour; and that labour, vigorously continued, has not often failed of its reward.

Rambler, vol. 1, p. 155.

Literature is a kind of intellectual light, which, like the light of the sun, may sometimes enable us to see what we do not like; but who would wish to escape unpleasing objects, by condemning himself to perpetual darkness?

Dissertation on Authors, p. 22.

It is the great excellence of learning, that it borrows very little from time or place. It is not confined to season or to climate; to cities or the country; but may be cultivated and enjoyed where no other pleasure can be obtained.

Idler, vol. 2, p. 234.

In respect to the loss and gain of literature, if letters were considered only as a means of pleasure, it might well be doubted in what degree of estimation they should be held; but when they are referred to necessity, the controversy is at an end. It soon appears, that though they may sometimes incommode us, yet human life would scarcely rise, without them, above the common existence of animal nature. We might, indeed, breathe and eat,

eat, in univerſal ignorance, but muſt want all that gives pleaſure or ſecurity, all the embelliſhments and delights, and moſt of the conveniencies and comforts of our preſent condition.

Diſſertation on **Authors**, p. 21.

LOVE.

It is not hard to love thoſe from whom nothing can be feared.

Life of **Addiſon**.

In love it has been held a maxim, that ſucceſs is moſt eaſily obtained by indirect, and unperceived approaches; he who too ſoon profeſſes himſelf a lover, raiſes obſtacles to his own wiſhes; and thoſe whom diſappointments have taught experience, endeavour to conceal their paſſion, till they believe their miſtreſs wiſhes for the diſcovery.

Rambler, vol. 1, p. 3.

Love being always ſubject to the operations of time, ſuffers change and diminution.

Notes upon **Shakeſpeare**, vol. 10, p. 366.

SELF-LOVE.

Partiality to ourſelves is ſeen in a variety of inſtances. The liberty of the preſs is a bleſſing, when we are inclined to write againſt others; and a calamity, when we find ourſelves overborne by the multitude of our aſſailants; as the power of the crown is always thought too great by thoſe who ſuffer through its influence, and too little by thoſe in whoſe favour it is exerted. A ſtanding army is generally accounted neceſſary, by thoſe who command, and dangerous and oppreſſive by thoſe who ſupport it.

Life of **Savage**.

To charge those favourable representations which every man gives of himself, with the guilt of hypocritical falsehood, would shew more severity than knowledge. The writer commonly believes himself. Almost every man's thoughts, whilst they are general, are right; and most hearts are pure, whilst temptation is away. It is easy to awaken generous sentiments in privacy; to despise death where there is no danger; to glow with benevolence where there is nothing to be given. Whilst such ideas are formed, they are felt, and self-love does not suspect the gleam of virtue to be the meteor of fancy.

Life of Pope.

LANGUAGE.

When the matter is low and scanty, a dead language, in which nothing is mean, because nothing is familiar, affords great convenience.

Life of Addison.

Language is only the instrument of science, and words are but the signs of ideas.

Preface to Dictionary, fol. p. 2.

However academies have been instituted to guard the avenues of their languages; to retain fugitives and repulse intruders; their vigilance and activity have hitherto been vain. Sounds are too volatile and subtle for legal restraints; to enchain syllables and lash the wind are equally the undertakings of pride, unwilling to measure its desires by its strength. Among a people polished by art, and classed by subordination, those who have much leisure to think, will always be enlarging the stock of ideas; and every increase of knowledge, whether real, or fancied, will produce new words, or combinations

combinations of words. When the mind is unchained from neceffity, it will range after convenience; when it is left at large in the fields of fpeculation, it will fhift opinions. As any cuftom is difufed, the words that expreffed it muft perifh with it; as any opinion grows popular, it will innovate fpeech in the fame proportion as it alters practice.

Ibid. p. 9.

It is incident to words, as to their authors, to degenerate from their anceftors, and to change their manners when they change their country.

Ibid. p. 3.

No nation can trace their language beyond the fecond period; and even of that it does not often happen that many monuments remain.

Idler, vol. 2, p. 62.

Commerce, however neceffary, however lucrative, as it depraves the manners, corrupts the language. They that have frequent intercourfe with ftrangers, to whom they endeavour to accommodate themfelves, muft in time learn a mingled dialect, like the jargon which ferves the traffickers on the Mediterranean and Indian coafts. This will not always be confined to the exchange, the warehoufe, or the port, but will be communicated by degrees to other ranks of the people, and be at laft incorporated with the current fpeech.

Preface to Johnfon's Dictionary, p. 81.

Every language has its anomalies, which, though inconvenient, and in themfelves once unneceffary, muft be tolerated among the imperfections of human things, and which require only to be regiftered,

tered, that they may not be increased, and ascertained, that they may not be confounded.

Ibid. p. 56.

Language is the dress of thought; and as the noblest mien, or most graceful action, would be degraded and obscured by a garb appropriated to the gross employments of rustics or mechanics, so the most heroic sentiments will lose their efficacy, and the most splendid ideas drop their magnificence, if they are conveyed by words used commonly upon low and trivial occasions, debased by vulgar mouths, and contaminated by inelegant applications.

Life of Cowley.

When languages are formed upon different principles, it is impossible that the same modes of expression should always be elegant in both.

Life of Dryden.

Language proceeds, like every thing else, thro' improvement to degeneracy.

Idler, vol. 2, p. 60.

Every man is more speedily instructed by his own language than by any other.

Ibid. p. 218.

Orthography is vitiated among such as learn first to speak, and then to write, by imperfect notions of the relations between letters and vocal utterance.

Western Islands, p. 382.

ENGLISH LANGUAGE.

There is not, perhaps, one of the liberal arts which may not be completely learned in the English language.

Idler, vol. 2, p. 219.

In our language *two negatives* did not originally *affirm*, but *strengthen the negation*.—This mode of speech was in time changed, but as the change was made in oppofition to long cuftoms, it proceeded gradually, and uniformity was not obtained but through an intermediate confufion.

Notes upon Shakefpeare, vol. 4, p. 346.

To our language may be, with great juftnefs, applied the obfervation of Quintilian, " that fpeech was not formed by an analogy fent from heaven." It did not defcend to us in a ftate of uniformity and perfection, but was produced by neceffity, and enlarged by accident, and is therefore compofed of diffimilar parts, thrown together by negligence, by affectation, by learning, or by ignorance.

Plan of an Englifh Dictionary, p. 41.

Such was the power of our language in the time of Queen Elizabeth, that a fpeech might be formed adequate to all the purpofes of life. If the language of theology were extracted from *Hooker*, and the tranflation of the Bible; the terms of natural knowledge from *Bacon*; the phrafes of policy, war, and navigation, from *Raleigh*; the dialect of poetry and fiction from *Spenfer* and *Sidney*; and the diction of common life from *Sdakefpeare*, few ideas would be loft to mankind for want of *Englifh words* in which they might be expreffed.

Preface to Johnfon's Dictionary, p. 74.

The affluence and comprehenfion of our language is very illuftrioufly difplayed in our poetical *tranflations of ancient writers*; a work which the French feem to relinquifh in defpair, and which we were long unable to perform with dexterity.

Life of Dryden.

From

From the time of *Gower* and *Chaucer*, the English writers have studied elegance, and advanced their language, by successive improvements, to as much harmony as it can easily receive, and as much copiousness as human knowledge has hitherto required, till every man now endeavours to excel others in accuracy, or outshine them in splendour of style; and the danger is, lest *care* should too soon pass to *affectation*.

Idler, vol. 2, p. 63.

LAWS.

It is, perhaps, impossible to review the laws of any country, without discovering many defects, and many superfluities. Laws often continue when their reasons have ceased. Laws made for the first state of the society, continue unabolished when the general form of life is changed. Parts of the judicial procedure, which were at first only accidental, become, in time, essential; and formalities are accumulated on each other, till the art of litigation requires more study than the discovery of right.

Memoirs of the King of Prussia, p. 112.

To embarrass justice by multiplicity of laws, or to hazard it by confidence in judges, seems to be the opposite rocks on which all civil institutions have been wrecked, and between which, legislative wisdom has never yet found an open passage.

Ibid.

It is observed, that a corrupt society has many laws.

Idler, vol. 2, p. 186.

Laws are often occasional, often capricious, made always by a few, and sometimes by a single voice.

Ibid. vol. 1, p. 60.

The firſt laws have no laws to enforce them—The firſt authority is conſtituted by itſelf.

Falſe Alarm, p. 12.

Laws that exact obedience, and yield no protection, contravene the firſt principles of the compact of authority.

Weſtern Iſlands, p. 209.

A man accuſtomed to ſatisfy himſelf with the obvious and natural meaning of a ſentence, does not eaſily ſhake off his habit; but a true-bred lawyer never contents himſelf with one ſenſe, when there is another to be found.

Marmor Norfolcienſe, p. 48.

PENAL LAWS.

Death is, as one of the antients obſerves, " of dreadful things the moſt dreadful." An evil beyond which nothing can be threatened by ſublunary power, or feared from human enmity or vengeance. This terror therefore ſhould be reſerved as the *laſt reſort of authority*, as the ſtrongeſt and moſt operative of prohibitory ſanctions, and placed before the treaſure of life to guard from invaſion what cannot be reſtored. To equal robbery with murder, is to reduce murder to robbery, to confound in common minds the gradations of iniquity, and incite the commiſſion of a greater crime, to prevent the detection of a leſs. If only murder was puniſhed with death, very few robbers would ſtain their hands in blood; but when, by the last act of cruelty, no new danger is incurred, and greater security may be obtained, upon what principle shall we forbid them forbear.

Rambler, vol. 3, p. 51.

If those whom the wisdom of our laws has condemned to die, had been detected in their rudiments of robbery, they might by proper discipline and useful labour, have been disentangled from their habits; they might have escaped all the temptations to subsequent crimes, and passed their days in reparation and penitence.

Ibid p. 53.

LIBERTY.

A zeal, which is often thought and called liberty, sometimes disguises from the world, and not rarely from the mind which it possesses, an envious desire of plundering wealth or degrading greatness; and of which the immediate tendency is innovation and anarchy, or imperious eagerness to subvert and confound, with very little care what shall be established.

Life of Akenside.

It has been observed that they who most loudly clamour for *liberty*, do not most liberally grant it.

Life of Milton.

LOYALTY.

As a man inebriated only by vapours, soon recovers in the open air, a nation discontented to madness, without any adequate cause, will return to its wits and allegiance, when a little pause has cooled it to reflection.

False Alarm, p. 53.

LETTER-WRITING.

Letters on public busines should be written with a mind more intent on *things* than *words*, and above the affectation of unseasonable elegance. The business of a statesman can be little forwarded by flowers of rhetoric.

Life of Cowley.

As letters are written on all subjects, in all states of mind, they cannot be properly reduced to settled rules, or described by any single characteristic; and we may freely disentangle our minds from critical embarrassments, by determining that a letter has no peculiarity but its form; and that nothing is to be refused admission, which would be proper in any other method of treating the same subject.

Rambler, vol. 3, p. 278.

LONDON.

London is a place too wide for the operation of petty competition, and private malignity; where merit might soon become conspicuous, and find friends as soon as it becomes reputable to befriend it.

Life of Thompson.

MARRIAGE.

M.

MARRIAGE.

Marriage has many pains, but celibacy has no pleasures.
Prince of Abyssinia; p. 158.

The infelicities of marriage are not to be urged against its inftitutution, as the miseries of life prove equally, that life cannot be the gift of heaven.
Ibid. p. 169.

Marriage is not commonly unhappy, but as life is unhappy, and moft of thofe who complain of connubial miferies, have as much fatisfaction as their natures would have admitted, or their conduct procured in any other condition.
Rambler, vol. 1, p. 272.

When we fee the avaricious and crafty taking companions to their tables and their beds, without any inquiry but after farms and money; or the giddy and thoughtlefs uniting themfelves for life to thofe whom they have only feen by the light of tapers; when parents make articles for children without enquiring after their confent; when fome marry for heirs to difappoint their brothers; and others throw themfelves into the arms of thofe whom they do not love, becaufe they have found themfelves rejected were they were more folicitous to pleafe; when fome marry becaufe their fervants cheat them; fome becaufe they fquander their own money; fome becaufe their houfes are peftered with company; fome becaufe they will live like other people; and fome becaufe they are fick of themfelves; we are not fo much inclined

clined to wonder that marriage is sometimes unhaypy, as that it appears so little loaded with calamity; and cannot but conclude, that society has something in itself eminently agreeable to human nature, when we find its pleasures so great, that even the ill-choice of a companion can hardly over-balance them. Those, therefore, of the above description, that should rail against matrimony, should be informed, that they are neither to wonder, or repine, that a contract begun on such principles, has ended in disappointment.

Ibid. p. 274 & 276.

Men generally pass the first weeks of matrimony, like those who consider themselves as taking the last draught of pleasure, and resolve not to quit the bowl without a surfeit.

Ibid. vol. 4, p. 41.

Marriage should be considered as the most solemn league of perpetual friendship; a state from which artifice and concealment are to be banished for ever; and in which every act of dissimulation is a breach of faith.

Ibid. p. 43.

A poet may praise many whom he would be afraid to marry, and, perhaps, marry one whom he would have been ashamed to praise. Many qualities contribute to domestic happiness, upon which poetry has no colours to bestow, and many airs and sallies may delight imagination, which he who flatters them, never can approve. There are charms made only for distant admiration—no spectacle is nobler than a blaze.

Life of Waller.

It is not likely that the married state is eminently miserable; since we see such numbers, whom the death of their partners has set free from it, enter it again.

Rambler, vol. 1, p. 273.

The happiness of some marriages are celebrated by their neighbours, because the married couple happen to grow rich by parsimony, to keep quiet by insensibility, and agree to eat and sleep together.

Ibid. vol. 4, p. 42.

A certain dissimilitude of habitudes and sentiments, as leaves each some peculiar advantages, and affords that *concordia discors*, that suitable disagreement, is always necessary to happy marriages. Such reasonings, though often formed upon different views, terminate generally in the same conclusion. Such thoughts, like rivulets issuing from distant springs, are each impregnated in its course with various mixtures, and tinged by infusions unknown to the other, yet at last easily unite into one stream, and purify themselves by the gentle effervescence of contrary qualities.

Ibid. p. 43.

To die with husbands, or to live without them, are the two extremes which the *prudence* and *moderation* of *European ladies* have in all ages equally declined.

Ibid. vol. 2, p. 198.

Most people marry upon mingled motives, between *convenience* and *inclination*.

Life of Sir T. Browne, p. 262.

EARLY MARRIAGES.

From early marriages proceeds the rivalry of parents and children. The son is eager to enjoy the world before the father is willing to forsake it; and there is hardly room at once for two generations. The daughter begins to bloom before the mother can be content to fade; and neither can forbear to wish for the absence of the other.

Prince of Abyssinia, p. 173.

LATE MARRIAGES.

Those who marry late in life will find it dangerous to suspend their fate upon each other, at a time when opinions are fixed and habits are established; when friendships have been contracted on both sides; when life has been planned into method, and the mind has long enjoyed the contemplation of its own prospects. They will probably escape the encroachment of their children; but, in diminution of this advantage, they will be likely to leave them, ignorant and helpless, to a guardian's mercy; or, if that should not happen, they must, at least, go out of the world, before they see those whom they love best, either wise or great. From their children, if they have less to fear, they have also less to hope; and they lose, without equivalent, the joys of early love, and the convenience of uniting with manners pliant, and minds susceptible of new impressions, which might wear away their dissimilitudes by long cohabitation, as soft bodies, by continual attrition, conform their surfaces to each other.

Ibid. p. 175 & 177.

COMPARISON BETWEEN EARLY AND LATE MARRIAGES.

It will be generally found, that those who marry late are best pleased with their children; and those who marry early, with their partners.
Ibid. p. 178.

MALICE.

We should not despise the malice of the weakest. We should remember, that venom supplies the want of strength; and that the lion may perish by the puncture of an asp.
Rambler, vol. 4, p. 163.

The natural discontent of inferiority will seldom fail to operate, in some degree of malice, against him who professes to superintend the conduct of others, especially if he seats himself uncalled in the chair of judicature, and exercises authority by his own commission.
Idler, vol. 1, p. 97.

MAN.

Man's study of himself, and the knowledge of his own station in the ranks of being, and his various relations to the innumerable multitudes which surround him, and with which his Maker has ordained him to be united, for the reception and communication of happiness, should begin with the first glimpse of reason, and only end with life itself. Other acquisitions are merely temporary benefits, except as they contribute to illustrate the knowledge, and confirm the practice, of morality and piety, which extend their influence beyond the grave, and increase our happiness through endless duration.
Preface to the Preceptor, p. 75.

There is an inequality happens to every *man*, in every mode of exertion, manual or mental. The mechanic cannot handle his hammer and his file, at all times, with equal dexterity; there are hours, he knows not why, *when his hand is out*.
Life of Milton.

There are *men* whose powers operate at leisure and in retirement, and whose intellectual vigour deserts them in conversation; whom merriment confuses, and objection disconcerts; whose bashfulness restrains their exertion, and suffers them not to speak till the time of speaking is past; or whose attention to their own character makes them unwilling to utter, at hazard, what has not been considered, and cannot be recalled.
Life of Dryden.

There are some men who, in a great measure, supply the place of reading by gleaning from accidental intelligence, and various conversation; by a quick apprehension, a judicious selection, and a happy memory; by a keen appetite for knowledge and a powerful digestion; by a vigilance that permits nothing to pass without notice, and a habit of reflection that suffers nothing useful to be lost.
Ibid.

It is not sufficiently considered, that men more frequently require to be *reminded* than *informed*.
Rambler, vol. 1, p. 12.

It was said by *Cujacius*, that he never read more than one book, by which he was not instructed: and he that shall enquire after virtue with ardour and attention, will seldom find a man by whose example or sentiments he may not be improved.

Ibid. vol. 4, p. 222.

Man is seldom willing to let fall the opinion of his own dignity. He is better content to want diligence than power, and sooner confesses the depravity of his will, than the imbecility of his nature.

Idler, vol. 2, p. 204.

Every man is obliged, by the Supreme Master of the universe, to improve all the opportunities of good which are afforded him, and to keep in continual activity such abilities as are bestowed upon him. But he has no reason to repine, though his abilities are small, and his opportunities few. He that has improved the virtue or advanced the happiness of one fellow-creature, he that has ascertained a single moral proposition or added one useful experiment to natural knowledge, may be contented with his own performance; and, with respect to mortals like himself, may demand, like Augustus, to be dismissed, at his departure, with applause.

Ibid. p. 205.

Man is made unwillingly acquainted with his own weakness; and meditation shews him only how little he can sustain and how little he can perform.

Western Islands, p. 88.

Such seems to be the disposition of man, that whatever makes a distinction produces rivalry.

Ibid. p. 96.

There are men who are always busy, though no effects of their activity ever appear; and always eager, though they have nothing to gain.

Memoirs of the K. of Pruffia, p. 95.

Every man's first cares are necessarily domestic.

Ibid. p. 102.

MANNERS.

The manners of a people are not to be found in the schools of learning, or the palaces of greatness, where the national character is obscured, or obliterated by travel or instruction, by philosophy or vanity; nor is public happiness to be estimated by the assemblies of the gay or the banquets of the rich. The great mass of nations is neither rich nor gay. They whose aggregate constitutes the people, are found in the streets and the villages; in the shops and farms; and from them, collectively considered, must the measure of general prosperity be taken. As they approach to delicacy, a nation is refined; as their conveniencies are multiplied, a nation, at least a commercial nation, must be denominated wealthy.

Western Islands, p. 45.

Such manners as depend upon standing relations and general passions, are co-extended with the race of man; but those modifications of life, and peculiarities of practice, which are the progeny of error and perverseness, or, at best, of some accidental influence or transient persuasion, must perish with their parents.

Life of Butler.

MADNESS.

MADNESS.

It is very common for madmen to catch an accidental hint and ſtrain it to the purpoſe predominant in their minds; hence Shakeſpeare makes Lear pick up a *flock*, who from this immediately thinks to ſurpriſe his enemies by a troop of horſe ſhod with *flocks*, or felt.

Notes upon Shakeſpeare, vol. 9, p. 527.

MEANNESS.

An infallible characteriſtic of meanneſs is cruelty.
Falſe Alarm, p. 49.

MERCHANT.

No mercantile man or mercantile nation has any friendſhip but for money; and alliance between them will laſt no longer than their common ſafety or common profit is endangered; no longer than they have an enemy who threatens to take from each more than either can ſteal from the other.
Political State of Great-Britain p. 50.

A merchant's deſire is not of glory, but of gain; not of public wealth, but of private emolument; he is therefore rarely to be conſulted about war and peace, or any deſigns of wide extent and diſtant conſequence.
Taxation no Tyranny, p. 9.

MEMORY.

It may be obſerved that we are apt to promiſe to ourſelves a more laſting memory than the changing ſtate of human things admits; late events obliterate the former; the civil wars have left in
this

this nation scarcely any tradition of more ancient history.

Notes upon Shakespeare, vol. 6, p. 124.

We suffer equal pain from the pertinacious adhesion of unwelcome images as from the evanescence of those which are pleasing and useful; and it may be doubted, whether we should be more benefited by the art of memory or the art of forgetfulness.

Idler, vol. 2, p. 110.

Forgetfulness is necessary to remembrance.

Ibid.

To forget or to remember at pleasure are equally beyond the power of man. Yet, as memory may be assisted by method, and the decays of knowledge repaired by stated times of recollection, so the power of forgetting is capable of improvement. Reason will, by a resolute contest, prevail over imagination; and the power may be obtained of transferring the attention as judgment shall direct.

Ibid. p. 112.

Memory is like all other human powers, with which no man can be satisfied who measures them by what he can conceive or by what he can desire. He, therefore, that, after the perusal of a book, finds few ideas remaining in his mind, is not to consider the disappointment as peculiar to himself, or to resign all hopes of improvement, because he does not retain what even the author has, perhaps, forgotten.

Ibid. p. 120.

The true art of memory is the art of attention. No man will read with much advantage, who is not able, at pleasure, to evacuate his mind, and who brings not to his author an intellect defecated and pure; neither turbid with care, nor agitated with pleasure. If the repositories of thought are already full, what can they receive? If the mind is employed on the past or future, the book will be held before the eyes in vain.

Ibid. p. 123.

Memory is the purveyor of reason, the power which places those images before the mind, upon which the judgment is to be exercised, and which treasures up the determinations that are once passed, as the rules of future action or grounds of subsequent conclusions.

Rambler, vol. 1, p. 248.

The two offices of memory are *collection* and *distribution*. By one, images are accumulated, and by the other, produced for use. Collection is always the employment of our first years, and distribution commonly that of our advanced age.

Idler, vol. 1, p. 246.

MIND.

An envious and unsocial mind, too proud to give pleasure and too sullen to receive it, always endeavours to hide its malignity from the world and from itself, under the plainness of simple honesty, or the dignity of haughty independence.

Notes upon Shakespeare, vol. 2, p. 270.

Of the powers of the mind, it is difficult to form an estimate. Many have excelled Milton in their first essays, who never rose to works like " *Paradise Lost.*"

Life of Milton.

Those who look upon the *mind* to depend on the seasons, and suppose the intellect to be subject to periodical ebbs and flows, may justly be derided as intoxicated by the fumes of a vain imagination. *Sapiens dominabitur astris.* The author that thinks himself *weather-bound*, will find, with a little help from hellebore, that he is only idle or exhausted. But while this notion has possession of the head, it produces the inability which it supposes.

Ibid.

Another opinion (equally ridiculous) wanders about the world, and sometimes finds reception among wife men; an opinion that restrains the operation of the *mind to particular regions,* and supposes that a luckless mortal may be born in a degree of latitude too high or too low for wisdom or for wit.

Ibid.

The natural flights of the human mind are not from pleasure to pleasure, but from hope to hope.

Rambler, vol. 1, p. 8.

There seem to be some minds suited to *great* and others to *little* employments; some formed to soar aloft and others to grovel on the ground, and confine their regard to a narrow sphere. Of these, the one is always in danger of becoming useless by a daring negligence; the other, by a scrupulous solicitude. The one collects many ideas, but confused and indistinct; the other is busied in minute accuracy, but without compass and without dignity.

Ibid. p. 260.

There are some minds so fertile and comprehensive, that they can always feed reflection with new supplies,

supplies, and suffer nothing from the preclusion of adventitious amusements; as some cities have, within their own walls, enclosed ground enough to feed their inhabitants in a siege.

Ibid. vol. 3, p. 179.

Such is the delight of mental superiority, that none on whom nature or study have conferred it, would purchase the gifts of fortune by its loss.

Ibid. p. 267.

Nothing produces more singularity of manners, and inconstancy of life, than the conflict of opposite vices in the same mind. He that uniformly pursues any purpose, whether good or bad, has a settled principle of action; and, as he may always find associates who are travelling the same way, is countenanced by example, and sheltered in the multitude; but a man actuated at once by different desires, must move in a direction peculiar to himself, and suffer that reproach which we are naturally inclined to bestow on those who deviate from the rest of the world, even without inquiring whether they are worse or better.

Ibid. vol. 4, p. 248.

To find the nearest way from truth to truth, or from purpose to effect; not to use more instruments where fewer will be sufficient; not to move by wheels and levers, what will give way to the naked hand, is the great proof of a healthful and vigorous mind, neither feeble with helpless ignorance, nor over-burdened with unwieldy knowledge.

Idler, vol. 1, p. 202.

PROGRESS.

PROGRESS OF THE MIND.

If we confider the exercifes of the human mind, it will be found, that in each part of life fome particular faculty is more eminently employed. When the treafures of knowledge are firft opened before us, while novelty blooms alike on either hand, and every thing equally unknown and unexamined, feems of equal value, the power of the foul is principally exerted in a vivacious and defultory curiofity. She applies, by turns, to every object, enjoys it for a fhort time, and flies with aqual ardour to another. She delights to catch up loofe and unconnected ideas, but ftarts away from fyftems and complications which would obftruct the rapidity of her tranfitions, and detain her long in the fame purfuit.

When a number of diftinct images are collected by thefe erratic and hafty furveys, the fancy is bufied in arranging them, and combines them into pleafing pictures with more refemblance to the realities of life, as experience advances, and new obfervations rectify the former. While the judgement is yet uninformed, and unable to compare the draughts of fiction with their originals, we are delighted with improbable adventures, impracticable virtues, and inimitable characters; but, in proportion as we have more opportunities of acquainting ourfelves with living nature, we are fooner difgufted with copies in which there appears no refemblance. We firft difcard abfurdity and impoffibility, then exact greater and greater degrees of probability, but at laft become cold and infenfible to the charms of falfehood, however fpecious; and, from the imitations of truth, which are never perfect, transfer our affection to truth itfelf.

Now commences the ruin of judgment or reason. We begin to find little pleasure but in comparing arguments, stating propositions, disentangling perplexities, clearing ambiguities, and deducing consequences. The painted vales of imagination are deserted, and our intellectual activity is exercised in winding through the labyrinths of fallacy, and toiling with firm and cautious steps up the narrow tracks of demonstration. Whatever may lull vigilance or mislead attention, is contemptuously rejected, and every disguise in which error may be concealed, is carefully observed, till, by degrees, a certain number of incontestible or unsuspected propositions are established, and at last concatenated into arguments or compacted into systems.

At length, weariness succeeds to labour, and the mind lies at ease in the contemplation of her own attainments, without any desire of new conquests or excursions. This is the age of recollection and narrative. The opinions are settled, and the avenues of apprehension shut against any new intelligence; the days that are to follow must pass in the inculcation of precepts already collected, and assertions of tenets already received; nothing is henceforward so odious as opposition, so insolent as doubt, or so dangerous as novelty.

Rambler, vol. 3, p. 271, 272, & 273.

MINUTENESS.

The parts of the greatest things are litttle: what is little can be but pretty, and by claiming dignity, becomes ridiculous.

Life of Cowley.

MISERY.

MISERY.

If misery be the effect of virtue, it ought to be reverenced; if of ill fortune, it ought to be pitied; and if of vice, not to be insulted; because it is, perhaps, itself a punishment adequate to the crime by which it was produced; and the humanity of that man can deserve no panegyric, who is capable of reproaching a criminal in the hands of the executioner.

Life of Savage.

The misery of man proceeds not from any single crush of overwhelming evil, but from small vexations continually repeated.

Life of Pope.

That misery does not make all virtuous, experience too certainly informs us; but it is no less certain, that of what virtue there is, misery produces far the greater part. Physical evil may be therefore endured with patience, since it is the cause of moral good; and patience itself is one virtue by which we are prepared for that state in which evil shall be no more.

Idler, vol. 2, p. 211.

MIRTH.

Merriment is always the effect of a sudden impression; the jest which is expected is already destroyed.

Idler, vol. 2, p. 32.

Any passion, too strongly agitated, puts an end to that tranquillity which is necessary to mirth. Whatever we ardently wish to gain, we must in the

the same degree be afraid to lose; and fear and pleasure, cannot dwell together.

Rambler, vol. 4, p. 244.

Real mirth must be always natural; and nature is uniform—Men have been wise in different modes, but they have always laughed the same way.

Life of Cowley.

The perverseness of mankind makes it often mischievous in men of eminence to give way to *merriment*. The idle and the illiterate will often shelter themselves under what they say in those moments.

Life of Blackmore.

MONEY.

To mend the world by banishing money is an old contrivance of those who did not consider that the quarrels and mischiefs which arise from money, as the sign, or ticket, of riches, must, if money were to cease, arise immediately from riches themselves; and could never be at an end till every man was contented with his own share of the goods of life.

Notes upon Shakespeare, vol. 6, p. 388.

MOTIVES.

Nothing is more vain than at a distant time to examine the motives of discrimination and partiality; for the enquirer, having considered interest and policy, is obliged, at last, to omit more frequent and more active motives of human conduct; such as caprice, accident, and private affections.

Life of Roger Ascham, p. 248.

METHOD.

METHOD.

As the end of method is perspicuity, that series is sufficiently regular that avoids obscurity; and where there is no obscurity, it will not be difficult to discover method.

Life of Pope.

MAXIMS.

There are *maxims* treasured up in the mind rather for show than use, and operate very little upon a man's conduct, however elegantly he might sometimes explain, or however forcibly he might inculcate them.

Life of Savage.

OLD MAIDS.

Old maids seldom give those that frequent their conversation any exalted notions of the blessings of liberty; for, whether it be that they are angry to see with what inconsiderate eagerness other heedless females rush into slavery, or with what absurd vanity the married ladies boast the change of their condition, and condemn the heroines who endeavour to assert the natural dignity of their sex; whether they are conscious that, like barren countries, they are free only because they were never thought to deserve the trouble of a conquest, or imagine that their sincerity is not always unsuspected, when they declare their contempt of men; it is certain that they generally appear to have some great and incessant cause of uneasiness, and that many of them have been at last persuaded, by *powerful rhetoricians*, to try the life which they had so long condemned, and put on the bridal ornaments at a time when they least became them.

Rambler, vol. 1, p. 236.

MODERATION.

Moderation is commonly firm; and firmness is commonly successful.
Falkland Islands, p. 32.

It was one of the maxims of the Spartans, not to press upon a flying army; and therefore their enemies were always ready to quit the field, because they knew the danger was only in opposing.
Letter to Douglas, p. 3.

N.

NATURE.

Nothing can please many, and please long, but just representations of general nature.
Preface to Shakespeare, p. 8.

The power of nature is only the power of using to any certain purpose the materials which diligence procures or opportunity supplies.
Ibid. p. 39.

ENGLISH NABOBS, &c.

Those who make an illegal use of power in foreign countries to enrich themselves and dependants, live with hearts full of that malignity which fear of detection always generates in them, who are to defend unjust acquisitions against lawful authority; and, when they come home with riches thus acquired, they bring minds hardened in evil, too proud for reproof, and too stupid for reflection. They

They offend the high by their insolence, and corrupt the low by their examples.

Falkland Islands, p. 11.

NEGLIGENCE.

No man can safely do that by others, which might be done by himself. He that indulges negligence, will quickly become ignorant of his own affairs; and he that trusts without reserve, will at last be deceived.

Rambler, vol. 4, p. 14.

NOVELTY.

To oblige the most fertile genius to say only what is *new*, would be to contract his volumes to a few pages.

Idler, vol. 2, p. 187.

Every novelty appears more wonderful as it is more remote from any thing with which experience or testimony have hitherto acquainted us; and if it passes further beyond the notions that we have been accustomed to form, it becomes at last incredible.

Idler, vol. 2, p. 195.

NUMBERS.

To count is a modern practice; the ancient method was to guess; and when numbers are guessed, they are always magnified.

Western Islands, p. 227.

NARRATION.

Nothing can be more disgusting than a narrative spangled with conceits; and conceits are all that some narratives supply.

Life of Cowley.

Every

Every one has so often detected the fallaciousness of hope, and the inconvenience of teaching himself to expect what a thousand accidents may preclude, that, when time has abated the confidence with which youth rushes out to take possession of the world, we endeavour, or wish, to find entertainment in the review of life, and to repose on real facts, and certain experience. This is, perhaps, one reason among many, why age delights in narratives.

Rambler, vol. 4, p. 232.

NOTES.

Notes to a literary work are often necessary; but they are necessary evils. Parts are not to be examined, till the whole has been surveyed: there is a kind of intellectual remoteness necessary for the comprehension of any great work in its full design, and its true proportions; a close approach shews the smaller niceties, but the beauty of the whole is discerned no longer.

Preface to Shakspeare, p. 148.

NATIONS.

Nations have changed their characters; slavery is now no where more patiently endured than in countries once inhabited by the zealots of liberty.

Idler, vol. 1, p. 160.

Such is the diligence with which, in nations completely civilized, one part of mankind labours for another, that wants are supplied faster than they can be formed, and the idle and luxurious find life stagnate, for want of some desire to keep it in motion. This species of distress furnishes a new set of occupations; and multitudes are busied, from

from day to day, in finding the rich and the fortunate something to do.

Ibid. p. 166.

It is, perhaps, the character of the English nation to despise trifles.

Ibid. vol. 2, p. 216.

All nations whose power has been exerted on the ocean, have fixed colonies in remote parts of the world; and while those colonies subsisted, navigation, if it did not increase, was always preserved from total decay.

Political State of Great Britain in 1756, p. 48.

It is ridiculous to imagine that the friendship of nations, whether civil or barbarous, can be gained or kept, but by *kind treatment*; and, surely, they who intrude *uncalled* upon the country of a distant people, ought to consider the natives as worthy of common kindness.

Ibid. p. 56.

It is observable, that most nations amongst whom the use of clothes is unknown, paint their bodies. Such was the practice of the first inhabitants of our own country; and from this custom did our earliest enemies, the Picts, owe their denomination. This practice contributes in some degree to defend them from the injuries of winter, and, in those climates where little evaporates by the pores, may be used with no great inconvenience; but in hot countries, where perspiration is in a great degree necessary, the natives only use unction to preserve them from the other extreme of weather. So well do either reason or experience supply the place of science in savage countries.

Life of Drake, p. 202.

It is observed, that among the natives of England is to be found a greater variety of humour than in any other country.

Origin and Importance of Fugitive Pieces, p. 3.

O.

OPINION.

The opinion prevalent in one age, as truths above the reach of controversy, are confuted and rejected in another, and rise again to reception in remoter times. Thus, the human mind is kept in motion without progress. Thus, sometimes, truth and error, and sometimes contrarieties of error, take each other's place by reciprocal invasion.

Preface to Shakespeare, p. 54.

Much of the pain and pleasure of mankind arises from the conjectures which every one makes of the thoughts of others. We all enjoy praise which we do not hear, and resent contempt which we do not see.

Idler, vol. 2, p. 280.

To think differently, at different times, of poetical merit, may be easily allowed. Such opinions are often admitted and dismissed without nice examination. Who is there that has not found reason for changing his mind about questions of greater importance?

Life of Savage.

When an opinion, to which there is no temptation of interest, spreads wide and continues long,
it

it may be reasonably presumed to have been infused by nature or dictated by reason.

Idler, vol. 1, p. 290.

OPPORTUNITY.

To improve the golden moment of opportunity, and catch the good that is within our reach, is the great art of life. Many wants are suffered which might have once been supplied, and much time is lost in regretting the time which had been lost before.

The Patriot, p. 1.

He that waits for an opportunity to do much at once, may breathe out his life in idle wishes, and regret, in the last hour, his useless intentions and barren zeal.

Idler, vol. 1, p. 22.

OATHS.

Rash oaths, whether kept or broken, frequently produce guilt.

Notes upon Shakespeare, vol. 2, p. 402.

OBLIGATION.

To be obliged, is to be in some respect inferior to another, and few willingly indulge the memory of an action which raises one whom they have always been accustomed to think below them, but satisfy themselves with faint praise and penurious payment, and then drive it from their own minds, and endeavour to conceal it from the knowledge of others.

Rambler, vol. 4, p. 37.

OBSERVATION.

An obferver, deeply impreffed by any remarkable fpectacle, does not fuppofe that the traces will foon vanifh from his mind, and having commonly no great convenience for writing, defers the defcription to a time of more leifure and better accommodation. But he who has made the experiment, or who is not accuftomed to require rigorous accuracy from himfelf, will fcarcely believe how much a few hours take from certainty of knowledge and diftinctnefs of imagery; how the fucceffion of objects will be broken, how feparate parts will be confufed, and how many particular features and difcriminations will be compreffed into one grofs and general idea.

Weftern Iflands, p. 343.

P.

PARENTS.

In general, thofe parents have moft reverence, who moft deferve it; for he that lives well cannot be defpifed.

Prince of Abyffinia, p. 155.

PATRIOT.

A Patriot is he, whofe public conduct is regulated by one fingle motive, viz. *the love of his country*; who, as an agent, in parliament, has for himfelf neither hope nor fear; neither kindnefs nor refentment; but refers every thing to the common intereft.

Patriot, p. 3.

The frowns of a prince and the loss of a pension have been found of wonderful efficacy to abstract men's thoughts from the present time, and fill them with zeal for the liberty and welfare of ages to come.

Marmor Norfolciense, p. 21.

PASSION.

The adventitious peculiarities of personal habits are only superficial dies, bright and pleasing for a while, yet soon fading to a dim tint, without any remains of former lustre. But the discrimination of true passion are the colours of nature; they pervade the whole mass, and can only perish with the body that exhibits them.

Preface to Shakespeare, p. 18.

Passion, in its first violence, controls interest, as the eddy, for a while, runs against the stream.

Taxation no Tyranny, p. 3.

Real passion runs not after remote allusions and obscure opinions. Where there is leisure for *fiction*, there is little grief.

Life of Milton.

Of any passion *innate* and *irresistible*, the existence may reasonably be doubted. Human characters are by no means constant; men change by change of place, of fortune, of acquaintance; he who is at one time a lover of pleasure, is at another a lover of money.

Life of Pope.

It is the fate of almost every passion, when it has passed the bounds which nature prescribes, to counteract its own purpose. Too much rage hinders

ders the warrior from circumspection; too much eagerness of profit hurts the credit of the trader; and too much ardour takes away from the lover that easiness of address with which ladies are delighted.

Rambler, vol. 1, p. 320.

PROGRESS OF THE PASSIONS.

The passions usurp the separate command of the successive periods of life. To the happiness of our first years, nothing more seems necessary than freedom from restraint. Every man may remember, that if he was left to himself, and indulged in the disposal of his own time, he was once content without the superaddition of any actual pleasure.

The new world is in itself a banquet, and till we have exhausted the freshness of life, we have always about us sufficient gratification. The sunshine quickens us to play, and the shade invites us to sleep.

But we soon become unsatisfied with negative felicity, and are solicited by our senses and appetites to more powerful delights, as the taste of him who has satisfied his hunger must be excited by artificial stimulations. The simplicity of natural amusements is now passed, and art and contrivance must improve our pleasures; but, in time, art, like nature, is exhausted, and the senses can no longer supply the cravings of the intellect.

The attention is then transferred from pleasure to interest, in which pleasure is perhaps included, though diffused to a wider extent, and protracted through new gradations. Nothing now dances before the eyes but wealth and power, nor rings in the ear but the voice of fame: wealth, to which, however variously denominated, every man at some time

time or other aspires; power, which all wish to obtain within their circle of action; and fame, which no man, however high or mean, however wise or ignorant, was yet able to despise. Now prudence and foresight exert their influence. No hour is devoted wholly to any present enjoyment, no act or purpose terminates in itself, but every motion is referred to some distant end; the accomplishment of one design begins another, and the ultimate wish is always pushed off to its former distance.

At length fame is observed to be uncertain, and power to be dangerous. The man whose vigour and alacrity begin to forsake him, by degrees contracts his designs, remits his former multiplicity of pursuits, and extends no longer his regard to any other honour than the reputation of wealth, or any other influence than his power. Avarice is generally the last passion of those lives, of which the first part has been squandered in pleasure, and the second in ambition. He that sinks under the fatigue of getting wealth, lulls his age with the milder business of saving it.

Rambler, vol. 3, p. 273 & 274.

PAIN.

Pain is less subject than pleasure to caprices of expression.

Idler, vol. 1, p. 282.

Our sense is so much stronger of what we suffer, than of what we enjoy, that the ideas of pain predominate in almost every mind. What is recollection, but a revival of vexation; or history, but a record of wars, treasons, and calamities? Death, which is considered as the greatest evil, happens to all; the greatest good, be it what it will, is the lot but of a part.

Western Islands, p. 250.

PATRONAGE.

A man conspicuous in a high station, who multiplies hopes, that he may multiply dependents, may be considered as a beast of prey.

Idler, vol. 1, p. 79.

To solicit patronage is, at least in the event, to set virtue to sale. None can be pleased without praise, and few can be praised without falsehood; few can be assiduous without servility, and none can be servile without corruption.

Rambler, vol. 2, p. 298.

PLEASURE.

Whatever professes to benefit by pleasing, must please at once. What is perceived by slow degrees, may gratify us with the consciousness of improvement, but will never strike us with the sense of pleasure.

Life of Cowley.

Pleasure is very seldom found where it is sought; our brightest blazes of gladness are commonly kindled by unexpected sparks. The flowers which scatter their odours from time to time in the paths of life, grow up without culture from seeds scattered by chance.

Idler, vol. 2, p. 31.

The great source of pleasure is variety. Uniformity must tire at last, though it be uniformity of excellence. We love to expect, and when expectation

pectation is disappointed or gratified, we want to be again expecting.
Life of Butler.

The merit of pleasing must be estimated by the means. Favour is not always gained by good actions or laudable qualities. Caresses and preferments are often bestowed on the auxillaries of vice, the procurers of pleasure, or the flatterers of vanity.
Life of Dryden.

Men may be convinced, but they cannot be *pleased* against their will. But though taste is obstinate, it is very variable, and time often prevails, when arguments have failed.
Life of Congreve.

Pleasure is only received, when we believe that we give it in return.
Rambler, vol. 2, p. 90.

Pleasure is seldom such as it appears to others, nor often such as we represent it to ourselves.
Idler, vol. 1, p. 99.

It is an unhappy state, in which danger is hid under pleasure.
Preface to Shakespeare, p. 146.

Pleasure in itself harmless, may become mischievous, by endearing us to a state which we know to be transient and probatory. Self-denial is no virtue in itself; nor is it of any other use, than as it disengages us from the allurements of sense. In the state of future perfection, to which we all aspire, there will be pleasure without danger, and security without restraint.
Prince of Abyssinia.

PLEASURES OF LOCAL EMOTION.

To abstract the mind from all local emotion would be impossible, if it were endeavoured; and would be foolish if it were possible. Whatever withdraws us from the power of our senses, whatever makes the past, the distant, or the future predominate over the present, advances us in the dignity of thinking beings. Far from me, and far from my friends, be such frigid philosoyhy as may conduct us indifferent and unmoved over any ground which has been dignified by wisdom, bravery, or virtue. That man is little to be envied whose patriotism would not gain force upon the plains of Marathon, or whose piety would not grow warmer among the ruins of Iona.

Western Islands, p. 346.

POETS AND POETRY.

In almost all countries, the most ancient poets are considered as the best. Whether it be that every other kind of knowledge is an acquisition gradually attained, and poetry is a gift conferred at once, or that the first poetry of every nation surprised them as a novelty, and retained the credit by consent, which it received by accident at first; or whether, as the province of poetry is to describe nature and passion, which are always the same, the first writers took possession of the most striking objects for description, and the most probable occurrences for fiction, and left nothing to those that followed them but transcriptions of the same events, and new combinations of the same images. Whatever be the reason, it is commonly observed, that the early writers are in possession of *nature*, and their followers of *art*.

Prince of Abyssinia, p. 64 & 65.

Compositions, merely pretty, have the fate of other pretty things, and are quitted in time for some thing useful. They are flowers fragrant and fair, but of short duration; or they are blossoms only to be valued as they foretel fruits.
Life of Waller.

It is a general rule in poetry, that all appropriated terms of art, should be sunk in general expressions; because poetry is to speak an universal language. This rule is still stronger with regard to arts not liberal, or confined to few, and therefore far removed from common knowledge.
Life of Dryden.

A mythological fable seldom pleases. The story we are accustomed to reject as false, and the manners are so distant from our own, that we know them not by sympathy, but by study.
Life of Smith.

No poem should be long, of which the purpose is only to strike the fancy, without enlightening the understanding by precept, ratiocination, or narrative.—A blaze first pleases, and then tires the sight.
Life of Fenton.

After all the refinements of subtilty, and the dogmatism of learning, all claim to poetical honours must be finally decided by the common sense of readers, uncorrupted with literary prejudices.
Life of Gray.

Though poets profess fiction, the legitimate end of fiction is the conveyance of truth, and he that has flattery ready for all whom the vicissitudes of the world happen to exalt, must be scorned as a prostituted mind, that may retain the glitter of wit, but has lost the dignity of virtue.

Life of Waller.

It does not always happen that the success of a poet is proportionate to his labour. The same observation may be extended to all works of imagination, which are often influenced by causes wholly out of the performer's power, by the hints of which he perceives not the origin, by sudden elevations of mind which he cannot produce in himself, and which sometimes rise when he expects them least.

Dissertation on the Epitaphs of Pope, p. 320.

Poets are scarce thought *freemen* of their company, without paying some *duties*, or obliging themselves to be true to love.

Life of Cowley.

The man that sits down to suppose himself charged with treason or peculation, and heats his mind by an elaborate purgation of his character from crimes which he never was within the possibility of committing, differs only by the *infrequency of his folly* from the poet who praises beauty which he never saw, complains of jealousy which he never felt, supposes himself sometimes invited, and sometimes forsaken, fatigues his fancy, and ransacks his memory for images which may exhibit the gaiety of hope, or the gloominess of despair; and dresses his imaginary Chloris, or Phillis, sometimes in flowers fading as her beauty, and sometimes in gems lasting as her virtues.

Ibid.

One of the greatest sources of poetical delight is description, or the powers of presenting pictures to the mind.
Ibid.

Waller's opinion concerning the duty of a poet was—" That he should blot from his works any line that did not contain some motive to virtue."
Life of Waller.

It is in vain for those who borrow too many of their sentiments and illustrations from the old mythology, to plead the example of the ancient poets. The deities which they produced so frequently were considered as realities, so far as to be received by the imagination, whatever sober reason might then determine. But of these images time has tarnished the splendor. A fiction not only detected but despised, can never afford a solid basis to any position, though sometimes it may furnish a transient allusion, or slight illustration. No modern monarch can be much exalted by hearing, that as Hercules has had his *club*, he has his *navy*.
Ibid.

Those who admire the beauties of a great poet, sometimes force their own judgment into a false approbation of his little pieces, and prevail upon themselves to think that admirable which is only singular. All that short compositions can commonly attain is neatness and elegance.
Life of Milton.

Bossu is of opinion, that the poet's first work is to find a *moral*, which his fable is afterwards to illustrate and establish.
Ibid.

Pleasure and terror are indeed the genuine sources of poetry; but poetical pleasure must be such as human imagination can at least conceive, and poetical terror such as human strength and fortitude may combat.

Ibid.

In every work one part must be for the sake of others; a palace must have its passages; a *poem* must have transitions. It is no more to be required that wit should be always blazing, than that the sun should stand at noon. In a great work there is a vicissitude of luminous and opaque parts, as there is in the world a succession of day and night.

Ibid.

The *occasional poet* is circumscribed by the narrowness of his subject. Whatever can happen to a man has happened so often, that little remains for fancy and invention. Not only matter, but time is wanting. The poem must not be delayed till the occasion is forgotten. Occasional compositions may however secure to a writer the praise both of learning and facility; for they cannot be the effect of long study, and must be furnished immediately from the treasures of the mind.

Life of Dryden.

Knowledge of the subject is to a poet what materials are to the architect.

Ibid.

Local poetry is a species of composition, of which the fundamental subject is some particular landscape to be poetically described, with the addition of such embellishments as may be supplied by historical retrospection, or incidental meditation.

tion. Sir John Denham's *Cooper's Hill* appears to claim the originality of this kind of poetry among us.

Life of Denham.

A poem fridgidly didactic without rhyme is so near to prose, that the reader only scorns it for pretending to be verse.

Life of Roscommon.

Those performances which strike with wonder, are combinations of skilful genius with happy casualty.

Life of Pope.

As men are often esteemed who cannot be loved, so the poetry of some writers may sometimes extort praise when it gives little pleasure.

Life of Collins.

For the same reason that *pastoral poetry* was the first employment of the human imagination, it is generally the first literary amusement of our minds.

Rambler, vol. 1, p. 218.

The occasions on which *pastoral* poetry can be properly produced, are few, and general. The state of a man confined to the employments and pleasures of the country, is so little diversified, and exposed to so few of those accidents which produce perplexities, terrors, and surprises, in more complicated transactions, that he can be shewn but seldom in such circumstances as attract curiosity. His ambition is without policy, and his love without intrigue. He has no complaints to make of his rival, but that he is richer than himself; nor any disasters to lament, but a cruel mistress, or a bad harvest.

Ibid. p. 220.

If we search the writings of Virgil, for the true definition of a *pastoral*, it will be found " A poem in which any action or passion is represented by its effects upon a country life."

Ibid. p. 224.

Every other power by which the understanding is enlightened, or the imagination enchanted, may be exercised in prose. But the poet has this peculiar superiority, that to all the powers which the perfection of every other composition can require, he adds the faculty of joining music with reason, and of acting at once upon the senses and the passions.

Ibid. vol. 2, p. 184.

Easy poetry is that in which natural thoughts are expressed, without violence to the language. Any epithet which can be ejected without diminution of the sense, any curious iteration of the same word, and all unusual, though not ungrammatical, structure of speech, destroy the grace of easy poetry.

Idler, vol. 2, p. 136.

It is the prerogative of *easy poetry*, to be understood as long as the language lasts ; but modes of speech, which owe their prevalence only to modish folly, or to the eminence of those that use them, die away with their inventors ; and their meaning, in a few years, is no longer known.

Ibid. p. 139.

Easy poetry, though it excludes pomp, will admit greatness.

Ibid.

The poets, from the time of Dryden, have gradually advanced in *embellishment*, and consequently departed from simplicity and ease.

Ibid. p. 140.

POVERTY.

Poverty has, in large cities, very different appearances. It is often concealed in splendor, and often in extravagance. It is the care of a very great part of mankind to conceal their indigence from the rest. They support themselves by temporary expedients, and every day is lost in contriving for to-morrow.

Prince of Abyssinia, p. 151.

It is the great privilege of poverty to be happy unenvied, to be healthful without physic, and secure without a guard. To obtain from the bounty of nature, what the great and wealthy are compelled to procure by the help of artists, and the attendance of flatterers and spies.

Rambler, vol. 4, p. 229.

There are natural reasons why poverty does not easily conciliate. He that has been confined from his infancy to the conversation of the lowest classes of mankind, must necessarily want those accomplishments which are the usual means of attracting favour; and though truth, fortitude, and probity, give an indisputable right to reverence and kindness, they will not be distinguished by common eyes, unless they are brightened by elegance of manners, but are cast aside, like unpolished gems, of which none but the artist knows the intrinsic value, till their asperities are smoothed, and their incrustrations rubbed away.

Ibid. p. 35.

Nature makes us poor only when we want necessaries, but custom gives the name of poverty to the want of superfluities.
Idler, vol. 1, p. 208.

In a long continuance of poverty, it cannot well be expected that any character should be exactly uniform. There is a degree of want, by which the freedom of agency is almost destroyed; and long associations with fortuitous companions, will, at last, relax the strictness of truth, and abate the fervor of sincerity.—Of such a man, it is surely some degree of praise to say, that he preserved the source of action unpolluted; that his principles were never shaken; that his distinctions of right and wrong were never confounded, and that his faults had nothing of malignity, or design, but proceeded from some unexpected pressure, or casual temptation. A man doubtful of his dinner, or trembling at a creditor, is not much disposed to abstracted meditation, or remote enquiries.
Life of Collins.

The poor are insensible of many little vexations which sometimes imbitter the possessions and pollute the enjoyments of the rich. They are not pained by casual incivility, or mortified by the mutilation of a compliment; but this happiness is like that of a malefactor, who ceases to feel the cords that bind him when the pincers are tearing his flesh.
Review of the Origin of Evil, p. 10.

Some men are poor by their own faults; some by the fault of others.
Life of Roger Ascham, p. 252.

Many

Many men are made the poorer by opulence.
Life of Sir T. Brown, p. 254.

POVERTY AND IDLENESS.

To be idle and to be poor have always been reproaches, and therefore every man endeavours, with his utmost care, to hide his poverty from others, and his idleness from himself.
Idler, vol. 1, p. 93.

POLITICS.

Political truth is equally in danger from the praises of courtiers, and the exclamation of patriots.
Life of Waller.

It is convenient, in the conflict of factions, to have that disaffection known which cannot safely be punished.
Ibid.

He that changes his party by his humour, is not more virtuous, than he that changes it by his interest. He loves himself rather than truth.
Life of Milton.

Faction seldom leaves a man honest, however it might find him.
Ibid.

A wise minister should conclude, that the flight of every honest man is a loss to the community. That those who are unhappy without guilt, ought to be relieved; and the life which is overburthened by accidental calamities, set at ease by the care of the public; and that those who by their misconduct have forfeited their claim to favour, ought rather

rather be made useful to the society which they have injured, than be driven from it.
Life of Savage.

There is reason to expect, that as the world is more enlightened, policy and morality will at last be reconciled, and that nations will learn not to do, what they would not suffer.
Falkland Island, p. 10.

The power of a political treatise depends much on the disposition of the people. When a nation is combustible, a spark will set it on fire.
Life of Swift.

When a political design has ended in miscarriage, or success; when every eye and every ear is witness to general discontent, or general satisfaction, it is then a proper time to disentangle confusion, and illustrate obscurity; to shew by what causes every event was produced, and in what effects it is likely to terminate; to lay down with distinct particularity what rumour always huddles in general exclamations, or perplexes by undigested narratives: to shew whence happiness or calamity is derived, and whence it may be expected, and honestly to lay before the people, what enquiry can gather of the past, and conjecture can estimate of the future.
Observations on the State of Affairs, 1756, p. 17.

It is not to be expected that physical and political truth should meet with equal acceptance, or gain ground upon the world with equal facility. The notions of the naturalist find mankind in a state of neutrality, or, at worst, have nothing to encounter but prejudice and vanity; prejudice without

without malignity, and vanity without interest. But the politician's improvements are opposed by every passion that can exclude conviction, or suppress it; by ambition, by avarice, by hope, and by terror, by public faction, and private animosity.

False Alarm, p. 4.

PRAISE.

Praise is so pleasing to the mind of man, that it is the original motive of almost all our actions.

Rambler, vol. 4, p. 178.

They who are seldom gorged to the full with praise, may be safely fed with gross compliments; for the appetite must be satisfied before it is disgusted.

Ibid. p. 180.

That praise is worth nothing of which the price is known.

Life of Waller.

Praise, like gold and diamonds, owes its value only to its scarcity: it becomes cheap as it becomes vulgar, and will no longer raise expectation, or animate enterprize. It is, therefore, not only necessary that wickedness, even when it is not safe to censure it, be denied applause, but that goodness be commended only in proportion to its degree; and, that the garlands due to the great benefactors of mankind, be not suffered to fade upon the brow of him, who can boast only petty services and easy virtues.

Rambler, vol. 3, p. 181.

The real satisfaction which praise can afford, is when what is repeated aloud, agrees with the whispers

pers of conscience, by shewing us that we have not endeavoured to deserve well in vain.

Ibid. p. 183.

Every man willingly gives value to the praise which he receives, and considers the sentence passed in his favour, as the sentence of discernment. We admire in a friend that understanding which selected us for confidence. We admire more in a patron that judgment, which instead of scattering bounty indiscriminately, directed it to us; and those performances which gratitude forbids us to blame, affection will easily dispose us to exalt.

Life of Halifax.

To be at once in any great degree *loved* and *praised*, is truly rare.

Notes upon Shakespeare, vol. 9, p. 176.

Men are seldom satisfied with praise, introduced or followed by any mention of defect.

Life of Pope.

Some are lavish of praise, because they hope to be repaid.

Rambler, vol. 2, p. 230.

To scatter praise or blame without regard to justice, is to destroy the distinction of good and evil. Many have no other test of actions than general opinion; and all are so influenced by a sense of reputation, that they are often restrained by fear of reproach, and excited by hope of honour, when other principles have lost their power.

Ibid. vol. 3, p. 181.

PRIDE.

PRIDE.

Small things make mean men proud.
Preface to Shakespeare, p. 280.

Pride is a vice, which pride itself inclines every man to find in others, and to overlook in himself.
Life of Sir T. Browne, p. 280.

PRIDE AND ENVY.

Pride is seldom delicate, it will please itself with very mean advantages; and envy feels not its own happiness, but when it may be compared with the misery of others.
Prince of Abyssinia, p. 60.

COMPARISON BETWEEN A DRAMATIC POET AND A STATESMAN.

Distrest alike the statesman with the wit,
When one a *Borough* courts—and one the *Pit*;
The busy candidates for power and fame
Have hopes, and fears, and wishes, just the same;
Disabled both, to combat or to fly,
Must hear all taunts, and hear without reply:
Uncheck'd, on both loud rabbles vent their rage,
As mongrels bay the lion in the cage.
Th' offended burgess hoards his angry tale
For that blest year when all that vote may rail;
Their schemes of spite the poet's foes dismiss
Till that glad night when all that hate may hiss.
This day the powdered curls and golden coat,
Says swelling *Crispin*, begged a cobler's vote.
This night our wit, the pert apprentice cries,
Lies at my feet; I hiss him and he dies:
The great, 'tis true, can damn th' electing tribe,
The bard can only supplicate——not bribe.
Prologue to the Good-natured Man.

PRAYER.

PRAYER:

(Its proper Objects.)

———————— Petitions yet remain
Which Heaven may hear—nor deem Religion vain;
Still raise for *good* the supplicating voice,
But leave to Heaven the measure and the choice;
Safe in his power whose eyes discern afar
The secret ambush of a specious prayer;
Implore his aid, in his decision rest,
Secure whate'er he gives, he gives the best.
  Yet when the sense of sacred presence fires,
And strong devotion to the skies aspires,
Pour forth thy fervours for a *healthful mind*,
Obedient passions, and a *will resign'd*;
For *Love* which scarce collective man can fill,
For *Patience* sovereign o'er transmuted ill,
For *Faith*, that panting for a happier seat,
Counts Death kind Nature's signal for retreat.
These goods for man the laws of Heaven ordain,
These goods he grants who grants the pow'r to gain;
With these, celestial wisdom calms the mind,
And makes the happiness she does not find.

Vanity of Human Wishes.

PROSPERITY.

  Prosperity, as is truly asserted by Seneca, very much obstructs the knowledge of ourselves. No man can form a just estimate of his own powers, by inactive speculation. That fortitude which has encountered no dangers, that prudence which has surmounted no difficulties, that integrity which has been attacked by no temptations, can, at best, be considered but as gold not yet brought to the test, of which, therefore, the true value cannot be assigned. Equally necessary is some variety of for-

tune to a nearer infpection of the manners, principles, and affections, of mankind.
Rambler, vol. 3, p. 268.

Moderation in profperity is a virtue very difficult to all mortals.
Memoirs of the K. of Pruffia, p. 137.

PEEVISHNESS.

Peevifhnefs, though fometimes it arifes from old age, or the confequence of fome mifery, it is frequently one of the attendants on the profperous, and is employed by infolence, in exacting homage; or by tyranny, in harraffing fubjection. It is the offspring of idlenefs or pride; of idlenefs, anxious for trifles, or pride, unwilling to endure the leaft obftruction of her wifhes. Such is the confequence of peevifhnefs, it can be borne only when it is defpifed.
Rambler, vol. 2, p. 114.

It is not eafy to imagine a more unhappy condition than that of dependence on a peevifh man. In every other ftate of inferiority, the certainty of pleafing is perpetually increafed by a fuller knowledge of our duty, and kindnefs and confidence are ftrengthened by every new act of truft and proof of fidelity. But peevifhnefs facrifices to a momentary offence, the obfequioufnefs or ufefulnefs of half a life, and, as more is performed, encreafes her exactions.
Ibid. vol. 3, p. 39.

Peevifhnefs is generally the vice of narrow minds, and except when it is the effect of anguifh
and

and difeafe, by which the refolution is broken, and the mind made too feeble to bear the lighteft addition to its miferies, proceeds from an unreafonable perfuafion of the importance of trifles. The proper remedy againft it is, to confider the dignity of human nature, and the folly of fuffering perturbation and uneafinefs, from caufes unworthy of our notice.

Ibid. p. 41.

He that refigns his peace to little cafualties, and fuffers the courfe of his life to be interrupted by fortuitous inadvertencies or offences, delivers up himfelf to the direction of the wind, and lofes all that conftancy and equanimity, which conftitute the chief praife of a wife man.

Ibid. vol. 3, p. 41.

PEOPLE.

No people can be great who have ceafed to be virtuous.

Political State of Great-Britain, p. 56.

The profperity of a people is proportionate to the number of hands and minds ufefully employed. To the community, fedition is a fever, corruption is a gangrene, and idlenefs an atrophy. Whatever body, and whatever fociety waftes more than it requires, muft gradually decay; and every being that continues to be fed, and ceafes to labour, takes away fomething from the public ftock.

Idler, vol. 1, p. 121.

Great regard fhould be paid to the voice of the people in cafes where knowledge has been forced upon

upon them by *experience*, without long deductions, or deep researches.

Rambler, vol. 1, p. 150.

PEDANTRY.

It is as possible to become pedantic by fear of pedantry, as to be troublesome by ill-timed civility.

Ibid. vol. 4, p. 76.

PUNCTUALITY.

Punctuality is a quality which the interest of mankind requires to be diffused through all the ranks of life, but which many seem to consider as a vulgar and ignoble virtue, below the ambition of greatness, or attention of wit, scarcely requisite amongst men of gaiety and spirit, and sold at its highest rate, when it is sacrificed to a frolic or a jest.

Ibid. p. 223.

PRUDENCE.

Prudence is of more frequent use than any other intellectual quality; it is exerted on slight occasions, and called into act by the cursory business of common life.

Idler, vol. 2, p. 25.

Prudence operates on life in the same manner as rules on composition; it produces vigilance rather than elevation, rather prevents loss than procures advantage, and often escapes miscarriages, but seldom reaches either power or honour.

Ibid.

PRUDENCE AND JUSTICE.

Aristotle is praised for naming fortitude, first of the cardinal virtues, as that without which no other virtue can steadily be practised; but he might with equal propriety, have placed *prudence* and *justice* before it; since without prudence fortitude is mad, without justice it is mischievous.

Life of Pope.

PREJUDICE.

To be prejudiced is always to be weak, yet there are prejudices so near to being laudable, that they have often been praised, and are always pardoned.

Taxation no Tyranny, p. 3.

PEACE.

Peace is easily made, when it is necessary to both parties.

Memoirs of the King of Prussia, p. 121.

PRACTICE.

In every art, *practice* is much; in arts manual, practice is almost the whole; precept can at most but warn against error, it can never bestow excellence.

Life of Roger Ascham, p. 240.

Uniformity of practice seldom continues long without good reason.

Western Islands. p. 361.

PIETY.

Piety is elevation of mind towards the Supreme Being, and extention of the thought to another life.

The other life is future, and the Supreme Being is invisible. None would have recourse to an invisible power, but that all other subjects had eluded their hopes. None would fix their attention upon the future, but that they are discontented with the present. If the senses were feasted with perpetual pleasure, they would always keep the mind in subjection. Reason has no authority over us, but by its power to warn us against evil.

Idler, vol. 2, p. 209.

PERFECTION.

To pursue perfection in any science, where perfection is unattainable, is like the first inhabitants of Arcadia to chase the sun, which, when they had reached the hill where he seemed to rest, was still beheld at the same distance from them.

Life of Waller.

It seldom happens that all the necessary causes concur to any great effect. Will is wanting to power, or power to will, or both are impeded by external obstructions.

Life of Dryden.

An imperial crown cannot be one continued diamond, the gems must be held together by some less valuable matter.

Ibid.

PERFIDY.

Combinations of wickedness would overwhelm the world, by the advantage which licentious principles afford, did not those who have long practised perfidy, grow faithless to each other.

Life of Waller.

PERSEVERANCE.

No terrestrial greatness is more than aggregate of little things, and to inculcate, after the Arabian proverb, " Drops added to drops, constitute the ocean.'

Plan of an English Dictionary, p. 49.

All the performances of human art, at which we look with praise or wonder, are instances of the resistless force of persevarance. It is by this that the quarry becomes a pyramid, and that distant countries are united with canals ; it is therefore of the utmost importance that those who have any intention of deviating from the beaten roads of life, and acquiring a reputation superior to names hourly swept away by time among the refuse of fame, should add to their reason and their spirit, *the power of persisting in their purposes*, acquire the art of sapping what they cannot batter, and the habit of vanquishing obstinate resistance by obstinate attacks.

Rambler, vol. 1, p. 261 & 262.

PRODIGALITY.

He seldom lives frugally who lives by chance. Hope is always liberal, and they that trust her promises, make little scruple of revelling to-day, on the profits of to-morrow.

Life of Dryden.

PATIENCE.

If what we suffer has been brought on us by ourselves, it is observed by an antient poet, that patience is eminently our duty, since no one ought to be angry at feeling that which he has deserved. If we are

are conscious that we have not contributed to our own sufferings, if punishment falls upon innocence, or disappointment happens to industry and prudence, patience, whether more necessary or not, is much easier, since our pain is then without aggravation, and we have not the bitterness of remorse to add to the asperity of misfortune.

Rambler, vol. 1, p. 195.

In those evils which are allotted us by Providence, such as deformity, privation of any of the senses, or old age, it is always to be remembered, that impatience can have no present effect, but to deprive us of the consolations which our condition admits, by driving away from us those, by whose conversation, or advice, we might be amused or helped ; and that with regard to futurity, it is yet less to be justified, since without lessening the pain, it cuts off the hope of that reward, which he, by whom it is inflicted, will confer upon them that bear it well.

Ibid.

In all evils which admit a remedy, impatience is to be avoided, because it wastes that time and attention in complaints, that, if properly applied, might remove the cause.

Ibid.

In calamities which operate chiefly on our passions, such as diminution of fortune, loss of friends, or declension of character, the chief danger of impatience is upon the first attack, and many expedients have been contrived by which the blow might be broken. Of these, the most general precept is, not to take pleasure in any thing of which it is not in our power to secure the possession to ourselves.

ourselves. This counsel, when we consider the enjoyment of any terrestrial advantage, as opposite to a constant and habitual solicitude for future felicity, is undoubtedly just, and delivered by that authority which cannot be disputed; but, in any other sense, is it not like advice not to walk, lest we should stumble, or not to see, lest our eyes should light on deformity?

It seems reasonable to enjoy blessings with confidence, as well as to resign them with submission, and to hope for the continuance of good which we possess without insolence or voluptuousness, as for the restitution of that which we lose without despondency or murmurs.

Rambler, vol. 1, p. 197.

The chief security against the fruitless anguish of impatience, must arise from frequent reflection on the wisdom and goodness of the God of Nature, in whose hands are riches and poverty, honour and disgrace, pleasure and pain, and life and death. A settled conviction of the tendency of every thing to our good, and of the possibility of turning miseries into happiness, by receiving them rightly, will incline us *to bless the name of the Lord, whether he gives or takes away.*

Ibid. p. 198.

The uncivilized, in all countries, have patience proportionate to their unskilfulness, and are content to attain their end by very tedious methods.

Western Islands, p. 161.

PITY.

Pity is to many of the unhappy, a source of comfort in hopeless distresses, as it contributes to recom-

recommend them to themselves, by proving that they have not lost the regard of others; and heaven seems to indicate the duty even of barren compassion, by inclining us to weep for evils which we cannot remedy.

Rambler, vol. 2, p. 35.

PHILOSOPHY.

One of the chief advantages derived by the present generation from the improvement and diffusion of philosophy, is deliverance from unnecessary terrors, and exemption from false alarms. The unusual appearances, whether regular or accidental, which once spread consternation over ages of ignorance, are now the recreations of inquisitive security. The sun is no more lamented when it is eclipsed, than when it sets, and meteors play their coruscations without prognostic or prediction.

False Alarm, p. 1.

The antidotes with which philosophy has medicated the cup of life, though they cannot give it salubrity and sweetness, have at least allayed its bitterness, and contempered its malignity; the balm which she drops upon the wounds of the mind, abates their pain, though it cannot heal them.

Ibid. p. 265.

PHYSICIAN.

A physician in a great city, seems to be the mere plaything of fortune; his degree of reputation is for the most part, totally casual. They that employ him know not his excellence; they that reject him, know not his deficience. By an accurate observer,

observer, who had looked on the transactions of the medical world for half a century, a very curious book might be written on the fortune of physicians.

Life of Akenside.

PERIODICAL PUBLICATIONS.

Nothing is so proper as the frequent publications of short papers, (like the Tatlers, Spectators, &c.) which we read, not as a study, but amusement. If the subject be slight, the treatise is likewise short. The busy may find time, and the idle may find patience.

Life of Addison.

He that condemns himself to compose on a *stated day*, will often bring to his task an attention dissipated, a memory embarrassed, an imagination overwhelmed, a mind distracted with anxieties, a body languishing with disease. He will labour on a barren topic, till it is too late to change it; or, in the ardour of invention, diffuse his thoughts into wild exuberance, which the pressing hour of publication cannot suffer judgment to examine or reduce.

Rambler, vol. 4, p. 262.

LITERARY PUBLICATIONS.

If nothing may be published but what civil *authority* shall have previously approved, power must always be the *standard of truth*; if every dreamer of innovations may propagate his projects, there can be no settlement; if every murmurer at government may diffuse discontent, there can be no peace; and if every sceptic in theology may teach his follies, there can be no religion. The remedy against these evils is to punish the authors; for
it

it is yet allowed, that every society may punish, though not prevent, the publication of opinions which that society shall think pernicious. But this punishment, though it may crush the author, promotes the book; and it seems not more reasonable to leave the right of printing unrestrained, because writers may be afterwards censured, than it would be to sleep with doors unbolted, because by our laws we can hang a thief.

Life of Milton.

OCCASIONAL PUBLICATIONS.

There is, perhaps, no nation in which it is so necessary as in our own, to assemble, from time to time, the small tracts, and fugitive pieces which are ocasionally published; for, beside the general subjects of enquiry which are cultivated by us in common with every other learned nation, our constitution in church and state, naturally gives birth to a multitude of performances, which would either not have been written, or could not have been made public, in any other place.

Origin and importance of Fugitive Pieces, p. 1

PLAYER.

A public performer is so much in the power of spectators, that all unnecessary severity is restrained by that general law of humanity which forbids us to be cruel where there is nothing to be feared.

Idler, vol. 1, p. 138.

In every new performer, something must be pardoned. No man can, by any force of resolution, secure to himself the full possession of his powers, under the eye of a large assembly. Variation of gesture, and flexion of voice, are to be obtained only by experience.

Ibid.

PAINTING.

An historical painter must have an action not successive, but instantaneous; for the time of a picture is a single moment.

Ibid. p. 252.

Though genius is chiefly exerted in historical pictures, and the art of the painter of portraits is often lost in the obscurity of his subject; yet it is in painting as in life, what is greatest is not always best. I should grieve to see *Reynolds* transfer to heroes and to goddesses, to empty splendour and to airy fiction, that art which is now employed in diffusing friendship, in reviving tenderness, in quickening the affections of the absent, and continuing the presence of the dead.

Ibid. p. 251.

PROVIDENCE.

If the extent of the human view could comprehend the whole frame of the universe, perhaps it would be found invariably true, that Providence has given that in greatest plenty which the condition of life makes of the greatest use; and that nothing is penuriously imparted, or placed far from the reach of men, of which a more liberal distribution, or more easy acquisition, would increase real and rational felicity.

Ibid. p. 207.

PUBLIC.

Whatever is found to gratify the public, will be multiplied by the emulation of venders beyond necessity

cessity or use. This plenty, indeed, produces cheapness; but cheapness always ends in negligence and depravation.

Idler, vol. 1, p. 36.

Every man is taught to consider his own happiness as combined with the public prosperity, and to think himself great and powerful in proportion to the greatness and power of his country.

Taxation no Tyranny, p. 19.

POLITENESS.

Politeness is one of those advantages which we never estimate rightly, but by the inconvenience of its loss. Its influence upon the manners is constant and uniform, so that, like an equal motion, it escapes perception. The circumstances of every action are so adjusted to each other, that we do not see where any error could have been committed, and rather acquiesce in its propriety, than admire its exactness.

Rambler, vol. 2, p. 261.

The true effect of genuine politeness seems to be rather *ease*, than *pleasure*. The power of delighting must be conferred by nature, and cannot be delivered by precept, or obtained by imitation; but though it be the privilege of a very small number to ravish and to charm, every man may hope, by rules and caution, not to give pain, and may, therefore, by the help of good breeding, enjoy the kindness of mankind, though he should have no claim to higher distinctions.

Ibid.

When the pale of ceremony is once broken, rudeness and insult soon enter the breach.

Ibid. vol. 4, p. 23.

PRECIPITANCY.

He that too early aspires to honours must resolve to encounter, not only the opposition of interest, but the malignity of envy. He that is too eager to be rich, generally endangers his fortune in wild adventures and uncertain projects; and he that hastens too speedily to reputation, often raises his character by artifices and fallacies, decks himself in colours which quickly fade, or in plumes which accident may shake off or competition pluck away.

Rambler, vol. 3, p. 33.

PLAGIARISM.

When the excellence of a new composition can no longer be contested, and malice is compelled to give way to the unanimity of applause, there is yet this one expedient to be tried—the *charge of plagiarism*. By this, the author may be degraded, though his work be reverenced; and the excellence which we cannot obscure, may be set at such a distance as not to overpower our fainter lustre.

Ibid. p. 224.

The author who imitates his predecessors, only by furnishing himself with thoughts and elegancies out of the same general magazine of literature, can with little more propriety be reproached as a *plagiary*, than the architect can be censured as a mean copier of Angelo, or Wren, because he digs his marble from the same quarry, squares his stones by the fame art, and unites them in columns o the fame orders.

Ibid. p. 225.

POWER.

Power and fuperiority are fo flattering and delightful, that, fraught with temptation, and expofed to danger, as they are, fcarcely any virtue is fo cautious, or any prudence fo timorous, as to decline them. Even thofe that have moſt reverence for the laws of right, are pleafed with fhewing, that not *fear*, but *choice*, regulates their behaviour; and would be thought to comply, rather than obey. We love to overlook the boundaries which we do not wifh to pafs; and, as the Roman fatyriſt remarks, "he that has no defign to take the life of another, is yet glad to have it in his hands."

Ibid. p. 48.

PROMISE.

Every fcholar knows the opinion of Horace concerning thofe that open their undertakings with magnificent promifes; but every man fhould know the dictates of common fenfe and common honefty, names of greater antiquity than that of Horace, who directs, *that no man fhould promife what he cannot perform*.

Review of the Memoirs of the Court of Auguſtus, p. 2.

R.

RAILLERY.

He who is in the exercife of raillery fhould prepare himfelf to receive it in turn. When Lewis the XIV. was asked why, with so much wit, he never attempted raillery, he answered, that he who practised raillery, ought to bear it in his turn, and that to stand the butt of raillery was not suitable to the dignity of a King.

Notes upon Shakespeare, vol. 5, p. 364.

RESOLUTION.

When desperate ills demand a speedy cure, distrust is cowardice, and prudence, folly.

Irene, p. 52.

Resolution and success reciprocally produce each other.

Life of Drake, p. 174.

Marshal Turenne, among the acknowledgements which he used to pay in conversation to the memory of those by whom he had been instructed in the art of war, mentioned one, with honour, who taught him *not to spend his time in regretting any mistake which he had made, but to set himself immediately, and vigorously, to repair it.* Patience and submission should be carefully distinguished from cowardice and indolence; we are not to repine, but we may lawfully struggle; for the calamities of life, like the necessities of nature, are calls to labour, and exercises of diligence.

Rambler, vol. 2, p. 195.

Some firmness and resolution is necessary to the discharge of duty, but it is a very unhappy state of life in which the necessity of such struggles frequently occurs; for no man is defeated without some resentment, which will be continued with obstinacy, while he believes himself in the right, and exerted with bitterness, if even to his own conviction, he is detected in the wrong.

Ibid. vol. 2, p. 17.

To have attempted much is always laudable, even when the enterprize is above the strength that undertakes it. To rest below his own aim, is incident to every one whose fancy is active, and whose views are comprehensive; nor is any man satisfied with himself, because he has done much, but because he can conceive little.

Preface to Dictionary, fol. p. 5.

There is nothing which we estimate so fallaciously as the force of our own resolutions, nor any fallacy which we so unwillingly and tardily detect. He that has resolved a thousand and a thousand times, deserted his own purpose, yet suffers no abatement of his confidence, but still believes himself his own master, and able, by innate vigour of soul, to press forward to his end, through all the obstructions that inconveniencies or delights can put in his way.

Idler, vol. 1, p. 150.

Nothing will ever be attempted if all possible objections must be first overcome.

Prince of Abyssinia, p. 40.

Most men may review all the lives that have passed within their observation, without remembering one efficacious resolution, or being able to tell a single instance of a course of practice suddenly changed, in consequence of a change of opinion, or an establishment of determination. Many, indeed alter their conduct, and are not at fifty, what they were at thirty; but they commonly va-

ried imperceptibly from themselves, followed the train of external causes, and rather suffered reformation than made it.
Idler, vol. 1, p. 151.

RELIGION.

To be of no church, is dangerous. Religion, of which the rewards are distant, and which is animated only by faith and hope, will glide by degrees out of the mind, unless it be invigorated and re-impressed by external ordinances, by stated calls to worship, and the salutary influence of example.
Life of Milton.

That conversion of religion will always be suspected, that apparently concurs with interest. He that never findsh is error, 'till it hinders his progress towards wealth and honour, will not be thought to love truth only for herself. Yet it may happen, information may come at a commodious time, and as truth and interest are not by any fatal necessity at variance, that one may, by accident, introduce the other.
Life of Dryden.

Philosophy may infuse stubbornness, but Religion only can give patience.
Idler, vol. 1, p. 234.

Malevolence to the clergy, is seldom at a great distance from irreverence to Religion.
Life of Dryden.

The great task of him who conducts his life by the precepts of religion, is to make the future predominate over the present, to impress upon his mind

mind so strong a sense of the importance of obedience to the divine will, of the value of the reward promised to virtue, and the terrors of the punishment denounced against crimes, as may overbear all the temptations which temporal hope or fear can bring in his way, and enable him to bid equal defiance to joy and sorrow, to turn away at one time from the allurements of ambition, and push forward at another against the threats of calamity.

Rambler, vol. 1, p. 38.

A man who has once settled his religious opinions, does not love to have the tranquillity of his conviction disturbed.

Western Islands, p. 280.

Men may differ from each other in many religious opinions, yet all may retain the essentials of christianity; men may sometimes eagerly dispute, and yet not differ much from one another. The rigorous persecutors of error should therefore enlighten their zeal with knowledge, and temper their orthodoxy with charity; that charity, without which, orthodoxy is vain; that charity " that thinketh no evil," but " hopeth all things, and endureth all things."

Life of Sir T. Browne, p. 248.

RICHES.

Poverty is an evil always in our view; an evil complicated with so many circumstances of uneasiness and vexation, that every man is studious to avoid it. Some degree of riches therefore is required, that we may be exempt from the gripe of necessity. When this purpose is once attained, we naturally wish for more, that the evil which is regarded

garded with so much horror, may be yet at a greater distance from us; as he that has at once felt, or dreaded the paw of a savage, will not be at rest, till they are parted by some barrier, which may take away all possibility of a second attack.

Rambler, vol. 1, p. 231.

Whoever shall look heedfully upon those who are eminent for their riches, will not think their condition such, as that he should hazard his quiet, and much less his virtue, to obtain it; for all that great wealth generally gives above a moderate fortune, is more room for the freaks of caprice, and more privilege for ignorance and vice; a quicker succession of flatteries, and a larger circle of voluptuousness.

Rambler, vol. 1, p. 232.

There is one reason seldom remarked, which makes riches less desirable. Too much wealth is generally the occasion of poverty. He whom the wantonness of abundance has once softened, easily sinks into neglect of his affairs; and he that thinks he can afford to be negligent, is not far from being poor. He will soon be involved in perplexities, which his inexperience will render insurmountable; he will fly for help to those whose interest it is that he should be more distressed; and will be, at last, torn to pieces by the vultures that always hover over our fortunes in decay.

Ibid. p. 233.

Wealth is nothing in itself; it is not useful but when it departs from us: its value is found only in that which it can purchase, which if we suppose it put to its best use, seems not much to deserve
the

the defire or envy of a wife man. It is certain that, with regard to corporal enjoyment, money can neither open new avenues to pleafure, nor block up the paffages of anguifh. Difeafe and infirmity ftill continue to torture and enfeeble, perhaps exafperated by luxury, or promoted by foftnefs.

Ibid. vol. 2, p. 29.

With regard to the mind, it has rarely been obferved, that wealth contributes much to quicken the difcernment, enlarge the capacity, or elevate the imagination; but may, by hiring flattery, or laying diligence afleep, confirm error, or harden ftupidity. Wealth cannot confer greatnefs; for nothing can make that great, which the degree of nature has ordained to be little. The bramble may be placed in a hot-bed, but can never become an oak.—Even Royalty itfelf is not able to give that dignity, which it happens not to find, but oppreffes feeble minds, though it may elevate the ftrong. The world has been governed in the name of Kings, whofe exiftence has fcarcely been perceived, by any real effects beyond their own palaces.— When, therefore, the defire of wealth is taking hold of the heart, let us look round and fee how it operates upon thofe whofe induftry or fortune has obtained it. When we find them oppreffed with their own abundance, luxurious without pleafure, idle without eafe, impatient and querulous in themfelves, and defpifed or hated by the reft of mankind, we fhall foon be convinced, that if the real wants of our condition are fatisfied, there remains little to be fought with folicitude, or defired with eagernefs.

Ibid. p. 30.

Though

Though riches often prompt extragavant hopes and fallacious appearances; there are purposes to which a wise man may be delighted to apply them. They may, by a rational distribution to those who want them, ease the pains of helpless disease, still the throbs of restless anxiety, relieve innocence from oppression, and raise imbecility to cheerfulness and vigour. This they will enable a man to perform; and this will afford the only happiness ordained for our present state, the consequence of divine favour, and the hope of future rewards.

Rambler, vol. 3, p. 94.

It is observed of gold, by an old epigrammatist, "that to have it, is to be in fear, and to want it, to be in sorrow."

Ibid. p. 155.

Every man is rich or poor, according to the proportion between his desires and enjoyments. Any enlargement of riches is therefore equally destructive to happiness with the diminution of possession; and he that teaches another to long for what he shall never obtain, is no less an enemy to his quiet, than if he had robbed him of part of his patrimony.

Ibid. vol. 4, p. 17.

Whosoever rises above those who once pleased themselves with equality, will have many malevolent gazers at his eminence. To gain sooner than others that which all pursue with the same ardour, and to which all imagine themselves entitled, will for ever be a crime. When those who started with us in the race of life, leave us so far behind, that we have little hope to overtake them, we revenge our disappointment by remarks on the arts of supplantation by which they gained the advantage, or on the folly and arrogance with which they possess it; of them whose rise we could not hinder, we solace ourselves by prognosticating the fall. Riches, therefore, perhaps do not so often produce crimes as incite accusers.

Ibid. p. 68.

It must, however, be confessed, that as all sudden changes are dangerous, a quick transition from poverty to abundance can seldom be made with safety. He that has long lived within sight of pleasures which he could not reach, will need more than common moderation not to lose his reason in unbounded riot, when they are first put into his power.

Ibid. p. 69.

Of riches, as of every thing else, the hope is more than the enjoyment. Whilst we consider them as the means to be used at some future time, for the attainment of felicity, we press on our pursuit ardently and vigorously, and that ardor secures us from weariness of ourselves; but no sooner do we sit down to enjoy our acquisitions, than we find them insufficient to fill up the vacuities of life.

Idler, vol. 2, p. 115.

It is surely very narrow policy that supposes money to be the chief good.

Life of Milton.

It is not hard to discover that riches always procure protection for themselves; that they dazzle the eyes of enquiry, divert the celerity of pursuit, or appease the ferocity of vengeance. When any

any man is incontestably known to have large possessions, very few think it requisite to enquire by what practices they were obtained: the resentment of mankind rages only against the struggles of feeble and timorous corruption; but when it has surmounted the first opposition, it is afterwards supported by favour, and animated by applause.

Rambler, vol. 3, p. 154.

Money, in whatever hands, will confer power. Distress will fly to immediate refuge, without much consideration of remote consequences.

Ibid. p. 222.

Though the rich very rarely desire to be thought poor, the poor are strongly tempted to assume the appearance of wealth.

Idler, vol. 2, p. 115.

One cause, which is not always observed, of the insufficiency of riches, is, that they very seldom make their owner rich. To be rich, is to have more than is desired, and more than is wanted; to have something which may be spent without reluctance, and scattered without care; with which the sudden demands of desire may be gratified, the casual freaks of fancy indulged, or the unexpected opportunities of benevolence improved.

Ibid. p. 116.

When the power of birth and station ceases, no hope remains but from the prevalence of money.

Western Islands, p. 216.

Money confounds subordination, by overpowering the distinctions of rank and birth; and weakens authority,

authority, by supplying power of resistance, or expedients for escape.

Ibid. p. 263.

Nothing is more uncertain than the estimation of wealth by denominated money. The precious metals never retain long the same proportion to real commodities, and the same names in different ages do not imply the same quantity of metal; so that it is equally difficult to know how much money was contained in any nominal sum, and to find what any supposed quantity of gold, or silver would purchase; both which are necessary to the commensuration of money, or the adjustment of proportion between the same sums at different periods of time. Bread-corn is the most certain standard of the necessaries of life.

Life of Roger Ascham, p. 243.

COMPARISON BETWEEN RICHES AND UNDERSTANDING.

As many more can discover that a man is richer than themselves, superiority of understanding is not so readily acknowledged, as that of fortune; nor is that haughtiness, which the consciousness of great abilities incites, borne with the same submission, as the tyranny of affluence.

Life of Savage.

COMPARISON BETWEEN RICHES AND POWER.

Power and wealth supply the place of each other. Power confers the ability of gratifying our desires without the consent of others; wealth enables us to obtain the consent of others to our gratification. Power, simply considered, whatever it confers on one, must take from another. Wealth enables its

owner

owner to give it to others, by taking only from himself. Power pleases the violent and the proud; wealth delights the placid and the timorous. Youth therefore flies at power, and age grovels after riches.

Western Islands, p. 216.

RIDICULE.

The assertion of Shaftesbury, that ridicule is the test of truth, is foolish. If ridicule be applied to any position as the test of truth, it will then become a question, whether such ridicule be just, and this can only be decided by the application of truth, as the test of ridicule. Two men fearing, one a real, and the other a fancied danger, will be, for awhile, equally exposed to the inevitable consequences of cowardice, contemptuous censure, and ludicrous representation; and the true state of both cases must be known, before it can be decided whose terror is rational, and whose is ridiculous, who is to be pitied, and who to be despised.

Life of Akenside.

He that indulges himself in ridiculing the little imperfections and weaknesses of his friends, will in time find mankind united against him. The man who sees another ridiculed before him, though he may, for the present, concur in the general laugh, yet, in a cool hour, will consider the same trick might be played against himself; but when there is no sense of this danger, the natural pride of human nature rises against him, who, by general censures, lays claim to general superiority.

Rambler, vol. 4, p. 81.

REFLECTION.

REFLECTION.

It may be laid down as a position which will seldom deceive, that when a man cannot bear his own company, there is something wrong. He must fly from himself, either because he finds a tediousness in the equipoise of an empty mind, which having no tendency to one motion more than another, but as it is impelled by some external power, must always have recourse to foreign objects; or he must be afraid of the intrusion of some unpleasing ideas, and perhaps is struggling to escape from the remembrance of a loss, the fear of a calamity, or some other thought of greater horror.

Ibid. vol. 1, p. 27.

There are fewer higher gatifications than that of reflection on surmounted evils, when they were not incurred nor protracted by our fault, and neither reproach us with cowardice nor guilt.

Ibid. vol. 4, p. 233.

All useless misery is certainly folly, and he that feels evils before they come, may be deservedly censured; yet surely to dread the future, is more reasonable than to lament the past. The business of life is to go forward; he who sees evils in prospect, meets it in his way; but he who catches it in retrospection, turns back to find it.

Idler, vol. 1, p. 111.

There is certainly no greater happiness than to be able to look back on a life usefully and virtuously employed; to trace our own progress in existence, by such tokens as excite neither shame nor sorrow. It ought therefore to be the care of those who wish to pass the last hours with comfort, to

lay up such a treasure of pleasing ideas, as shall support the expences of that time, which is to depend wholly upon the fund already acquired.
Rambler, vol. 1, p. 250 & 252.

The remembrance of a crime committed in vain, has been considered as the most painful of all reflections.
Life of Pope.

REBELLION.

To bring misery on those who have not deserved it, is part of the aggregated guilt of rebellion.
Taxation no Tyranny, p. 61.

Nothing can be more noxious to society, than that erroneous clemency, which, when a rebellion is suppressed, exacts no forfeiture, and establishes no securities, but leaves the rebels in their former state.
Ibid. p. 87.

REFINEMENT.

He that pleases himself too much with minute exactness, and submits to endure nothing in accomodations, attendance, or address, below the point of perfection, will, whenever he enters the croud of life, be harrassed with innumerable distresses, from which those who have not, in the same manner, increased their sensations, find no disturbance. His exotic softness will shrink at the coarseness of vulgar felicity, like a plant transplanted to Northern nurseries, from the dews and sun-shine of the tropical regions. It is well known, that exposed to a microscrope, the smoothest polish of the most solid bodies discovers cavities and prominencies; and that the softest bloom of roseate virginity
repels

repels the eye with excrescencies and discolorations. Thus the senses, as well as the perceptions, may be improved to our own disquiet; and we may, by diligent cultivation of the powers of dislike, raise in time an artificial fastidiousness, which shall fill the imagination with phantoms of turpitude, shew us the naked skeleton of every delight, and present us only with the pains of pleasure, and the deformities of beauty.

Rambler, vol. 3, p. 37.

RECOLLECTION.

That which is obvious is not always known; and what is known, is not always present. Sudden fits of inadvertancy will surprise vigilance; slight avocations will seduce attention; and casual eclipses of the mind will darken learning; so that the writer shall often, in vain, trace his memory at the moment of need, for that which yesterday he knew with intuitive readiness, and which will come uncalled into his thoughts to-morrow.

Preface to Dictionary, fol. p. 10.

RETIREMENT.

There is a time when the claims of the public are satisfied; then a man might properly retire to review his life, and purify his heart.

Prince of Abyssinia, p. 135.

Some suspension of common affairs, some pause of temporal pain and pleasure, is doubtless necessary to him that deliberates for eternity, who is forming the only plan in which miscarriage cannot be repaired, and examining the only question in which mistake cannot be rectified.

Rambler, vol. 3, p. 29.

RESENTMENT.

It is too common for those who have unjustly suffered pain, to inflict it likewise in their turn with the same injustice, and to imagine they have a right to treat others as they themselves have been treated.

Life of Savage.

Resentment is an union of sorrow with malignity; a combination of a passion which all endeavour to avoid, with a passion which all concur to detest. The man who retires to meditate mischief, and to exasperate his own rage; whose thoughts are employed only on means of distress, and contrivances of ruin; whose mind never pauses from the remembrance of his own sufferings, but to indulge some hope of enjoying the calamities of another, may justly be numbered among the most miserable of human beings, among those who are guilty without reward, who have neither the gladness of prosperity, nor the calm of innocence.

Rambler, vol. 4, p. 137.

RELAXATION.

After the exercises which the health of the body requires, and which have themselves a natural tendency to actuate and invigorate the mind, the most eligible amusement of a rational being, seems to be that interchange of thoughts which is practised in free and easy conversation, where suspicion is banished by experience, and emulation by benevolence; where every man speaks with no other restraint than unwillingness to offend, and hears with no other disposition than desire to be pleased.

Ibid. vol. 2, p. 204.

REPENTANCE.

REPENTANCE.

Repentance is the change of the heart, from that of an evil to a good disposition; it is that disposition of mind by which " the wicked man turneth away from his wickedness, and doth that which is lawful and right;" and when this change is made, the repentance is complete.

Convicts Address, p. 14 & 15.

Repentance, however difficult to be practised, is, if it be explained without superstition, easily understood. *Repentance is the relinquishment of any practice, from the conviction that it has offended God.* Sorrow, and fear, and anxiety, are properly not parts, but adjuncts of repentance; yet they are too closely connected with it, to be easily separated; for they not only mark its sincerity, but promote its efficacy.

No man commits any act of negligence or obstinacy, by which his safety or happiness in this world is endangered, without feeling the pungency of remorse. He who is fully convinced, that he suffers by his own failure, can never forbear to trace back his miscarriage to its first cause, to image to himself a contrary behaviour, and to form involuntary resolutions against the like fault, even when he knows that he shall never again have the power of committing it. Danger, considered as imminent, naturally produces such trepidations of impatience, as leave all human means of safety behind him: he that has once caught an alarm of terror, is every moment seised with useless anxieties, adding one security to another, trembling with sudden doubts, and distracted by the perpetual occurrence of new expedients. If, therefore, he whose crimes have deprived him of the favour of

God, can reflect upon his conduct without disturbance, or can at will banish the reflection; if he who considers himself as suspended over the abyss of eternal perdition only by the thread of life, which must soon part by its own weakness, and which the wing of every minute may divide, can cast his eyes round him without shuddering with horror, or panting with security; what can he judge of himself, but that he is not yet awakened to sufficient conviction, since every loss is more lamented than the loss of the divine favour, and every danger more dreaded than the danger of final condemnation?

Rambler, vol. 3, p. 28 & 29.

The completion and sum of repentance is a change of life. That sorrow which dictates no caution, that fear which does not quicken our escape, that austerity which fails to rectify our affections, are vain and unavailing. But sorrow and terror must naturally precede reformation; for what other cause can produce it? He, therefore, that feels himself alarmed by his conscience, anxious for the attainment of a better state, and afflicted by the memory of his past faults, may justly conclude, that the great work of repentance is begun, and hope, by retirement and prayer, the natural and religious means of strengthening his conviction, to impress upon his mind such a sense of the divine presence, as may overpower the blandishments of secular delights, and enable him to advance from one degree of holiness to another, till death shall set him free from doubt and contest, misery and temptation.

What better can we do than prostrate fall
Before him reverent; and there confess
Humbly

Humbly our faults, and pardon beg, with tears
Wat'ring the ground, and with our sighs the air
Frequenting, sent from hearts contrite, in sign
Of sorrow unfeign'd, and humiliation meek?

Ibid. p. 30.

REVENGE.

Forbearance of revenge, when revenge is within reach, is scarcely ever to be found among princes.

Memoirs of the King of Prussia, p. 137.

RESPECT.

Respect is often paid in proportion as it is claimed.

Idler, vol. 1, p. 276.

LITERARY REPUTATION.

Of the decline of literary reputation, many causes may be assigned. It is commonly lost because it never was deserved, and was conferred at first, not by the suffrage of criticism, but by the fondness of friendship, or servility of flattery. Many have lost the final reward of their labours, because they were too hasty to enjoy it. They have laid hold on recent occurrences and eminent names, and delighted their readers with allusions and remarks, in which all were interested, and to which therefore all were attentive; but the effect ceased with its cause; the time quietly came when new events drove the former from memory, when the vicissitudes of the world brought new hopes and fears, transferred the love and hatred of the public to other agents, and the writers whose works were no longer assisted by gratitude or resentment, was left to the cold regard of idle curiosity.

curiosity. But he that writes upon general principles, or delivers universal truths, may hope to be often read, because his work will be equally useful at all times, and in every country; but he cannot expect it to be received with eagerness, or to spread with rapidity, because desire can have no particular stimulation. That which is to be loved long, is to be loved with reason, rather than with passion.

Ibid. vol. 2. p. 36 & 37.

REASON AND FANCY.

Reason is like the sun, of which the light is constant, uniform and lasting. Fancy, a meteor of bright, but transitory lustre, irregular in its motion, and delusive in its direction.

Prince of Abyssinia, p. 116.

RHYME.

Rhyme, says Milton, and says truly, is *no necessary adjunct of true poetry*. But, perhaps, of poetry, as a mental operation, metre or music is no necessary adjunct; it is, however, by the music of metre that poetry has been discriminated in all languages; and in languages melodiously constructed, by a due proportion of long and short syllables, metre is sufficient. But one language cannot communicate its rules to another. Where metre is scanty and imperfect, some help is necessary. The music of the English heroic line strikes the ear so faintly, that it is easily lost, unless all the syllables of every line co-operate together. This co-operation can be only obtained by the preservation of every verse, unmingled with another, as a distinct system of sounds; and this distinctness

tinctness is obtained, and preserved, by the *artifice of rhyme*.
Life of Milton.

To attempt any further improvement of *versification*, beyond what Pope has given us in his translation of Homer's Iliad, will be dangerous. Art and diligence have now done their best; and what shall be added, will be the effort of tedious toil, and needless curiosity.
Life of Pope.

RHETORICIAN.
There is no credit due to a rhetorician's account either of good or evil.
Life of Roger Ascham, p. 247.

REPROOF.
Reproof should not exhaust its power upon petty failings; let it watch diligently against the incursion of vice, and leave foppery and futility to die of themselves.
Idler, vol. 1, p. 141.

RULES.
Rules may obviate faults, but can never confer beauties.
Idler, vol. 2, p. 26.

CHARACTER OF THE ANCIENT ROMANS.
While they were poor, *they robbed mankind*; and as soon as they became rich, *they robbed one another*.
Review of the Memoirs of the Court of Augustus, p. 6.

RIGHT.
The utmost exertion of right is always invidious; and where claims are not easily determinable, is always dangerous.
Falkland Islands, p. 59.

S.

SATIRE.

Personal resentment, though no laudable motive to satire, can add great force to general principle. Self-love is a busy prompter.

Life of Dryden.

All truth is valuable, and satyrical criticism may be considered as useful, when it rectifies error, and improves judgment. He that refines the public taste, is a public benefactor.

Life of Pope.

SATYRIST.

In defence of him who has satyrized the man he has once praised, it may be alledged, that the object of his satire has changed his principles, and that he who was once deservedly commended, may be afterwards satyrized with equal justice, or that the poet was dazzled with the appearance of virtue, and found the man whom he had celebrated, when he had an opportunity of examining him more nearly, unworthy of the panegyric which he had too hastily bestowed; and that, as false satire ought to be recanted, for the sake of him whose reputation may be injured, false praise ought likewise to be obviated, lest the distinction between vice and virtue should be lost, lest a bad man, should be trusted upon the credit of his encomiast, or lest others should endeavour to obtain the like praises by the same means.——But though these excuses may be often plausible, and sometimes just, they are seldom satisfactory to mankind; and the writer who is not constant to his subject, quickly sinks into contempt; his satire loses its force, and his panegyric its value; and he is only considered at one time as a flatterer, and as a calumniator at another. To avoid these imputations, it is only necessary to follow the rules of virtue, and to preserve an unvaried regard to truth. For though it is undoubtedly possible, that a man, however cautious, may be sometimes deceived by an artful appearance of virtue, or a false appearance of guilt, such errors will not be frequent; and it will be allowed, that the name of an author would never have been made contemptible, had no man ever said what he did not think, or misled others but when he was himself deceived.

Life of Savage.

SECRETS.

Secrets are so seldom kept, that it may be with some reason doubted, whether a secret has not some subtle volatility by which it escapes, imperceptibly, at the smallest vent, or some power of fermentation, by which it expands itself, so as to burst the heart that will not give it way.

Rambler, vol. 1, p. 75.

To tell our own secrets is generally folly, but that folly is without guilt. To communicate those with which we are entrusted, is always treachery, and treachery for the most part combined with folly.

Ibid. p. 76.

The vanity of being known to be trusted with a secret, is generally one of the chief motives to disclose it; for, however absurd it may be thought to boast an honour by an act which shews that it was conferred without merit, yet most men seem rather inclined to confess the want of virtue than of importance, and more willingly shew their influence, though at the expence of their probity, than glide through life with no other pleasure than the private conscioufness of fidelity, which, while it is preserved, must be without praise, except from the single person who tries and knows it.

Ibid. p. 75.

The whole doctrine, as well as the practice of secrecy, is so perplexing and dangerous, that next to him who is compelled to trust, that man is unhappy who is *chosen to be trusted*; for he is often involved in scruples, without the liberty of calling in the help of any other understanding; he is frequently drawn into guilt, under the appearance of friendship and honesty; and sometimes subjected to suspicion by the treachery of others, who are engaged without his knowledge in the same schemes: for he that has *one* confident, has generally *more*; and when he is, at last, betrayed, is in doubt on whom he shall fix the crime.

Ibid. p. 79.

The rules that may be proposed concerning secrecy, and which it is not safe to deviate from, without long and exact deliberation, are,

First, *Never to solicit the knowledge of a secret*; nor *willingly*, nor *without many limitations*, accept such confidence, when it is offered.

Second, when a secret is once admitted, to consider the trust as of a very high nature, *important as society*—and *sacred as truth*—and therefore not to be violated for *any incidental convenience*, or *slight appearance of contrary fitness*.

Ibid. p. 80.

SCEPTICISM.

There are some men of narrow views and groveling conceptions, who, without the instigation of personal malice, treat every new attempt as wild and chimerical, and look upon every endeavour to depart from the beaten track, as the rash effort of a warm imagination, or the glittering speculation of an exalted mind, that may please and dazzle for a time, but can produce no real, or lasting advantage.

Life of Blake, p. 191.

To play with important truths, to disturb the repose of established tenets, to subtilize objections, and elude proof, is too often the sport of youthful vanity, of which maturer experience commonly repents. There is a time when every man is weary of raising difficulties only to task himself with the solution, and desires to enjoy truth, without the labour, or hazard, of contest.

Life of Sir T. Browne, p. 279.

SEDUCTION.

There is not perhaps, in all the stores of ideal anguish, a thought more painful than the consciousness of having propagated corruption by vitiating principles; of having not only drawn others from the paths of virtue, but blocked up the way by which they should return; of having blinded them to every beauty but the paint of pleasure; and deafened them to every call, but the alluring voice of the syrens of destruction.

Rambler, vol. 1, p. 191.

SOLITUDE.

In solitude, if we escape the example of bad men, we likewise want the counsel and conversation of the good.
Prince of Abyssinia, p. 133.

The life of a Solitary man will be certainly miserable, but not certainly devout.
Ibid.

To those who pass their time in solitude and retirement, it has been justly objected, that if they are happy, they are happy only in being useless; that mankind is one vast republic, where every individual receives many benefits from the labour of others; which by labouring in his turn for others, he is obliged to repay; and that where the united efforts of all are not able to exempt all from misery, none have a right to withdraw from their task of vigilance, or be idulged in idle wisdom and solitary pleasures.
Idler, vol. 1, p. 102.

SORROW.

The sharpest and most melting sorrow is that which arises from the loss of those whom we have loved with tenderness. But friendship between mortals can be contracted on no other terms, than that one must sometimes mourn for the other's death; and this grief will always yield to the survivor, one consolation proportionate to his affliction; for the pain, whatever it be, that he himself feels, his friend has escaped.
Rambler, vol. 1. p. 104.

It is urged by some, as a remedy for sorrow, to keep our minds always suspended in such indifference,

erence, that we may change the Objects about us without emotion. An exact compliance with this rule might perhaps contribute to tranquillity, but surely it would never produce happiness. He that regards none so much as to be afraid of losing them, must live for ever without the gentle pleasures of sympathy and confidence. He must feel no melting confidence, no warmth of benevolence, nor any of those honest joys which nature annexes to the power of pleasing. And as no man can justly claim more tenderness than he pays, he must forfeit his share in that officious and watchful kindness which love only can dictate, and those lenient endearments by which love only can soften life.

Ibid. p. 285.

The safe and general antidote against sorrow, is, employment. It is commonly observed, that among soldiers and seaman, though there is much kindness, there is little grief. They see their friend fall without any of that lamentation which is indulged in security and idleness, because they have no leisure to spare from the care of themselves; and whoever shall keep his thoughts equally busy, will find himself equally unaffected with irretrievable losses.

Ibid. p. 287.

Sorrow is a kind of rust to the Soul, which every new idea contributes in its passage to scour away. It is the putrefaction of stagnant life, and is remedied by exercise and motion.

Ibid.

STYLE.

The polite are always catching at modish innovations, and the learned depart from established forms

forms of speech, in hopes of finding or making better. But propriety resides in that kind of conversation which is above grossness and below refinement.

Preface to Shakespeare, p. 18.

Words being arbitrary, must owe their power to association, and have the influence, and that only, which custom has given them.

Life of Cowley.

Words too familiar, or too remote, defeat the purpose of a poet. From these sounds, which we hear on small, or coarse occasions, we do not easily receive strong impressions or delightful images; and words to which we are nearly strangers, whenever they occur, draw that attention on *themselves*, which they should convey to *things*.

Life of Dryden.

An epithet, or metaphor, drawn from nature, ennobles art; an epithet or metaphor drawn from art, degrades nature.

Life of Gray.

There is a mode of style for which the masters of oratory have not as yet found a name; a style, by which the most evident truths are so obscured, that they can no longer be perceived, and the most familiar propositions so disguised, that they cannot be known. Every other kind of eloquence is the dress of sense, but this is the mask by which a true master of his art will so effectually conceal it, that a man will as easily mistake his own positions, if he meets them thus transformed, as he may pass, in a masquerade, his nearest acquaintance.

Idler, vol. 1, p. 203.

Few

Few faults of style, whether real or imaginary, excite the malignity of a more numerous class of readers, than the use of hard words --- But words are only hard to those who do not understand them; and the critic ought always to enquire, whether he is incommoded by the fault of the writer, or by his own.
Ibid. vol. 2, p. 96.

Every language of a learned nation necessarily divides itself into diction, scholastic and popular, grave and familiar, elegant and gross; and, from a nice distinction of these different parts, arises a great part of the beauties of style.
Life of Dryden.

It is not easy to distinguish affectation from habit; he that has once studiously formed a style, rarely writes afterwards with complete ease.
Life of Pope.

SINGULARITY.

Singularity, as it implies a contempt of general practice, is a kind of defiance, which justly provokes the history of ridicule. He, therefore, who indulges peculiar habits, is worse than others if he be not better.
Life of Swift.

SUBORDINATION.

He that encroaches on another's dignity, puts himself in his power; he is either repelled with helpless indignity, or endured by clemency and condescension. A great mind disdains to hold any thing by courtesy, and therefore never usurps what a lawful claimant may take away.
Ibid.

No man can pay a more servile tribute to the great, than by suffering his liberty, in their presence, to aggrandize him in his own esteem. Between different ranks of the community, there is necessarily some distance. He who is called by his superior to pass the interval, may very properly accept the invitation; but petulence and obtrusion, are rarely produced by magnanimity, nor have often any nobler cause, than the pride of importance, and the malice of inferiority. He who knows himself necessary, may set, while that necessity lasts, a high value upon himself; as in a lower condition, a servant eminently skilful may be saucy, but he is saucy, because he is servile.

Ibid.

A due regard to subordination is the power that keeps peace and order in the world.

Notes upon Shakespeare, vol. 9, p. 290.

SOLICITATION.

Every man of known influence has so many petitions which he cannot grant, that he must necessarily offend more than he gratifies; as the preference given to one, affords all the rest a reason for complaint " When I give away a place, (said Lewis the XIVth) I make an hundred discontented, and one ungrateful."

Life of Swift.

SUSPICION.

Suspicion is no less an enemy to virtue, than to happiness. He that is already corrupt is naturally suspicious; and he that becomes suspicious, will quickly be corrupt.

Rambler, vol. 2, p. 145.

He that suffers by imposture, has too often his virtue more impaired than his fortune. But as it is necessary not to invite robbery by supineness, so it is our duty not to suppress tenderness by suspicion. It is better to suffer wrong than to do it; and happier to be sometimes cheated, than not to trust.

Ibid. p. 147.

He who is spontaneously suspicious, may be justly charged with radical corruption; for if he has not known the prevalence of dishonesty by information, nor had time to discern it with his own eyes, whence can he take his measures of judgment but from himself?

Ibid. vol. 4, p. 86.

SUPERIORITY.

The superiority of some is merely local. They are *great*, because their associates are *little*.

Life of Swift.

SCRIPTURE.

Idle and indecent applications of sentences taken from scripture, is a mode of merriment which a good man dreads for its profaneness, and a witty man disdains for its easiness and vulgarity.

Life of Pope.

All *amplification of sacred history* is *frivolous* and *vain*; all addition to that which is already sufficient for the purposes of religion, seems not only *useless*, but in some degree *profane*.

Life of Cowley.

SIMILE.

A simile, to be perfect, must both illustrate and ennoble the subject; must shew it to the understanding

standing in a clearer view, and display it to the fancy with greater dignity; but either of these qualities may be sufficient to recommend it. In didactic poetry, of which the great purpose is instruction, a simile may be praised which illustrates, though it does not enoble. In heroics, that may be admitted which enobles, though it does not illustrate. That it may be complete, it is required to exhibit, independently of its references, a pleasing image; for a simile is said to be a short episode.

Life of Pope.

SHAME.

Shame, above every other passion, propagates itself.

Rambler, vol. 3, p. 309.

It is, perhaps, kindly provided by nature, that as the feathers and strength of a bird grow together, and her wings are not completed till she is able to fly; so some proportion should be observed in the human mind, between judgment and courage. The precipitation of experience is therefore restrained by *shame*, and we remain shackled by timidity, till we have learned to speak and act with propriety.

Ibid. p. 316.

Shame operates most strongly in our earliest years.

Notes upon Shakespeare, vol. 5, p. 79.

STUDY.

As in life, so in study, it is dangerous to do more things than one at a time; and the mind is not to be harrassed with unnecessary obstructions, in a way of which the natural and unavoidable asperity is such, as too frequently produces despair.

Preface to the Preceptor, p. 65.

The predominance of a favourite study, affects all subordinate operations of the intellect.

Life of Cowley.

SOBRIETY.

Sobriety, or temperance, is nothing but the forbearance of pleasure; and if peasure was not followed by pain, who would forbear it!

Idler, vol. 2, p. 208.

SCARCITY.

Value is more frequently raised by *scarcity* than by use. That which lay neglected when it was common, rises in estimation as its quantity becomes less. We seldom learn the true want of what we have, till it is discovered that we can have no more.

Ibid. p. 280.

SENTENCES.

In all pointed sentences, some degree of accuracy must be sacrificed to concifeness.

Bravery of English Common Soldiers, p. 324.

SUCCESS AND MISCARRIAGE.

Success and miscarriage have the same effects in all conditions. The prosperous are feared, hated, and flattered; and the unfortunate avoided, pitied, and despised.

Idler, vol. 2, p. 277.

SHAKESPEARE.

Of all the disputed plays of Shakespeare, except *Titus Andronicus*, it may be asked, if they are taken from him, *to whom shall they be given?* for it will be found more credible that Shakespeare might sometimes sink below his *highest flights*, than that any other should rise up to his *lowest*.

Notes upon Shakespeare, vol. 1, p. 216.

Each change of many-coloured life he drew,
Exhausted worlds, and then imagin'd new:
Existence saw him spurn her bounded reign,
And panting Time toil'd after him in vain.

Prologue at the opening of Drury-lane Theatre.

SUPERFLUITIES.

Nothing gives so much offence to the lower ranks of mankind, as the sight of superfluities merely ostentatious.

Notes upon Shakespeare, vol. 6, p. 339.

GOOD-SENSE.

Good-sense is a sedate and quiescent quality, which manages its possessions well, but does not encrease them; it collects few materials for its own operations, and preserves safety, but never gains supremacy.

Life of Pope.

RURAL SPORTS.

It is probable all the sports of the field are of Gothic original; the antients neither hunted by the scent, nor seem much to have practised horsemanship as an exercise; and though in their works there is mention of *Aucupium* and *Piscatio*, they
seem

seem no more to have been considered as diversions, than agriculture, or any other manual labour.

Life of Sir T. Brown, p. 269.

SEASONS.

It is observed by *Milton*, that he who neglects to visit the country in *spring*, and rejects the pleasures that are then in their first bloom and fragrance, is guilty of "*sullenness against nature.*" If we allot different duties to different seasons, he may be charged with equal disobedience to the voice of nature, who looks on the bleak hills, and leafless woods, without seriousness and awe. Spring is the season of gaiety, and winter of terror. In spring, the heart of tranquillity dances to the melody of the groves, and the eye of benevolence sparkles at the sight of happiness and plenty; in the winter, compassion melts at universal calamity, and the tear of softness starts at the wailings of hunger, and the cries of creation in distress.

Rambler, vol. 2, p. 149.

SUBLIMITY.

Sublimity is produced by *aggregation*, and *littleness* by *dispersion*.—Great thoughts are always general, and consist in positions not limitted by exceptions, and in descriptions not descending to minuteness.

Life of Cowley.

SCIENCE.

Divide and *conquer*, is a principle equally just in science as in policy.

Rambler, vol. 3, p. 187.

Every science has its difficulties which yet call for solution, before we attempt new systems of knowledge;

knowledge; as every country has its forests and marshes, which it would be wise to cultivate and drain, before distant colonies are projected as a necessary discharge of the exuberance of inhabitants.

Ibid. p. 292.

It is sometimes difficult to prove the principles of science, because notions cannot always be found more intelligible than those which are questioned.

Taxation no Tyranny, p. 1.

STATESMEN.

I know not whether statesmen and patrons, do not sometimes suffer more reproaches than they deserve from their dependants, and may not rather themselves complain that they are given up a prey to pretensions without merit, and to importunity without shame. The truth is, that the inconveniencies of attendance are more lamented than felt. To the greater number, solicitation is its own reward: to be seen in good company, to talk of familiarities with men of power, to be able to tell the freshest news, to gratify an inferior circle with predictions of increase or decline of favour, and to be regarded as a candidate for high offices, are compensations more than equivalent to the delay of favours, which, perhaps, he that begs them has hardly confidence to expect.

Idler, vol. 1, p. 79.

SEPARATION.

There are few things not purely evil, of which we can say, without some emotion of uneasiness---"*This is the last.*" Those who never could agree together, shed tears when mutual discontent has determined them to final seperation; of a place which

which has been frequently visited, though without pleasure, the *last look* is taken with heaviness of heart.

Ibid. vol. 2, p. 281.

T.

TIME.

He that runs against time, has an antagonist not subject to casualties.

Life of Pope.

The story of Melancthon affords a striking lecture on the value of time, which was, that whenever he made an appointment, he expected not only the *hour*, but the *minute* to be fixed, that the day might not run out in the idleness of suspense.

Rambler, vol. 2, p. 39.

When we have deducted all that is absorbed in sleep, all that is inevitably appropriated to the demands of nature, or irresistably engrossed by the tyranny of custom; all that passes in regulating the superficial decorations of life, or is given up in the reciprocations of civility to the disposal of others; all that is torn from us by the violence of disease, or stolen imperceptibly away by lassitude and languor; we shall find that part of our duration very small, of which we can truly call ourselves masters, or which we can spend wholly at our own choice.

Ibid. vol. 3, p. 13.

Time, like money, may be lost by unreasonable avarice.

Life of Burman, p. 295.

Time is the inflexible enemy of all false hypotheses.

Treatise on the Longitude, p. 10.

An Italian philosopher expressed in his motto, "That time was his estate." An estate, indeed, which will produce nothing without cultivation, but will always abundantly repay the labours of industry, and satisfy the most extensive desires, if no part of it be suffered to lie waste by negligence, to be over-run with noxious plants, or laid out for show rather than for use.

Rambler, vol. 3, p. 18.

Time, amongst other injuries, diminishes the power of pleasing.

Ibid. p. 216.

Time ought, above all other kinds of property, to be free from invasion; and yet there is no man who does not claim the power of wasting that time which is the right of others.

Idler, vol. 1, p. 78.

Life is continually ravaged by invaders; one steals away an hour, and another a day; one conceals the robbery by hurrying us into business, another by lulling us with amusement: the depredation is continued through a thousand vicissitudes of tumult and tranquillity, till, having lost all, we can lose no more.

Ibid.

To put every man in possession of his own time, and rescue the day from a succession of usurpers, is beyond hope; yet, perhaps, some stop might be put to this unmerciful persecution, if all would seriously reflect, that whoever pays a visit that is not desired,

desired, or talks longer than the hearer is willing to attend, is guilty of an injury which he cannot repair, and takes away that which he cannot give.

Ibid. p. 81.

Time, with all its celerity, moves flowly to him whose whole employment is to watch its flight.

Ibid. p. 118.

Time is, of all modes of existence, most obsequious to the imagination.

Preface to Shakespeare, p. 114.

TIME PAST.

Whether it be that life has more vexations than comforts, or what is in event just the same, that evil makes deeper impressions than good, it is certain that few can review the time past, without heaviness of heart. He remembers many calamities incurred by folly; many opportunities lost by negligence. The shades of the dead rise up before him, and he laments the companions of his youth, the partners of his amusements, the assistants of his labours, whom the hand of death has snatched away.

Idler, vol. 1, p. 249.

TRIFLES.

It may be frequently remarked of the studious and speculative, that they are proud of trifles, and that their amusements seem frivolous and childish; whether it be that men, conscious of great reputation, think themselves above the reach of censure, and safe in the admission of negligent indulgencies, or that mankind expect, from elevated genius, an uniformity of greatness, and watch its degradation

with

with malicious wonder, like him, who having followed with his eye an eagle into the clouds, should lament that she ever descended to a perch.

Life of Pope.

Trifles always require exuberance of ornament. The building which has no strength, can be valued only for the grace of its decorations. The pebble must be polished with care, which hopes to be valued as a diamond, and words ought surely to be laboured, when they are intended to stand for things.

Rambler, vol. 3, p. 280.

To proportion the eagerness of contest to its importance, seems too hard a task for human wisdom. The pride of wit has kept ages busy in the discussion of useless questions; and the pride of power has destroyed armies to gain or to keep unprofitable possessions.

Falkland Islands, p. 1.

TRAVELLING.

All travel has its advantages; if the passenger visits better countries, he may learn to improve his own; and if fortune carries him to worse, he may learn to enjoy it.

Western Islands, p. 322.

He that would travel for the entertainment of others, should remember, that the great object of remark is HUMAN LIFE. Every nation has something in its manufactures, its works of genius, its medicines, its agriculture, its customs, and its policy. He only is a useful traveller, who brings home something by which his country may be benefited, who procures some supply of want, or some

some mitigation of evil, which may enable his readers to compare their condition with that of others; to improve it wherever it is worse, and wherever it is better, to enjoy it.

Idler, vol. 2, p. 253.

It is by studying at home, that we must obtain the ability of travelling with intelligence and improvement.

Life of Gray.

TRADE.

Nothing dejects a trader like the interruption of his profits.

Taxation no Tyranny, p. 3.

The theory of trade is yet but little understood, and therefore the practice is often without real advantage to the public; but it might be carried on with more general success, if its principles were better considered.

Preface to the Preceptor, p. 77.

TRUTH.

Truth is scarcely to be heard, but by those from whom it can serve no interest to conceal it.

Rambler, vol. 3, p. 269.

Truth has no gradations; nothing which admits of increase can be so much what it is, as *truth is truth*. There may be a *strange thing*, and a thing *more strange*. But if a proposition be *true*, there can be none *more true*.

Notes upon Shakespeare, vol. 2, p. 136.

Malice often bears down truth.

Ibid. vol. 3, p. 222.

Truth, like beauty, varies its fashions, and is best recommended by different dresses, to different minds.

Idler, vol. 2, p. 186.

There is no crime more infamous than the violation of truth: it is apparent, that men can be sociable beings no longer than they can believe each other. When speech is employed only as the vehicle of falsehood, every man must disunite himself from others, inhabit his own cave, and seek prey only for himself.

Ibid. vol. 1, p. 108.

Truth is the basis of all excellence.

Life of Cowley.

Truth is always truth, and reason is always reason; they have an intrinsic and unalterable value, and constitute that intellectual gold which defies destruction: but gold may be so concealed in baser matter, that only a chymist can recover it; sense may be so hidden in unrefined and plebeian words, that none but philosophers can distinguish it; and both may be so buried in impurities, as not to pay the cost of their extraction.

Ibid.

To doubt whether a man of eminence has told the *truth* about his own birth, is, in appearance, to be very deficient in candour; yet nobody can live long without knowing, that falsehoods of convenience or vanity, falsehoods from which no evil immediately visible ensues, except the general degradation

gradation of human teſtimony, are very lightly uttered, and, once uttered, are ſullenly ſupported. Boileau, who deſired to be thought a rigorous and ſteady moraliſt, having told a petty lie to Lewis XIV. continued it afterwards by falſe dates; thinking himſelf obliged, *in honour*, (ſays his admirer,) to maintain what, when he ſaid it, was well received.

Life of Congreve.

It were doubtleſs to be wiſhed, that truth and reaſon were univerſally prevalent; that every thing were eſteemed according to its real value, and that men would ſecure themſelves from being diſappointed in their endeavours after happineſs, by placing it only in virtue, which is always to be obtained. But, if adventitious and foreign pleaſures muſt be purſued, it would be, perhaps, of ſome benefit, ſince that purſuit muſt frequently be fruitleſs, if it could be taught, that folly might be an antidote to folly, and one fallacy be obviated by another.

Life of Savage.

Where truth is ſufficient to fill the mind, fiction is worſe than uſeleſs; the counterfeit debaſes the genuine.

Life of Gray.

To the poſition of Tully, " that if virtue could be ſeen, ſhe muſt be loved," may be added, that if TRUTH could be heard, ſhe muſt be obeyed.

Rambler, vol. 2, p. 194.

Truth finds an eaſy entrance into the mind, when ſhe is introduced by deſire, and attended by pleaſure. But when ſhe intrudes uncalled, and brings only fear and sorrow in her train, the passes of the intellect are barred against her by prejudice and passion; if she sometimes forces her way by the batteries of argument, she seldom long keeps possession of her conquests, but is ejected by some favoured enemy, or at best obtains only a nominal sovereignty, without influence, and without authority.

Ibid. vol. 4, p. 29.

There are many truths which every human being acknowledges and forgets.

Ider, vol. 1, p. 6.

Truth, when it is reduced to practice, easily becomes subject to caprice and imagination, and many particular acts will be wrong, though their general principle be right.

Ibid. p. 291.

The most useful truths are always universal, and unconnected with accidents and customs.

Ibid. vol. 2, p. 76.

Between falsehood and useless truth there is little difference. As gold, which he cannot spend, will make no man rich, so knowledge, which he cannot apply, will make no man wise.

Ibid. p. 179.

He that contradicts acknowledged truth, will always have an audience; he that vilifies established authority, will always find abettors.

Falkland Islands, p. 54.

There are truths, which, as they are always necessary, do not grow stale by repetition.

Review of the Origin of Evil, p. 17.

Truth

Truth is best supported by virtue.
Introduction to the Proceedings of the Committee for Clothing French Prisoners, p. 160.

TEMPTATION.

It is a common plea of wickedness to call *temptation* destiny.
Notes upon Shakespeare, vol. 1, p. 51.

THOUGHTS.

It is the odd fate of some thoughts, to be the *worse* for being *true*.
Life of Cowley.

Levity of thought naturally produces familiarity of language, and the familiar part of language continues long the same; the dialogue of Comedy, when it is transcribed from popular manners, and real life, is read from age to age with equal pleasure. The artifices of inversion, by which the established order of works is changed, or of innovation, by which *new words*, or *new meanings of words*, are introduced, is practised, not by those who talk to be understood, but by those who write to be admired.
Ibid.

Though we have many examples of people existing without thought, it is certainly a state not much to be desired. He that lives in torpid insensibility, wants nothing of a carcase but putrefaction. It is the part of every inhabitant of the earth, to partake the pains and pleasures of his fellow beings; and, as in a road through a country desert and uniform, the traveller languishes for want of amusement, so the passage of life will be tedious

tedious and irksome to him who does not beguile it by diversified ideas.

Idler, vol. 1, p. 136.

TREATIES.

In forming stipulations, the commissaries are often ignorant, and often negligent. They are sometimes weary with debate, and contract a tedious discussion into general terms, or refer it to a former treaty which was never understood. The weaker part is always afraid of requiring explanations; and the stronger always has an interest in leaving the question undecided. Thus will it happen, without great caution on either side, that after long treaties, solemnly ratified, the rights that had been disputed, are still equally open to controversy.

Observations on the State of Affairs, 1756, p. 21.

THEORY.

It is true, that of far the greater part of things, we must content ourselves with such knowledge as description may exhibit, or analogy supply; but it is true, likewise, that those ideas are always incomplete, and that, at least till we have compared them with *realities*, we do not know them to be just. As we see more, we become possessed of more certainties, and consequently gain more principles of reasoning, and found a wider basis of analogy.

Western Islands, p. 85.

THINGS.

Things may be not only too little, but too much known, to be happily illustrated. To explain, requires the use of terms less abstruse than that which is to be explained, and such terms cannot

not always be found; for, as nothing can be proved but by suppofing fomething intuitively known, and evident without proof, fo nothing can be defined but by the ufe of words too plain to admit a definition.

Preface to Johnfon's Dictionary, p. 67.

TIMIDITY.

Timidity is a difeafe of the mind, more obftinate and fatal than prefumption; as every experiment will teach prefumption caution, and mifcarriages will hourly fhew that attempts are not always rewarded with fuccefs. But the timid man perfuades himfelf that every impediment is infuperable; and, in confequence of thinking fo, has given it, in refpect to himfelf, that ftrength and weight which it had not before.

Rambler, vol. 1, p. 152.

TRANSLATION.

Of every other kind of writing, the antients have left us models, which all fucceeding ages have laboured to imitate; but *tranflation* may juftly be claimed, by the moderns, as their own.

Idler, vol. 2, p. 86.

The Arabs were the firft nation who felt the ardour of tranflation. When they had fubdued the Eaftern provinces of the Greek empire, they found their captives wifer than themfelves, and made hafte to relieve their wants by imported knowledge.

Ibid. p. 89.

The firft book printed in Englifh (about the year 1490) was a *tranflation*; Caxton was both the tranflator and printer of it; it was the *Deftruccion of Troye*, a book which, in that infancy of learning, was confidered as the beft account of the fabulous ages; and which, though now driven out of notice by authors of no greater ufe or value, ftill continued to be read, in Caxton's Englifh, to the beginning of the prefent century.

Ibid. p. 92.

Literal tranflation, which fome carried to that exactnefs, " *that the lines fhould neither be more nor fewer than thofe of the original*, prevailed in this country, with very few examples to the contrary, till the age of Charles II. when the wits of that time no longer confined themfelves to fuch fervile clofenefs, but tranflated with freedom, fometimes with licentioufnefs. There is, undoubtedly, a mean to be obferved, between a *rigid clofenefs* and *paraphraftic liberties*. Dryden faw, very early, that clofenefs beft preferved an author's fenfe, and that freedom beft exhibited his fpirit: he, therefore, will deferve the higheft praife, who can give a reprefentation at once faithful and pleafing, who can convey the fame thoughts with the fame graces, and who, when he tranflates, changes nothing but the language.

Ibid. p. 94 & 99.

The greateft peft of fpeech, is frequency of tranflation. No book was ever turned from one language into another, without imparting fomething of its native idiom. This is the moft mifchievous and comprehenfive innovation: fingle words may enter by thoufands, and the fabric of the tongue continue the fame; but new phrafeology changes much at once; it alters not the single stones of the building, but the order of the columns.

Preface to Johnson's Dictionary, p. 83.

TRAGEDY.

The reflection that strikes the heart at a tragedy, is not that the evils before us are real evils, but that they are evils to which we ourselves may be exposed. If there be any fallacy, it is not that we fancy the players, but that we fancy ourselves, unhappy for a moment; but we rather lament the possibility than suppose the presence of misery; as a mother weeps over her babe, when she remembers that death may take it from her. In short, the delight of tragedy proceeds from our consciousness of fiction; if we thought murders and treasons real, they would please no more.

Preface to Shakespeare, p. 114.

V.

VANITY.

Those whom their virtue restrains from deceiving others, are often disposed, by their vanity, to deceive themselves.

Life of Blackmore.

The vanity of men, in advanced life, is generally strongly excited by the amorous attention of young women.

Life of Swift.

When any one complains of the want of what he is known to possess in an uncommon degree, he

he certainly waits with impatience to be contradicted.
Rambler, vol. 4, p. 130.

Vanity is often no less mischievous than negligence or dishonesty.
Idler, vol. 2, p. 72.

The greatest human virtue bears no proportion to human vanity.
Rambler, vol. 2, p. 296.

VIRTUE.

" Be virtuous ends pursu'd by virtuous means,
" Nor think th' intention sanctifies the deed."
That maxim publish'd in an impious age,
Would loose the wild enthusiast to destroy,
And fix the fierce usurper's bloody title.
Then bigotry might send her slaves to war,
And bid success become the test of truth.
Unpitying massacre might waste the world,
And persecution boast the call of heaven.
Irene, p. 42.

He who desires no virtue in his companion, has no virtue in himself. Hence, when the wealthy and the dissolute connect themselves with indigent companions, for their powers of entertainment, their friendship amounts to little more than paying the reckoning for them. They only desire to drink and laugh; their fondness is without benevolence, and their familiarity without friendship.
Life of Otway.

Many men mistake the love for the practice of virtue, and are not so much good men, as the friends of goodness.
Life of Savage.

Virtue

Virtue is undoubtedly most laudable in that state which makes it most difficult.

Ibid.

Virtue is the surest foundation both of reputation and fortune, and the first step to greatness is to be honest.

Life of Drake, p. 160.

He that would govern his actions by the laws of virtue, must regulate his thoughts by the laws of reason; he must keep guilt from the recesses of his heart, and remember that the pleasures of fancy and the emotion of desire, are more dangerous as they are more hidden, since they escape the awe of observation, and operate equally in every situation, without the concurrence of external opportunities.

Rambler, vol. 1, p. 48.

To dread no eye and to suspect no tongue, is the great prerogative of innocence; an exemption granted only to invariable virtue. But guilt has always its horrors and solicitudes; and to make it yet more shameful and detestable, it is doomed often to stand in awe of those, to whom nothing could give influence or weight, but their power of betraying.

Ibid. vol. 2, p. 85.

Virtue may owe her panegyrics to morality, but must derive her authority from religion.

Preface to the Preceptor, p. 76.

Virtue is too often merely local. In some situations, the air diseases the body; and in others, poisons the mind.

Idler, vol. 2, p. 2.

There are some who, though easy to commit small crimes, are quickened and alarmed at atrocious villainies. Of these, virtue may be said to sit *loosely*, but not *cast off*.
Notes upon Shakespeare, vol. 10, p. 629.

Where there is yet shame, there may in time be virtue.
Western Islands, p. 10.

There are some interior and secret virtues which a man may sometimes have, without the knowledge of others; and may sometimes assume to himself, without sufficient reasons for his opinion.
Life of Sir T. Browne, p. 280.

ROMANTIC VIRTUE.

Narrations of romantic and impracticable virtue, will be read with wonder; but that which is unattainable is recommended in vain. That good may be endeavoured, it must be shewn to be possible.
Life of Pope.

INTENTIONAL VIRTUE.

Nothing is more unjust, however common, than to charge with hypocrisy, him that expresses zeal for those virtues which he neglects to practise; since he may be sincerely convinced of the advantages of conquering his passions, without having yet obtained the victory; as a man may be confident of the advantages of a voyage or a journey, without having courage or industry to undertake it, and may honestly recommend to others, those attempts which he neglects himself.
Rambler, vol. 1, p. 83.

EXCESS

EXCESS OF VIRTUE.

It may be laid down as an axiom, that it is more easy to take away superfluities, than to supply defects; and therefore he that is culpable, because he has passed the *middle point of virtue*, is always accounted a fairer object of hope, than he who fails by falling short; as rashness is more pardonable than cowardice, profusion than avarice.

Ibid. p. 151.

VICE.

Vices, like diseases, are often hereditary. The property of the one is to infect the manners, as the other poisons the springs of life.

Idler, vol. 1, p. 238.

BLANK VERSE.

The exemption which blank verse affords from the necessity of closing the sense with the couplet, betrays luxurious and active minds into such indulgence, that they pile image upon image, ornament upon ornament, and are not easily persuaded to close the sense at all. Blank verse will, it is to be feared, be too often found in description, exuberant; in argument, loquacious; and in narration, tiresome.

Life of Akenside.

Blank verse makes some approach to that which is called "*the lapidary style.*" It has neither the easiness of prose, nor the melody of numbers.

Life of Milton.

Blank Verse, said an ingenious critic, *seems to be verse only to the eye*.

Ibid.

He that thinks himself capable of astonishing, may write blank verse; but those that hope only to please, must condescend to rhyme.
Ibid.

VAUNTING.
Large offers, and sturdy rejections are among the most common topics of falsehood.
Ibid.

U.

UNIVERSALITY.
What is fit for every thing, can fit nothing well.
Life of Cowley.

UNDERSTANDING.
As the mind must govern the hands, so in every society, the man of intelligence must direct the man of labour.
Western Islands, p. 201.

GREAT UNDERTAKINGS.
A large work is difficult, because it is large, even though all its parts might singly be performed with facility. Where there are many things to be done, each must be allowed its share of time and labour, in the proportion only which it bears to the whole; nor can it be expected that the stones which form the dome of the temple, should be squared and polished like the diamond of a ring.
Preface to Dictionary, fol. p. 9.

UTILITY.
The value of a work must be estimated by its use: it is not enough that a dictionary delights the critic,

critic, unless at the same time it instructs the learner. It is to little purpose that an engine amuses the philosopher by the subtlety of its mechanism, if it requires so much knowledge in its application, as to be of no advantage to the common workman.

Plan of an English Dictionary, p. 33.

UNITIES OF TIME AND PLACE.

The time required by a dramatic fable elapses, for the most part, between the acts; for of so much of the action as is represented, the real and poetical duration is the same. If, therefore, in the first act, preparations for war against *Mithridates*, are represented to be made at Rome, the event of the war, may, without absurdity, be represented in the catastrophe as happening in Pontus. We know that we are neither in Rome, nor Pontus; that neither *Mithridates*, nor *Lucullus*, are before us. The drama exhibits successive imitations of successive actions; and why may not the second imitation represent an action that happened years after the first, if it be so connected with it, that nothing but time can be supposed to intervene?

The lines, likewise, of a play, relate to some action, and an action must be in some place; but the different actions that complete a story may be in places very remote from each other: and where is the absurdity of allowing that space to represent, first Athens, and then Sicily, which was always known to be neither Sicily, nor Athens, but a modern theatre?

Yet he that, without diminution of any other excellence, shall preserve all the unities unbroken, deserves the like applause with the architect who shall display all the orders of architecture in a
citadel,

citadel, without any deduction from its strength. But the principal beauty of a citadel is to exclude the enemy; and the greatest graces of a play are to copy nature, and instruct life.

Preface to Shakespeare, p. 113 & 116.

W.

WAR.

As war is the extremity of evil, it is surely the duty of those whose station entrusts them with the care of nations, to avert it from their charge. There are diseases of a nanimal nature which nothing but amputation can remove; so there may, by the depravation of human passions, be sometimes a gangrene in collected life, for which fire and the sword are the necessary remedies; but in what can skill or caution be better shewn, than in preventing such dreadful operations, while there is room for gentler methods.

Falkland Islands, p. 41.

The wars of civilized nations make very slow changes in the system of empire. The public perceives scarcely any alteration, but an increase of debt; and the few individuals who are benefited, are not supposed to have the clearest right to their advantages. If he that shared the danger, enjoyed the profit; if he that bled in the battle, grew rich by victory; he might shew his gains without envy. But, at the conclusion of a long war, how are we recompensed for the death of multitudes, and the expence of millions; but by contemplating the sudden glories of pay-masters and agents, contractors

tors and commissioners, whose equipages shine like meteors, and whose palaces rise like exhalations?
Ibid. p. 43.

Princes have yet this remnant of humanity, that they think themselves obliged not to make war without reason, though their reasons are not always very satisfactory.
Memoirs of the K. of Prussia, p. 127.

He must certainly meet with obstinate opposition, who makes it equally dangerous to yield as to resist, and who leaves his enemies no hopes, but from victory.
Life of Drake, p. 191.

Among the calamities of war, may be justly numbered the diminution of the love of truth, by the falsehoods which interest dictates, and credulity encourages.
Idler, vol. 1, p. 169.

The lawfulness and justice of the holy wars have been much disputed; but perhaps there is a principle on which the question may be easily determined. If it be part of the religion of the Mahometans to extirpate by the sword all other religions, it is by the laws of self-defence, lawful for men of every other religion, and for Christians among others, to make war upon Mahometans, simply as Mahometans, as men obliged by their own principles to make war upon Christians, and only lying in wait till opportunity shall promise them success.
Notes upon Shakespeare, vol. 5, p. 254.

That conduct which betrays designs of future hostility, if it does not excite violence, will always generate malignity; it must for ever exclude confidence

fidence and friendship, and continue a cold and sluggish rivalry, by a sly reciprocation of indirect injuries, without the bravery of war, or the security of peace.

Falkland Island, p. 9.

War has means of destruction more formidable than the cannon and the sword. Of the thousands, and ten thousands that perished in our late contests with France and Spain, a very small part ever felt the stroke of an enemy; the rest languished in tents and ships, amidst damps and putrefactions, pale, torpid, spiritless and helpless, gasping and groaning, unpitied among men, made obdurate by long continuance of hopeless misery, or whelmed in pits, or heaved into the ocean, without notice, and without remembrance. By incommodious encampments, and unwholesome stations, where courage is useless, and enterprise impracticable, fleets are silently dispeopled, and armies sluggishly melted away.

Ibid. p. 43.

The revolutions of war are such as will not suffer human presumption to remain long unchecked.

Memoirs of the K. of Prussia, p. 138.

There are no two nations confining on each other, between whom a war may not always be kindled with plausible pretences on either part; as there is always passing between them a reciprocation of injuries, and fluctuation of encroachments.

Observations on the State of Affairs, 1756, p. 23.

WIT.

Wit is that which is at once natural and new, and which, though not obvious, is, upon its first production, acknowledged to be just.

Life of Cowley.

Wit will never make a man rich, but there are places where riches will always make a wit.
Idler, vol. 1, p. 268.

Wit, like every other power, has its boundaries. Its succefs depends on the aptitude of others to receive impreffions; and that as fome bodies, indiffoluble by heat, can fet the furnace and crucible at defiance, there are minds upon which the rays of fancy may be pointed without effect, and which no fire of fentiment can agitate or exalt.
Rambler, vol. 4, p. 78.

It is a calamity incident to *grey headed wit*, that his merriment is unfafhionable. His allufions are forgotten facts, his illuftrations are drawn from notions obfcured by time, his wit therefore may be called *fingle*, fuch as none has any part in but himfelf.
Notes upon Shakefpeare, vol. 5, p. 462.

Wit, like all other things fubject by their nature to the choice of man, has its changes and fafhions, and at different times takes different forms.
Life of Cowley.

The pride of wit and knowledge is often mortified, by finding that they confer no fecurity againft the common errors which miflead the weakeft and meaneft of mankind.
Rambler, vol. 1, p. 32.

It is common to find men break out into a rage at any infinuations to the difadvantage of their *wit*, who have borne with great patience *reflections on their morals*.
Ibid. p. 241.

Wit

Wit being an unexpected copulation of ideas, the discovery of some occult relation between images in appearance remote from each other; an effusion of wit, therefore, pre-supposes an accumulation of knowledge; a memory stored with notions, which the imagination may cull out to compose new assemblages. Whatever may be the native vigour of the mind, she can never form many combinations from few ideas; as many changes can never be rung upon a few bells.

Ibid. vol. 4, p. 187.

Nothing was ever said with uncommon felicity, but by the co-operation of chance; and therefore *wit*, as well as valour, must be content to share its honours with fortune.

Idler, vol. 2, p. 32.

WISDOM.

The first years of man must make provision for the last. He that never thinks, can never be wise.

Prince of Abyssinia, p. 113.

To be of grave mien, and slow of utterance; to look with solicitude, and speak with hesitation, is attainable at will; but the show of wisdom is ridiculous, when there is nothing to cause doubt, as that of valour, where there is nothing to be feared.

Idler, vol. 1, p. 288.

The two powers which, in the opinion of Epictetus, constitute a *wise man*, are those of *bearing* and *forbearing*.

Life of Savage.

Wisdom comprehends at once the end and the means, estimates easiness or difficulty, and is cautious or confident in due proportion.

Idler, vol. 2, p. 223.

WORLD.

The world is generally willing to support those who solicit favour, against those who command reverence. He is easily praised, whom no man can envy.

Preface to Shakespeare, p. 51.

Of things that terminate in human life, the world is the proper judge. To despise its sentence, if it were possible, is not just; and if it were just, is not possible.

Life of Pope.

To know the world, is necessary, since we were born for the help of one another; and to know it early, is convenient, if it be only that we may learn early to despise it.

Idler, vol. 2, p. 159

WOMEN.

Women are always most observed, when they seem themselves least to observe, or to lay out for observation.

Rambler, vol. 2, p. 254.

It is observed, that the unvaried complaisance which women have a right of exacting, keeps them generally unskilled in human nature.

Ibid. vol. 3, p. 269.

Our best poet seems to have given this character to women: " That they think ill of nothing that raises

raises the credit of their beauty, and are ready, however virtuous, to pardon any act which they they think excited by their own charms.

Notes upon Shakespeare, vol. 2, p. 156.

It is said of a woman who accepts a worse match than those which she had refused, that she has passed through the *wood*, and at last has taken a *crooked stick*.

Ibid. p. 286.

Nothing is more common than for the younger part of the sex, upon certain occasions, to say in a pet what they do not think, or to think for a time on what they do not finally resolve.

Ibid. vol. 4, p. 105.

As the faculty of writing has been chiefly a *masculine endowment*, the reproach of making the world miserable, has been always thrown upon the WOMEN; and the grave and the merry have equally thought themselves at liberty to conclude either with declamatory complaints or satirical censures of female folly or fickleness.

Rambler, vol. 1, p. 108.

Of women it has been always known, that no censure wounds so deeply, or rankles so long, as that which charges them with want of beauty.

Ibid. p. 242.

It may be particularly observed, of women, that they are for the most part good or bad, as they fall among those who practice vice or virtue; and that neither education nor reason gives them much security against the influence of example. Whether it be, that they have less courage to stand against opposition, oppofition, or that their defire of admiration makes them facrifice their principles to the poor pleafure of worthlefs praife, it is certain, whatever be the caufe, that female goodnefs feldom keeps its ground againft laughter, flattery, or fafhion.

Ibid. vol. 2, p. 95.

The wifdom of thofe by whom our female education was inftituted, fhould always be admired for having contrived that every woman, of whatever condition, fhould be taught fome arts of manufacture, by which the vacuities of reclufe and domeftic leifure may be filled up. Thofe arts are more neceffary, as the weaknefs of their fex, and the general fyftem of life, debar ladies from many employments, which, by diverfifying the circumftances of men, preferve them from being cankered by the ruft of their own thoughts.

Ibid. p. 180.

Women, by whatever fate, always judge abfurdly of the intellects of boys. The vivacity and confidence which attract female admiration, are feldom produced in the early part of life; but by ignorance, at leaft, if not by ftupidity; for they proceed not from *confidence of right*, but *fearlefsnefs of wrong*. Whoever has a clear apprehenfion, muft have quick fenfibility; and where he has no fufficient reafon to truft his own judgment, will proceed with doubt and caution, becaufe he perpetually dreads the difgrace of error.

Ibid. vol. 4, p. 186.

FEMALE WEAKNESS.

The weaknefs they lament, themfelves create;
Inftructed from their infant years to court,
With counterfeited fears, the aid of man,
They feem to fhudder at the ruftling breeze,

Start

Start at the light, and tremble in the dark;
Till affectation, ripening to belief,
And folly, frighted at her own chimeras,
Habitual cowardice usurps the soul.

Irene, p. 28.

WEALTH.

Some light might be given to those who shall endeavour to calculate the increase of English wealth, by observing that Latymer, in the time of Edward VI. mentions it, as a proof of his father's prosperity—That though but a yeoman he gave his daughters *five pounds* each for her portion. At the latter end of Elizabeth, *seven hundred pounds* were such a temptation to courtship, as made all other motives suspected.—Congreve makes *twelve thousand pounds* more than a counterbalance to the affectation of Belinda.—No poet would *now* fly his favourite character at less than *fifty thousand*.

Notes upon Shakespeare, vol. 1, p. 317.

WICKEDNESS.

There is always danger lest wickedness, conjoined with abilities, should steal upon esteem, though it misses of approbation.

Ibid. vol. 10, p. 628.

WINE.

In the bottle, discontent seeks for comfort, cowardice for courage, and bashfulness for confidence; but whoever asked succour from Bacchus, that was able to preserve himself frrom being enslaved by his auxiliary?

Life of Addison.

WRONGS.

WRONGS.

Men are wrong for want of sense, but they are wrong by halves for want of spirit.
Taxation no Tyranny, p. 42.

Men easily forgive wrongs which are not committed against themselves.
Notes upon Shakespeare, vol. 4, p. 158.

The power of doing *wrong* with impunity, seldom waits long for the will.
Observation on the State of Affairs, 1756, p. 22.

LETTER-WRITING.

The importance of writing letters with propriety, justly claims to be considered with care, since next to the power of pleasing with his presence, every man should wish to be able to give delight at a distance.
Preface to the Preceptor, p. 68.

MECHANICAL WRITING.

The mechanical art of writing began to be cultivated amongst us in the reign of Queen Elizabeth, and was at that time so highly valued, that it contributed much to the fame and fortune of him who wrote his pages with neatness, and embellished them with elegant draughts and illuminations; it was partly, perhaps, to this encouragement, that we now surpass all other nations in this art.
Life of Roger Ascham, p. 238.

NEWS-WRITER.

In Sir Henry Wotton's jocular definition, "an ambassador is said to be a man of virtue, sent abroad to tell lies for the advantage of his country." A *news-*

A *news-writer* is a man without virtue, who writes lies at home for his own profit.

Idler, vol. 3, p. 31.

SPLENDID WICKEDNESS.

There have been men splendidly wicked, whose endowments threw a brightness on their crimes, and whom scarce any villainy made perfectly detestable, because they never could be wholly divested of their excellencies: but such have been in all ages, the great corrupters of the world; and their resemblance ought no more to be preserved than the art of murdering without pain.

Rambler, vol. 1, p. 22.

WONDER.

All wonder is the effect of novelty upon ignorance.

Life of Yalden.

Wonder is a pause of reason, a sudden cessation of the mental progress, which lasts only while the understanding is fixed upon some single idea, and is at an end when it recovers force enough to divide the object into its parts, or mark the intermediate gradations from the first agent to the last consequence.

Rambler, vol. 3, p. 186.

Y.

YOUTH.

Youth is of long duration; and in maturer age, when the enchantments of fancy shall cease, and phantoms of delight dance no more about us, we shall have no comforts but the esteem of wise men, and the mean of doing good. Let us therefore

fore stop, while to stop is in our power. Let us live as men, who are some time to be old, and to whom it will be the most dreadful of all evils, to count their former luxuriance of health, only by the maladies which riot has produced.

Prince of Abyssinia, p. 113.

That the highest degree of reverence should be paid to youth, and that nothing indecent should be suffered to approach their eyes, or ears, are precepts extorted by sense and virtue from an ancient writer, by no means eminent for chastity of thought. The same kind, though not the same degree of caution is required in every thing which is laid before them, to secure them from unjust prejudices, perverse opinions, and incongruous combinations of images.

Rambler, vol. 1, p. 20.

Youth is the time of enterprise and hope: having yet no occasion for comparing our force with any opposing power, we naturally form presumptions in our own favour, and imagine that obstruction and impediment will give way before us.

Ibid. vol. 3, p. 31.

Youth is the time in which the qualities of *modesty* and *enterprise* ought chiefly to be found. Modesty suits well with inexperience, and enterprise with health and vigour, and an extensive prospect of life.

Ibid. vol. 1, p. 75.

THE PROGRESS OF YOUTH.

The youth has not yet discovered how many evils are continually hovering about us, and, when he is set free from the shackles of discipline, looks abroad into the world with rapture; he sees an Elysian

Elysian region open before him, so variegated with beauty, and so stored with pleasure, that his care is rather to accumulate good than to shun evil; he stands distracted by different forms of delight, and has no other doubt than which path to follow of those which all lead equally to the bowers of happiness.

He who has seen only the superficies of life, believes every thing to be what it appears, and rarely suspects that external splendour conceals any latent sorrow or vexation. He never imagines that there may be greatness without safety, affluence without content, jollity without friendship, and solitude without peace. He fancies himself permitted to cull the blessings of every condition, and to leave its inconveniencies to the idle and to the ignorant. He is inclined to believe no man miserable but by his own fault; and seldom looks with much pity upon failings or miscarriages, because he thinks them willingly admitted, or negligently incurred.

It is impossible without pity and contempt to hear a youth of generous sentiments, and warm imagination, declaring in the moment of openness and confidence, his designs and expectations; because long life is possible he considers it as certain, and therefore promises himself all the changes of happiness, and provides gratification for every desire.

He is for a time to give himself wholly to frolick and diversion, to range the world in search of pleasure, to delight every eye, and to gain every heart, and to be celebrated equally for his pleasing levities and solid attainments, his deep reflections and sporting repartees.

He then elevates his views to nobler enjoyments, and finds all the scattered excellencies of the female world united in a woman, who prefers his addresses to wealth and titles. He is afterwards to engage in bufinefs; to diffipate difficulty, and overpower oppofition; to climb, by the mere force of merit, to fame and greatnefs, and reward all thofe who countenanced his rife, or paid due regard to his early excellence. At laft he will retire in peace and honour, contract his views to domeftic pleafures, form the manners of his children like himfelf, obferve how every year expands the beauty of his daughters, and how his fons catch ardour from their father's hiftory; he will give laws to the neighbourhood, dictate axioms to pofterity, and leave the world an example of wifdom and of happinefs.

With hopes like thefe he fallies jocund into life: to little purpofe is he told that the condition of humanity admits no pure and unmingled happinefs; that the exuberant gaiety of youth ends in poverty or difeafe; that uncommon qualifications, and contrarieties or excellence, produce envy equally with applaufe; that whatever admiration and fondnefs may promife him, he muft marry a wife, like the wives of others, with fome virtues and fome faults, and be as often difgufted with her vices, as delighted with her elegance; that if he adventures into the circle of action, he muft expect to encounter men as artful, as daring, as refolute as himfelf; that of his children fome may be deformed, and others vicious; fome may difgrace him by their follies, fome offend him by their infolence, and fome exhauft him by their profufion. He hears all this with obftinate incredulity, and wonders by what malignity old age is influenced, that it cannot forbear to fill his ears with predictions of mifery.

Among other pleafing errors of young minds is the opinion of their own importance. He that has not yet remarked how little attention his contemporaries can fpare from their own affairs, conceives all eyes turned upon himself, and imagines every one that approaches him to be an enemy or a follower, an admirer or a spy. He therefore considers his fame as involved in the event of every action. Many of the virtues and vices of youth proceed from this quick sense of reputation. This it is that gives firmness and constancy, fidelity and disinterestedness, and it is this that kindles resentment for slight injuries, and dictates all the principles of sanguinary honour.

But, as time brings him forward in the world, he soon discovers that he only shares fame or reproach with innumerable partners; that he is left unmarked in the obscurity of the croud; and that what he does, whether good or bad, soon gives way to new objects of regard.

He then easily sets himself free from the anxieties of reputation, and considers praise or censure as a transient breath, which, while he hears it, is passing away, without any lasting mischief or advantage.

Rambler, vol. 4, p. 195, 196, 197 & 198.

YOUTH AND AGE.

When we are young we busy ourselves in forming schemes for succeeding time, and miss the gratifications that are before us; when we are old we amuse the langour of age, with the recollection of youthful pleasures or performances; so that our life, of which no part is filled with the business of the present time, resembles our dreams after dinner, when the events of the morning are mingled with the designs of the evening.

Notes upon Shakespeare, vol. 2, p. 74.

The End of the Beauties.

A CATALOGUE

OF

Dr. JOHNSON's WORKS.*

TRANSLATION of the Voyages of Lobo, published 1735

A Complete Vindication of the Licensers of the Stage, from the malicious and scand. lous aspersions of Mr. Brooke, author of *Gustavus Vasa*, with a Proposal for making the Office of Licenser more extensive and effectual, by an impartial Hand, 4to, 1739

Marmor Norfolciensis, pamphlet, 1739. Re printed, with notes, 1775

Parliamentary Debates, from 1740 to 1744, in the Gentleman's Magazine

Life of Savage, 1 vol. 12mo. 1744

Miscellaneous Observations on the Tragedy of Mackbeth, with Remarks on Sir Thomas Hanmer's Edition of Shakespeare, and Proposals for a new Edition of Shakespeare, with a Specimen, 1745

Rambler, 4 vols. originally published in numbers, 1750

Dictionary of the English Language, in 2 vols. folio, published 1755

Ditto abridged, in 2 vols. octavo

Occasional Papers in the Universal Visitor, 1756

Ditto in the Literary Magazine, 1756 and 1757

Idler, 2 vols. duodecimo, originally published in numbers, 1758

Prince of Abyssinia, 1 vol. duodecimo, 1759

Edition of Shakespeare, 8 vols. octavo, 1765

Ditto in conjunction with Mr. Steevens, 10 vols. octavo, published 1778

Falkland Islands, False Alarm, Patriot, and Taxation no Tyranny — Pamphlets published from 1769 to 1775

Tour to the Western Islands of Scotland, 1775

Convicts Address, 1777

Lives of the British Poets, 10 vols. small octavo, 1780

Ditto, 4 vols. large octavo.

---

* *When the first edition of the Beauties of Johnson appeared, he enquired of Mr Kearsley how he had procured a list of his works? who replied that he had obtained it by diligent enquiry among the literary world. He observed that he could not remember half the titles of what he had written. Mr. K. a few days after presented him with a copy, at which he expressed much satisfaction.*

MISCEL-

MISCELLANEOUS PIECES of Dr. JOHNSON,
published in Three Volumes, by T. Davies.

Pieces in the First Volume.

Review of the Enquiry into the Origin of Evil
Political State of Great Britain
Review of Letters from Sir Isaac Newton to Dr. Bentley
Preface to the Preceptor
Vision of Theodore
Memoirs of the King of Prussia

Life of Barretier
——— Dr. Sydenham
——— Sir Francis Drake
——— Roger Ascham
——— Sir Thomas Browne
——— Peter Burman
——— Edward Cave

Pieces in the Second Volume.

Origin and Importance of small Tracts and Fugitive Pieces, Written for the Introduction to the Harleian Miscellany
An Account of the Harleian Library
Plan of an English Dictionary, in a Letter to the Earl of Chesterfield, 1747
Preface to the folio of Johnson's Dictionary
Proposals for printing the Dramatic Works of Shakespeare
Preface to Shakespeare, published in 1765

Preliminary Discourse to the London Chronicle
Introduction to Proceedings of the Committee to make Contributions for clothing French Prisoners
Thoughts on Agriculture, Ancient and Modern
Introduction to the World Displayed
Dissertation on Pope's Epitaphs
Life of Boerhave
Character of Dr. William Collins

Pieces in the Third Volume.

Review of the Court of Augustus
A Letter from a French Refugee in America, to his Friend, a Gentleman in England
Observations on the State of Affairs in 1756
A Description of the Grotto of Antiparos
A Review of a Philosophical Enquiry into the Origin of our Ideas.

Ideas of the Sublime and Beautiful
The Life of Father Paul Sarpi, Author of the History of the Council of Trent
Preface to a Dictionary of Commerce
Some Account of the Life of Benvenuto Cellini
Some Account of the Life and Writings of Dr. John Eachard.

Original Papers in behalf of the late Dr. Dodd.

POEMS

POEMS of Dr. JOHNSON, juſt publiſhed in One Volume, by C. and G. KEARSLEY.

London: A Satire, in imitation of the Third Satire of Juvenal
The Vanity of Human Wiſhes, in imitation of the Tenth ditto of ditto
Prologue on the Opening of Drury Lane Theatre
Ditto to Comus, for the Benefit of Milton's Grand daughter
Ditto to the Comedy of the Good-natured Man
Ditto to the Comedy of The Word to the Wife
Verſes written at the requeſt of a Gentleman to whom a Lady had given a Sprig of Myrtle.
Irene, a Tragedy
A Latin Verſion of Pope's Meſſiah
Spring, an Ode
The Midſummer's Wiſh
Autumn
Winter
The Winter's Walk

A Song
An Evening Ode to Stella
The Natural Beauty, to Stella
Stella in Mourning
To Lyce, an elderly Lady
To Lady Firebrace, at Bury Aſſizes
The Vanity of Wealth
To Miſs ———, on her giving the Author a Gold and Silk network Purſe of her own weaving
To Miſs ———, on her playing on the Harpſicord
On the Death of Dr. Robert Levet
Latin Epitaph on Sir Thomas Hanmer
Tranſlation of the Latin Epitaph on Sir Thomas Hanmer
Latin Epitaph and Tranſlation on Dr. Goldſmith
Ditto on Henry Thrale, Eſq.
Latin ditto on Maria Saliſbury

POSTHUMOUS PIECES.

Tranſlation of the *Bellum Catilinarium*, from Salluſt
One Volume of Latin Poems

One ditto of Memoirs of his own Life *
And ſome Greek Epigrams.

* *Conſiſting of looſe memorandums. Another volume was burned by Dr. Johnſon in a miſtake, a few days before his death, along with other manuſcripts.*

ENTERTAINING

ENTERTAINING BOOKS
Lately published by
C. and G. KEARSLEY.
Johnson's Head, Fleet street.

An ABRIDGMENT of the HISTORY of SCOTLAND, from ROBERTSON, STUART, &c.
In the Manner of Goldsmith's Abridgment of the Histories of England, Rome, and Greece,
Price 3s. 6d. bound,

The Success which has attended the Abridgment of Goldsmith's History of England has encouraged the Author to offer to the Public the preceding Work: nor does he conceive the History of a Kingdom so long connected, and now blended with England under the Title of Great Britain, can be considered either as unentertaining or uninstructive to the rising Generation.

The following Work is intended to supply that Deficiency in Schools long complained of; and when the Editor affirms, that he has made Goldsmith's Abridgement of the History of England his Model of Execution, he doubts not but the Public will consider his Endeavours in promoting the Study of History, in our seminaries of Education, as deserving Encouragement.

An ABRIDGMENT of the HISTORY of FRANCE,

From the first establishment of that Monarchy to the present Time
Price 3s. 6d. bound.

NEW EDITIONS, MUCH IMPROVED.
In Two Volumes.

The FLOWERS of ANCIENT and MODERN HISTORY:
Comprehending, on a new Plan, the most remarkable and interesting Events, as well as ancient and modern Characters. Designed for the Improvement and Entertainment of Youth.

By the Rev. JOHN ADAMS, A. M.
Price 6s.

The following Abridgment is executed with a sufficient Degree of Judgment and Accuracy, to afford Young People Amusement and Instruction; and it is to be observed, that while these Volumes are sold at a moderate Price, and are easily consulted, it would be very expensive to purchase, and would require much Time to peruse the whole Stock of original Works from which they are compiled.

MONTHLY REVIEW, March 1791.

In Two Volumes, Price Six Shillings,
MODERN VOYAGES:
Containing a Variety of ufeful and entertaining Facts refpecting the expeditions and the principal Difcoveries of the moft celebrated Circumnavigators, as well as thofe of Briffon, White, Wilfon, Meares, Philip, &c. &c.

By the Rev. JOHN ADAMS, A. M.

With an ELEGANTLY ENGRAVED PORTRAIT of CAGLIOSTRO.

THE LIFE of JOSEPH BALSAMO, commonly called COUNT CAGLIOSTRO, containing the fingular and uncommon Adventures of that extraordinary Perfonage, from his Birth till his Imprifonment in the Caftle of Sr. Angelo. To which are added the particulars of his Trial before the Inquifition, the Hiftory of his Confeffions concerning Common and Egyptian Mafonry, and a variety of other interefting Particulars;

Tranflated from the Original Proceedings publifhed at Rome, by Order of the Apoftolic Chamber, with Notes by the Tranflator, containing many CURIOUS ANECDOTES of ENORMOUS DEPREDATIONS, never before made Public.

⁎ Compared with other Villains who have at different periods infefted the World, Caglioftro raifes a degree of wonder at the fubtilty of his Schemes, the enormity of his Depredations, and his hazardous Efcapes, which no others are entitled to.

Price 3s. 6d.

A new Edition, much enlarged, of
ORIGINAL ANECDOTES BON MOTS, and CHARACTERISTIC TRAITS.

Of the greateft Princes, Politicians, Philofophers, Poets, Orators, and Wits of modern Times; fuch as the Emperor Charles V. King of Pruffia, Peter the Great, Henry IV. Charles XII. Lewis XIV. Voltaire, Swift, Garrick, Dr. Johnfon, &c. &c.

By the Rev. JOHN ADAMS, M. A.

Price 4s.

An HISTORY of the CHRISTIAN CHURCH,
From the earlieft Periods to the prefent Time.
Compiled from the beft Authors, principally with a View to the Ufe of the younger Clergy.

By G. GREGORY, D. D. F. A. S.

Two Volumes, 12mo. Price 8s. in Boards.

The POETICAL WORKS of SAMUEL JOHNSON, LL. D.

Containing London, a Satire, and The Vanity of Human Wishes, both imitated from Juvenal; Irene, a Tragedy; The Winter's Walk; Stella in Mourning; The Midsummer's Wish; An Evening Ode to Stella; Vanity of Wealth; The Natural Beauty; Translation of Pope's Messiah, and sundry other Pieces.

A new Edition, Price 3s. in Boards.

(With a PORTRAIT of the AUTHOR, by WALKER.)
The tenth Edition, enlarged and corrected, of
The GENTLEMAN's STABLE DIRECTORY;
Or, MODERN SYSTEM OF FARIERY.

Comprehending every useful instruction for Equestrian Management in Sickness or in Health; Diseases are traced to their Origin, and the Causes explained; proper Modes of Prevention are particularly pointed out, and the direct Methods of Cure clearly confirmed. Occasional Observations are introduced upon the erroneous Treatment, and almost absolute Prescriptions of Gibson, Bracken, Bartlet, Osmer, and others; with general Directions for buying and Selling, Feeding, Bleeding, Purging, and getting into Condition, for their various Purposes, Horses of every Denomination.

To which are added,

Applicable and Experimental Remarks upon the proper Treatment of Draught Horses, the Qualifications and dangerous Practice of Country Farriers, and the destructive Infatuation of Farmer's Servants.

By WILLIAM TAPLIN, Surgeon.

In two Volumes. Price 12s. 6d. in Boards.

The POEMS of Mr. GRAY.

With Notes by Gilbert Wakefield, B. A. late Fellow of Jesus College, Cambridge.

Ingenium cui sit, cui mens divinior, atque os
Magna sonaturum, des nominis hujus honorem   Horat.

Creative Genius; and the Glow divine,
That warms and melts th' enthusiastic soul;
A pomp and prodigality of phrase;
These form the poet, and these shine in thee!

Price four Shillings in Boards.

A TOUR in ITALY,

By the Rev. THOMAS MARTYN, B. D. F. R. S. and Professor of Botany in the University of Cambridge;
With a Coloured Chart of the Post-Roads.

Price 7s. in Boards.

www.ingramcontent.com/pod-product-compliance
Lightning Source LLC
Chambersburg PA
CBHW050846300426
44111CB00010B/1151